D0765732

LIVERIGHT PUBLISHING CORPORATION

A Division of W. W. Norton & Company

Independent Publishers Since 1923

NEW YORK • LONDON

To librarians everywhere who, through hard work and dedication, support writers, researchers, learners, and book lovers alike. This writer couldn't have done it without you.

CONTENTS

===

REBELS
AT SEA

INTRODUCTION

———

Marblehead privateer *Argo*, painted by Ashley Bowen, 1783.

———

A TALL, ANGULAR MAN WITH A ROMAN NOSE AND A COOL demeanor stood on the quarterdeck of the American privateer *Pickering* peering through a spyglass at the British privateer *Achilles*. It was late in the day on June 3, 1780, and Captain Jonathan Haraden was in sight of the friendly port city of Bilbao, Spain, where the *Pickering* had been expecting to sell goods and to resupply. The *Achilles*, however, stood in the way. Nobody would have faulted Haraden had he fled in the face of this superior foe: while the *Pickering* had a crew of thirty-eight and sixteen six-pounder cannons, the *Achilles*, according to one of Haraden's British prisoners, bristled with one hundred thirty men and forty-three cannons, many of which were nine- and eighteen-pounders.* Hardly a fair fight. But that's not how Haraden saw it. He relished the chance to confront the enemy and strike a blow for the revolutionary cause. Turning to the prisoner who had informed him of the *Achilles'* might, Haraden calmly said, "I shan't run from her."

As with many men of the time who were not from wealthy or prominent families, we know little about Haraden's early life. Born in Gloucester, Massachusetts, in 1745, he was sent to Salem as a boy to apprentice as a cooper in the employ of Joseph Cabot, a successful merchant. Haraden must have gained some experience at sea in the years leading up to the American Revolution, because in June 1776 he was commissioned as first lieutenant on the aptly named sloop *Tyrannicide*, which Massachusetts sent out as part of its colonial (soon to be state) navy. The idea was to protect its merchantmen and seize British ones. As first lieutenant and later captain of the *Tyrannicide*, Haraden did just that, earning the respect of the Massachusetts Board of War, which called him a "brave officer" who "always acquitted himself with spirit and honor." Disagreements over pay, however, led him to leave the Massachusetts navy and become a privateersman. On September 30, 1778, he took command of the *Pickering*.

The *Pickering* was one of more than a thousand American privateers, and Haraden was one of tens of thousands of privateersmen who served during the American Revolution. (Often both the vessels and the men who served on them are called "privateers." Because that can lead to confusion, here the vessels will be referred to as "privateers" and the men sailing them "privateersmen.") Privateers were armed vessels owned and outfitted by private individuals who had government permission to capture enemy ships in times of war. That permission came in the form of a letter of marque, a formal legal document issued by the government that gave the bearer the right to seize vessels belonging to belligerent nations and to claim those vessels and their cargoes, or prizes, as spoils of war. The proceeds from the auction of these prizes were in turn split between the men who crewed the privateers and the owners of the ship. Typically, gov-

---

* The term "pounder" refers to the weight of the solid shot fired by a cannon (that shot or projectile is typically referred to as a cannonball). A six-pounder cannon or gun fires a ball that weighs six pounds.

Photograph of a miniature painting of Jonathan Haraden by an unknown artist, circa late 1700s–early 1800s.

ernments used privateers to amplify their power on the seas, most notably when their navies were not large enough to effectively wage war. More specifically, by attacking the enemy's maritime commerce and, when possible, its naval forces, privateers could inflict significant economic and military pain at no expense to the government that commissioned them. Privateers were like a cost-free navy. One late nineteenth-century historian dubbed them "the militia of the sea."

There were two types of privateers. Some were heavily armed with large crews, their sole purpose to seek out and capture enemy ships. The large crew was needed to work the cannons and fight enemy sailors and marines with muskets and swords but also to man the newly acquired prizes and sail them back to port—while allowing the privateer to continue on, now with a smaller but still sufficient crew, searching for the next prey. Other privateers were primarily merchant vessels intent on trade; these traveled between ports to buy and sell goods but also had permission to attack enemy shipping, and would do so when the opportunity arose. This latter type of privateer was often referred to as a "letter of marque"—not to be confused with the authority described above—whereas the first type of privateer was called just that, a privateer. Because the letter of marque's main purpose was trade, it generally had fewer cannons and a smaller crew than a conventional privateer, although it usually took along enough crewmen to man a few prizes. One other crucial difference concerned pay. While the crews of privateers earned money only if they took prizes, those on letters of marque were paid a base salary, which was supplemented by any prize money they earned. Privateers brought in the vast majority of the prizes during the Revolution, as compared to letters of marque. Some vessels alternated between the two statuses. The *Pickering* sailed variously as a privateer and a letter of marque; and it was a letter of marque on its trading voyage between Salem and Bilbao when it sighted the *Achilles*. (This book uses the term "privateer" to cover both types of vessels, except where differentiating between the two is necessary.)

As captain of the *Pickering* from the fall of 1778 to early 1780, Haraden took numerous prizes. A particularly spectacular success came in October 1779 off of Sandy Hook, New Jersey, when he came upon three British privateers, armed with fourteen, ten, and eight cannons, respectively. One of Haraden's officers, "though a brave man, advised him not to engage them as it would be imprudent, on account of their force." Haraden evenly replied that the officer was free to go below, but with or without him, he was going to do "his duty" and attack. In an engagement lasting one and a half hours, the *Pickering* captured all three ships. The speed with which Haraden accomplished this feat was a function of his fighting style. As one of his crewmen said, Haraden liked to "go alongside, and do what was to be done in a short time."

Haraden's encounter with the *Achilles* came at the end of a voyage that began in the spring of 1780 when the *Pickering*, loaded with West Indian sugar, sailed for Bilbao. Upon entering the Bay of Biscay on June 1, Haraden spied a British privateer named the *Golden Eagle*, which had a crew of fifty-seven and twenty-two cannons, fourteen of which were nine-pounders. A furious battle ensued, with the *Pickering* emerging victorious. Haraden put first mate Jonathan Carnes on the *Golden Eagle*, as prize master, along with nine other crewmen from the *Pickering*. While some of the *Golden Eagle*'s crew were imprisoned on the lower decks of their own ship, the captain, Robert Scott, along with the balance of his men, were brought onto the *Pickering*.

Two days later, as the *Pickering* made its final approach to Bilbao,

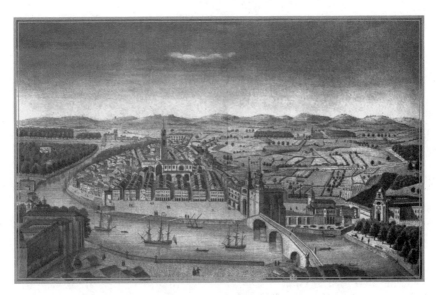

A West View of the Town of Bilbao in Vizcaya, circa 1756.

Haraden saw a large lugger* in the distance, closing in fast. Scott identified it as the *Achilles*. When he told Haraden about its size and strength, and that it "was the largest of its kind that had ever been fitted out from Great Britain," he assumed the American would try to escape. Instead, Haraden decided to stand and fight.

On its way toward the *Pickering*, the *Achilles* easily recaptured the *Golden Eagle* and placed a prize crew of its own on board. As the sky turned overcast and the night grew darker, Haraden surmised that the *Achilles* would put off its attack until morning. He retired to his cabin, ordering the watch to keep a sharp eye on the enemy ship and wake him should it approach.

As dawn broke, the *Achilles* began its advance, and a crewman rushed to alert Haraden. He "calmly rose and went up on deck, as if it had been some ordinary occasion," and surveyed his ship to make sure his men were prepared for the confrontation. Concerned about his diminished ranks, he offered a healthy reward to any of the British prisoners who would fight alongside him. Ten stepped forward.

---

* A lugger is a sailing vessel named for its rig, which uses lugsails fore-and-aft. Such sails have four corners and are suspended from a spar or yard that hangs from the masts. Luggers were typically fast ships, and were often used for smuggling.

Haraden told his newly augmented crew "that though the lugger appeared to be superior to them in force, he had no doubt that they should beat her off if they were firm and steady, and did not throw away their fire." Meanwhile, in Bilbao word quickly spread that two vessels just offshore were about to fight, and about a thousand people rushed to the water's edge to watch the spectacle.

Booming broadsides* and a staccato of musket fire filled the air, as the vessels engaged in their deadly dance, each trying valiantly to gain the upper hand. Robert Cowan, one of Haraden's crew, later remarked that the *Pickering* "looked like a longboat by the side of" the *Achilles*. He added that Haraden "fought with an energy and determination that seemed superhuman," and that while "shot flew around him" he was "as calm and steady as amidst a shower of snowflakes."

The men on the *Golden Eagle*, American and British alike, watched the pitched contest intently, knowing that their fate hung in the balance. When the British prize master asked Jonathan Carnes to describe the *Pickering*'s crew size and armaments, he didn't believe the response. How, he wondered, could such a lightly manned vessel with so few cannons put up such a spirited and effective fight against a much more powerful foe? "If you knew Captain Haraden as well as I do," Carnes replied, "you would not be surprised at this—it is just what I expected."

The battle raged for more than two hours, with no clear advantage on either side. Then, Haraden ordered his men to fill the cannons with bar shot—two iron balls or hemispheres connected by a solid rod. These projectiles, violently spinning as they flew through the air, were devastating, slashing through the *Achilles*' rigging and sails. Having had enough, the *Achilles* turned and fled, with the rebel commander close behind. But the *Achilles* was too fast despite its injuries, and Haraden soon spun about to reclaim the *Golden Eagle*. All told, one of the *Pickering*'s crew had been killed—his head sheared off by a cannonball—and another eight men were wounded. The number of British killed or maimed is unknown.

News of the American victory circulated in Bilbao. According to an eyewitness, after the *Pickering* came to anchor, Haraden and his men "could have walked a mile from the ship, stepping from boat to boat. So

---

* A broadside is the coordinated, nearly simultaneous, firing of all of the cannons on one side of a vessel, a fusillade intended to gravely damage or disable an enemy ship.

great was the admiration with which the battle and victory were witnessed that when the captain landed, he was surrounded by this vast throng of strangers, and borne in triumph into the city, where he was received with public honors and favors."

Haraden remained in Bilbao for two months, refitting the ship, taking on a new cargo, and selling the *Golden Eagle*, before heading back across the Atlantic to Salem. On the return voyage, Haraden captured three more British prizes and brought them safely into port. To honor their intrepid captain, the owners of the *Pickering* presented him with a silver tankard and two identical mugs, each engraved with his initials and an image of the ship.

During his tenure in the Massachusetts navy and as a privateer on multiple ships, Haraden took many prizes and brought back hundreds of British cannons and at least as many prisoners, if not more. He died of consumption (tuberculosis) at the age of fifty-nine, on November 23, 1803, and his obituary in the *Salem Gazette* lauded him as "one of the most able and valiant naval commanders that the war produced." Many historians

The silver tankard presented to Jonathan Haraden upon his return from Bilbao in the privateer *Pickering*. The ribbon of text beneath the image of the *Pickering* says, "The gift of the owners of the ship *Pickering*." Below that are Haraden's initials. The tankard was made by Benjamin Burt, a famous Boston silversmith. Haraden's privateer was called both the *General Pickering* and the *Pickering* during the Revolution and beyond, but *Pickering* is correct.

over the years have come to the same conclusion, with one late nineteenth-century writer claiming that Haraden's "desperate actions and wonderful triumphs, his consummate courage and severe intrepidity, entitle him to a place in history by the side of John Paul Jones," the legendary naval officer. Israel Thorndike, the first lieutenant of the *Tyrannicide*, when reflecting on the career of his former captain, gave perhaps the most succinct judgment of Captain Jonathan Haraden's maritime service during the American Revolution: "He was a perfect hero."

DESPITE THE CONTRIBUTIONS made by Haraden and thousands of other privateersmen during the Revolution, many believed then and have believed since that privateering was a sideshow in the war. Privateering has long been given short shrift in general histories of the conflict, where privateers are treated as a minor theme if they are mentioned at all. The coverage in maritime and naval histories of the Revolution is not much better, with privateering often overshadowed by the exploits of the Continental navy. As John Lehman, former secretary of the navy under President Ronald Reagan, observed, "From the beginning of the American Revolution until the end of the War of 1812, America's real naval advantage lay in its privateers. It has been said that the battles of the American Revolution were fought on land, and independence was won at sea. For this we have the enormous success of American privateers to thank even more than the Continental Navy." Yet even in the face of plenty of readily available evidence, "the official canon of naval history in both Britain and the United States virtually ignores" privateers.

The relatively small number of books that focus specifically on privateering during the Revolution do succeed in showing how it contributed to the American victory. But none of these books offers a comprehensive picture of the full extent of privateering, and just how important it actually was to the American cause. *Rebels at Sea* fills that void and demonstrates that privateering was critical to winning the war.

American privateersmen took the maritime fight to the British and made them bleed. In countless daring actions against British merchant ships and not a few warships, privateers caused British maritime insurance rates to precipitously rise, diverted critical British resources and naval assets to protecting their vessels and to attacking privateers, added to British weariness over the war, and played a starring role in bringing France into the war on the side of the United States, a key turning point in the conflict. On the domestic front, privateering brought much-needed goods and military supplies into the new nation, provided cash infusions for the war effort, boosted coastal economies through the building, outfitting, and manning of privateers, and bolstered America's confidence that it might succeed in its seemingly quixotic attempt to defeat the most powerful military force of the day.

Critics of privateering have admitted its influence but characterized that influence as largely negative, if not deleterious. These claims come mainly from those who blame privateering for siphoning valuable manpower and munitions from the Continental navy and army and for contributing to a coarsening of American morals and republican ideals by purportedly offering a means for men to place profit over patriotism. But such arguments lose much of their sting and persuasive power when considered within the actual context of the war. And whatever drawbacks came with privateering, they pale in comparison to its positive contribution to the Revolution.

The importance of privateering can only be grasped when the practice is set against the precarious nature of the war. At the outset, there were few reasons for the rebellious colonies to be confident of a good outcome. As William Moultrie, South Carolina's most famous Revolutionary War hero, would write years after the conflict, Americans were rising up against "a rich and powerful nation, with numerous fleets, and experienced admirals sailing triumphant over the ocean; with large armies and able generals in many parts of the globe: This great nation we dared to oppose, without money; without arms; without ammunition; no generals; no armies; no admirals; and no fleets; this was our situation when the contest began." Every year of the Revolution, there was cause to doubt that the colonies would be able to hold on, much less win. George Washington later reflected that the American victory in the war "was little short of a standing miracle." At many points during the Revolution, the war might have ended in American defeat had different decisions been made or different actions taken, and had various elements not been in place. Yet throughout, privateering provided a source of strength that helped the rebels persevere.

Although privateering was not the single, decisive factor in beating the British—there was no one cause—it was extremely important nonetheless.

THE EXACT NUMBER of privateers and privateersmen who operated during the Revolution is unknowable, but the figures we do have suggest that they were pivotal to the war. Records are incomplete and often duplicative—many were logged both at the congressional and state level. Further complicating any attempt to arrive at reliable figures is that contemporary accounts often applied the term "privateer" to vessels that were most certainly not privateers. As a result, many Continental navy vessels as well as state navy vessels were incorrectly labeled as privateers in newspapers, letters, and official government documents printed during or just after the Revolution. Some historians have perpetuated the error. Haraden's sloop *Tyrannicide*, which was a Massachusetts navy vessel, is frequently called a privateer in modern accounts.

The best single source of basic facts on privateering during the war is the Library of Congress's *Naval Records of the American Revolution*. It lists 1,697 armed vessels that received letters of marque from the Continental Congress and which were manned by 58,400 men and carried 14,872 cannons. Yet these numbers cannot be taken at face value. Quite a few of the listed vessels received multiple letters of marque, for different cruises in different years, and thus were double- or triple-counted; many men served on more than one privateer; and a considerable portion of the cannons saw service on more than one ship as well. Even as they are, in part, duplicative, the Library of Congress records are also incomplete: a few states, notably Massachusetts and New Hampshire, issued their own letters of marque independent of Congress, but it is not clear exactly how many of these state privateers there were. Some sources claim the number was relatively low, perhaps around one hundred, while others say that there was as many as one thousand. Although the overall number of privateers cannot be precisely known, it was large, and most likely within a few hundred of 1,697. Similarly, the number of privateersmen certainly was in the tens of thousands, and the privateers upon which they served carried many thousands of cannons. Reflecting on the sheer size of such a fleet, historian John Franklin Jameson claimed that privateering during the

Revolution "assumed such proportions as to make it . . . one of the leading American industries."

Privateers were not evenly distributed across the states. Based again on the available, imperfect data, Massachusetts launched the largest number of privateers, with approximately six hundred, followed by Pennsylvania, with around five hundred. Connecticut and Maryland each provided about two hundred. Rhode Island had nearly one hundred fifty, while Virginia and New Hampshire came in well below one hundred. There were a few North Carolina and New Jersey privateers, while South Carolina and New York, which was partially under British control from the summer of 1776 to the fall of 1783, sent out only one each. As far as is known, Georgia and Delaware didn't commission any privateers.

BEFORE PROCEEDING any further, a common misconception must be laid to rest. Many observers before, during, and since the Revolution have argued that privateersmen were virtually indistinguishable from pirates, those enemies of all mankind who pillaged any merchant vessels they came upon, often torturing victims while leaving a wake of terror on the high seas purely for personal gain. Claiming that it bears more than a passing resemblance to piratical behavior, some have called privateering "licensed" or "legalized" piracy. And in truth, given the origins of privateering, it is easy to understand why so many viewed privateering and piracy as two sides of the same coin.

The first recorded instance of privateering was sponsored by England in 1243 during the reign of Henry III. From that point of origin, the legally sanctioned practice blossomed and spread, appearing in virtually every European war of consequence through the 1700s, being employed by the English as well as the French, Dutch, and Spanish. But some countries, especially England, stretched the limits of privateering beyond what was generally deemed acceptable, helping give it a dark name.

For example, in the sixteenth century Elizabeth I issued letters of marque to her so-called sea dogs to attack her sworn enemy, the Spanish, and divest them of the riches they were violently looting from the Aztec and Incan Empires of Central and South America. This would have been in accord with the laws of privateering if England and Spain were at war, but Elizabeth often issued the letters when the two countries were nominally at peace.

One such letter of marque was given to Francis Drake before he left England on his circumnavigation of the globe in 1577. Drake attacked multiple Spanish towns and ships along the western coast of South America, amassing a fortune in silver and gold. His ship, the *Golden Hind*, returned triumphant to England, anchoring in Plymouth Harbor on September 26, 1580. While the irate Spanish king, Philip II, labeled Drake a pirate, which he undoubtedly was, the English viewed him as a privateersmen and a national hero—lending support to poet and literary critic Samuel Taylor Coleridge's trenchant observation some 250 years later that "no man is a *pirate*, unless his contemporaries agree to call him so."

Another egregious example of piratical privateering occurred during the Nine Years' War (1689–1697), known as King William's War in America, which saw most of Europe arrayed against the French. In the British colonies in North America, particularly New York and Rhode Island, governors issued letters of marque to armed ships giving them permission to attack French vessels. But the governors knew full well that these "privateers" had no intention of fighting the French, and that they instead planned to sail to the Indian Ocean and prey on ships from the Mughal Empire

Engraved portrait of Sir Francis Drake, circa 1583.

traveling between India and the Red Sea ports of Jeddah and Mocha laden with coins, textiles, and other exotic East Indian goods. These so-called Red Sea Men were nothing more than pirates who viciously plundered Mughal shipping and brought their riches back home. And it wasn't only the pirates who profited but also the governors themselves, who charged for privateering licenses and took a cut of the lucrative hauls.

Then there were privateersmen turning to piracy once a war ended. This happened after the War of the Spanish Succession (1702–1713), when suddenly out-of-work privateersmen became pirates and launched the most notorious phase of what is called the golden age of piracy, during which thousands of pirates, including Blackbeard, terrorized sea-lanes from the North Atlantic to the West Indies.

With such a history, it is no wonder that so many have viewed privateering and piracy as synonymous. The popular historian Barbara Tuchman wrote that "privateers were essentially ships with a license to rob" that engaged in the "business of maritime breaking and entering . . . equivalent to a policeman giving his kind permission to a burglar." But while there might be truth in this, particularly with respect to an earlier period of history, it does not apply to privateering during the American Revolution. By that time, laws had been better codified, government oversight of the practice was more effective, and legitimate privateersmen had less incentive to veer into piracy. As we will see, privateersmen operating during the American Revolution were not pirates, and the vast majority acted honorably, observing international law and the laws and regulations laid down by the Continental Congress during the war. The few exceptions only served to prove the rule.

THE CAST OF CHARACTERS in *Rebels at Sea* includes some of the most famous Americans of the time, and since. John Adams, Benedict Arnold, Benjamin Franklin, Elbridge Gerry, Nathanael Greene, John Hancock, Thomas Jefferson, John Paul Jones, Robert Morris, and George Washington, to name a few, all appear in significant roles. Beyond these well-known personages, there are numerous privateersmen who are central to the story. In addition to Haraden, their ranks include Offin Boardman, James Forten, David Ropes, Luke Ryan, and Andrew Sherburne.

Rebels at Sea does not focus solely on the achievements of American privateering. It also highlights when American privateersmen failed in their missions, and it details how the British viewed their scrappy seafaring opponents, and what steps they took to defeat them. Another dramatic and tragic thread of the story involves the prisons in England and the prison ships in New York's Wallabout Bay, where most of the inmates were former privateersmen. While the prisons in England were bad enough, Americans who ended up on the crowded and pestilential prison ships experienced conditions so horrific that they beggar belief.

Thousands of books have approached the Revolution from every possible angle: diplomatic history, military history, the economic incentives on each side, social relations in the colonies, the fate of loyalists, and much more. There have also been countless biographies of the many leading individuals who played critical roles in the conflict. *Rebels at Sea* places privateersmen, most of whom were not famous or even well-known individuals, at the very center of the war effort. It demonstrates that, when the United States was only a tenuous idea, they stepped forward and risked their lives to help make it a reality.

REBELS AT SEA

Massachusetts First

Marblehead's Elbridge Gerry, the man in charge of
drafting Massachusetts's seminal privateering law.

IT WAS WAR, BUT IT BEGAN AS A VERY STRANGE WAR, INITIALLY WAGED
without complete conviction. On April 19, 1775, the Battles of Lexington
and Concord shattered the increasingly tense standoff between Britain
and its American colonies. Fired by patriotic zeal, a motley assemblage
of colonial militiamen rushed to the outskirts of British-controlled Boston, laying siege to the city. Soon after, in Philadelphia, the Second Con-

tinental Congress appointed George Washington as commander in chief of the Continental army. Before he arrived in Cambridge to assume his duties, the bloody Battle of Bunker Hill had further ruptured the relationship between the colonies and Britain, making any attempt to secure a late peace appear even more improbable.

Yet despite these momentous events, and prior flashpoints including the Boston Massacre, the Boston Tea Party, and the Intolerable Acts, and notwithstanding the energizing rallying cry of "no taxation without representation," the delegates to the Continental Congress would not make a clean break with Britain. Instead of promptly announcing their independence and launching all-out war, the deeply divided delegates, who represented an equally divided populace, sent the Olive Branch Petition to King George III in early July, affirming their loyalty to the sovereign and imploring him to repeal the unjust and punitive laws that had riled the colonies so that peace could be restored. The delegates, however, knew that merely waiting for a response was not enough. The colonies were being attacked, and they needed to fight back. The petition had made that choice clear. As delegate John Adams stated, Congress's goal was to "prepare for

Boston Tea Party engraving, circa 1789. On the evening of December 16, 1773, American colonists disguised as Indians boarded the merchant ships *Dartmouth*, *Eleanor*, and *Beaver*, which contained a total of 342 chests of British East India Company tea, smashed the chests, and dumped the tea—roughly 90,000 pounds—into Boston Harbor.

a vigorous defensive war, but at the same time to keep open the door of reconciliation—to hold the sword in one hand and the olive branch in the other." The colonies would defend themselves on land and at sea. And on the seas, privateers would play a critical role, with Massachusetts leading the way.

That Massachusetts should pursue privateering was little surprise. One reason had to do with history and familiarity. In every war Britain waged in the early to mid-1700s, most notably the Seven Years' War (1756–63), it sent forth fleets of privateers to attack its enemies, with many of those privateers sailing from the American colonies. In these wars, New York and Rhode Island pursued privateering with the most eagerness and success, sending out hundreds of vessels that captured an even more impressive number of prizes, netting millions of pounds in profits. Massachusetts sent out scores of successful ventures as well. Thus in the earliest days of the American Revolution, many of the men who would be making decisions about Massachusetts's war footing were quite knowledgeable about privateering. And for their splendid education in the art and practice of privateering, the colonists had the expert tutelage of Britain to thank.

Another reason Massachusetts turned so quickly to privateering was that its residents felt aggrieved. It had been the rebellious thorn in Britain's side for many years before the revolution, with Boston serving as the locus of much of the action, earning it the appellation "the metropolis of sedition." As a result, Massachusetts had borne the brunt of the punishment when Britain lashed out at its "children" across the sea. The British believed that if the rabble-rousers in Massachusetts could be crushed any further, resistance would be squelched (a premise that proved to be woefully misguided). To that end, the Boston Port Act (effective June 1, 1774) brought a naval blockade. It was followed by the broader New England Restraining Act, also called the New England Trade and Fisheries Act (effective July 1, 1775), intended to "starve New England" by restricting the trade of its colonies to Great Britain, Ireland, and the British West Indies. The act also prohibited the colonists from fishing anywhere in the North Atlantic Ocean.

Three groups of individuals were particularly upset about these acts: the Massachusetts merchants, fishermen, and sailors whose ships were tied up to the docks as a result. Pierre-Augustin Caron de Beaumarchais, the French diplomat, spy, arms dealer, and playwright who penned *The Barber of Seville*, wrote a letter from London to King Louis XVI in Sep-

Engraving by Paul Revere entitled *A view of the town of Boston with several ships of war in the harbour*, 1774.

tember 1775 that attested to anger felt on the waterfront. Based on intelligence he had gathered, he said that "all those persons who took part in maritime commerce, which the English have brought to an end, have joined the fishermen to make war on their common persecutors [the British]; all the persons who worked in the harbors have increased the army of furious men, whose actions are all animated by a spirit of vengeance and hatred." Those "furious" Massachusetts men wanted to strike back at their oppressors and replace the earnings that had been lost. One way to do so was privateering.

A final reason Massachusetts engaged in privateering had to do with its exceptionally strong connection to the sea, and the proven willingness of its mariners to fight against tyranny and in defense of their liberty. Massachusetts was one of the most maritime-centric of all the colonies. Ports large and small up and down the coast harbored fleets of vessels devoted to all manner of fishing and commerce. Boatbuilding in the colony employed many thousands of men. Massachusetts seafarers and their vessels were the raw material needed for privateering. And those men—and their fathers and grandfathers—had already demonstrated that they were ready to defend any attempt to infringe their

This November 19, 1774, British print shows Bostonians, held captive in a cage suspended from the Liberty Tree, a stately old elm near Boston Common that was used by colonists as a rallying point for resistance against British laws and actions. The image shows the Bostonians being tormented by three British sailors. Around the tree and in the distance is military evidence of Britain's stranglehold on Boston in the wake of the Boston Port Act.

rights. Nowhere was this inclination more evident than in their resistance to impressment.

For more than one hundred years, the perpetually shorthanded Royal Navy had impressed American sailors, forcing them to serve on naval ships against their will. The navy pleaded necessity. Without such reinforcements, it would have been unable to adequately man its ships and, therefore, it would have been considerably weakened. As the self-proclaimed "lords of the ocean," the Royal Navy could not let that happen.

Massachusetts was a regular target of impressment raids, and it also had a history of violent defiance. The most famous instance occurred on April 22, 1769, when the brig *Pitt Packet* was returning to its home port of Marblehead, Massachusetts, with a load of salt from Cadiz. The British frigate HMS *Rose* stopped the *Pitt Packet* ostensibly to search for contraband but in reality to impress its crew. Four Irishmen who called Marblehead home hid in the forepeak to avoid detection but were discovered. They told the head of the press gang, Lieutenant Henry Gibson

Panton, that "they wanted nothing but their liberty," adding that "they were resolved to die, sooner than be pressed on board a man of war."* To demonstrate their seriousness, the four men armed themselves with "a fish gig,† harpoon, musket, and axe." According to John Adams, who would later defend the men in court, one of the four, Michael Corbet, spread a line of salt across the deck and told Panton, "If you step over that line, I shall consider it as a proof that you are determined to impress me, and by the eternal God of Heaven, you are [a] dead man." Unmoved by the threat, Panton replied, "Aye! My lad . . . I have seen many a brave fellow before now." Then he took his snuffbox out of his pocket, placed a pinch in his nostril, and boldly stepped forward across the line, attempting to seize Corbet. True to his word, Corbet drove his harpoon into Panton's neck, severing his jugular vein and carotid artery. A short fight ensued, ending with the four Irishmen taken prisoner, one of whom was severely injured. In the meantime, Panton bled out in the cabin of the *Pitt Packet*.

Adams's recollection of the events was recorded many years later and differs somewhat from some of the testimony at the trial. In that telling, there was an angry back-and-forth, and the Irishmen did threaten Panton with death should he try to impress them. But there was no line of salt, and Panton did not stride into danger. Instead, Panton sat on a pile of salt patiently trying to convince the Irishmen to surrender, noting that they were greatly outnumbered, and only after his repeated remonstrances failed did Panton's men attempt to break down the bulkhead and haul the Irishmen out. During the attempt, shots were fired, and Corbet thrust the harpoon home.

Regardless of the truth, the four Irishmen were tried in the court of the vice admiralty in Boston for murder and piracy. Adams believed that "in law, truth, and conscience, the commander of the *Rose* frigate ought to have been prosecuted for piracy and murder on the high seas, in illegally sending a pressgang to enslave freemen." But he knew that wouldn't be a winning argument, so he took a different tack, getting the charges dropped by proving that the men had acted in self-defense and their actions constituted justifiable homicide. Reflecting on the *Pitt Packet* affair many years

---

* In the interest of readability, lower- and upper-casing and spelling have been modernized throughout in all quotes.

† A multipronged spear used in fishing.

later, Adams said that it "contributed largely to render the sovereignty of parliament odious, detestable, and horrible to the people."

One of the most dramatic examples of mariners defending themselves against what they perceived as British overreach occurred in June 1775 in Maine, which was part of Massachusetts at the time. On June 2, the armed British schooner *Margaretta*, with a crew of about forty men, accompanied by two smaller sloops, the *Unity* and the *Polly*, sailed into the harbor of the sparsely populated town of Machias. They were there to obtain timber for the British military and for civilians in Boston, who were fast running out of firewood, a necessity for baking bread and for heating water to wash clothes and boil salted beef to make it palatable.

The voyage was organized by Tory merchant Ichabod Jones, who owned the sloops. He had an agreement with General Thomas Gage, commander in chief of the British forces in Boston, to sell wood to the British after trading barrels of flour and pork for it in Machias. The people of Machias had long supplied wood to Boston, but these were different times. It was just a few months after the Battles of Lexington and Concord, and even though the locals were low on food owing to a recent drought and therefore should have been eager to trade, Jones thought there might be trouble. So, Gage had sent the *Margaretta* to make a show of force and ensure that the transaction went smoothly.

Engraving of John Adams, circa 1784, by John Norman.

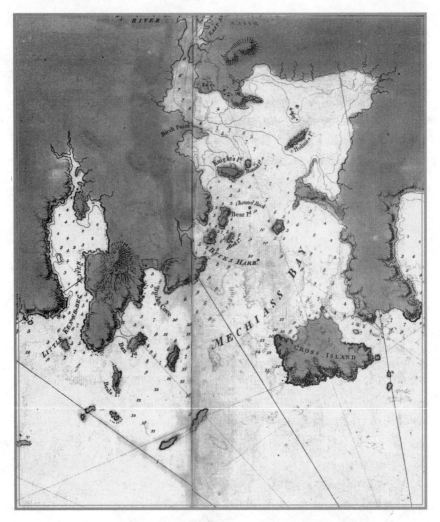

Detail of map of the coast of Maine
showing Machias Bay, circa 1776.

The patriotic inhabitants of Machias were indeed irate over the recent clashes and extremely reluctant to aid the enemy. Their hunger, however, was very real. After vigorously debating their options for a few days, they relented. A majority of the town agreed to terms laid out by Jones, and the exchanges began. However, Jones made a major miscalculation. Placing too much faith in the agreement and in the *Margaretta*'s cannons to keep colonial tempers in check, he offloaded the food and imperiously and foolishly announced that it would only be given to those who had voted in favor of his stipulations.

Those who had voted no were furious and quickly armed themselves, "determined to take Capt. Jones, if possible, and put a final stop to his supplying the King's troops with anything." On Sunday, June 11, scores of Americans from Machias and surrounding settlements rushed a church in which Jones, the *Margaretta*'s commander, James Moore, and some of his officers were attending services. Hearing the advancing mob, Moore and his men jumped to their feet. When the attackers burst through the church door, the British sailors leapt out the windows and ran toward the harbor. They made it to the *Margaretta* just as the Americans were about to close in. Jones, for his part, had run into the woods.

Over the course of the next day, the rebels, valiantly led by Jeremiah O'Brien and Benjamin Foster, commandeered the two sloops and a schooner and fiercely attacked the *Margaretta* twice. Each time, before the shooting began, the Americans hailed Moore, urging him to surrender and be treated well or to fight and die. And each time, Moore refused to give in.

During the second assault, the Americans, who greatly outnumbered the British, swarmed onto the *Margaretta*, firing muskets and swinging pitchforks and axes. Moore was shot in the belly and the chest, and five of his men were wounded before the British surrendered. The Americans suffered one dead and six wounded (one of whom later died). When an American asked Moore why he hadn't struck his colors* either of the times they hailed him, he said "he preferred death before yielding to such a set of villains." Moore lingered for another day before succumbing to his wounds. As for Jones, he finally emerged from the woods, was arrested, and was sent to Cambridge to be put on trial as an enemy of the province. Found guilty, he was briefly jailed, and his property in Machias was seized.

James Fenimore Cooper, in an early naval history of the United States, called the Machias affair "the Lexington of the sea, for like that celebrated land conflict, it was a rising of the people against a regular force, was characterized by a long chase, a bloody struggle, and a triumph." Those who battled the *Margaretta* were not privateersmen, but they demonstrated the

---

* When a ship lowers its flag, indicating that it has surrendered.

privateering spirit, and offered a clarion signal that Massachusetts men and, more broadly, Americans were ready and able to fight at sea.

THE FIRST TALK OF privateering in Massachusetts began in the summer of 1775. As early as July 5, Thomas Jefferson expressed delight at what he had heard was underway in Massachusetts and other nearby colonies. "The New Englanders," he wrote to his friend and physician George Gilmer, "are fitting out privateers, with which they expect to be able to scour the seas and bays of everything below ships of war; and may probably go to the European coasts, to distress the British trade there. The enterprising genius and intrepidity of these people are amazing."

Jefferson's "privateers" were still prospective, since at this early date no colony was distributing letters of marque. Nevertheless, these unofficial privateers were having an impact. On September 1, Vice Admiral Samuel Graves, British commander in chief of his nation's North American station, which was headquartered in Boston, wrote that he was "impatient . . . to scourge the inhabitants of" the seaport towns that had harbored privateers. They had done "so much mischief to" British transports and tenders, and "were continually popping in and out as soon as a merchant ship appeared off" the coast.

Throughout the summer, an increasing number of individuals in Massachusetts pleaded with the colony's legislature, the General Court, to authorize privateering. On July 19, Edward Emerson requested that the court allow him to fix up a "schooner for a privateer . . . enlist thirty men to serve on board . . . and use and improve said vessel for the defense of the sea coasts in the eastern part" of the colony. A few weeks later, Agreen Crabtree, a resident of Hancock, Maine, informed the court that he had already outfitted his schooner, the *Hannah and Molly*, "as a privateer to distress the enemies of the United Colonies," and had captured two British vessels that were taking supplies to British forces in Boston. To secure retrospective legitimacy for his actions, Crabtree asked that the court give him a letter of marque. At the end of August, a committee was established to deliberate over these requests, and then after another month had passed, yet another committee was tasked with considering "the expediency of fitting out a number of armed vessels."

The appointment of multiple committees that debated but recommended no action rankled many. William Tudor, judge advocate of the Continental army and a former clerk in John Adams's law office, wrote to his old boss on September 30, expressing exasperation at the court's dilatory stance. He complained that just a week earlier, British naval forces in Boston Harbor had "carried eleven sail of [colonial] vessels into Boston, where after the formality of a trial in admiralty court, they are confiscated, to the use of Graves and his harpies. Notwithstanding these continual depredations, our [provincial] assembly will not be prevailed upon to fit out privateers. The delicacy is absurd surely."

Tudor did not have to wait much longer. On October 9 the court appointed a committee, not to debate the need for privateers but rather to prepare a bill that would put Massachusetts into the privateering business. The person in charge of the bill-drafting committee was Elbridge Gerry.

BORN AND RAISED in Marblehead, one of America's foremost fishing communities, Gerry was part of a family that owned a fleet of ships engaged in coastal and transatlantic trade. He was thus keenly aware of the devastating impact of the British blockade on the economy of Massachusetts. On the same day the committee was formed, he wrote about his new task to Samuel Adams, second cousin of John Adams and one of the most outspoken and radical of revolutionaries. "My attention is directed to the fitting out of privateers, which I hope will make them swarm here. Is it not time to encourage individuals to exert themselves this way?"

The resulting bill—An Act & Resolve for Encouraging the Fixing out of Armed Vessels, to Defend the Sea Coast of America, and for Erecting a Court to Try and Condemn All Vessels, That Shall Be Found Infesting the Same—was passed by the General Court on November 1. Massachusetts officials understood its significance: International law dictated that only a sovereign nation could grant letters of marque. If Massachusetts authorized privateers, that would necessarily mean that the colony was assuming sovereign status. But Massachusetts, like the other colonies, was not yet ready to officially declare independence, and Gerry was given the delicate task of writing the preamble to the bill, in which he had to justify the law without going too far.

Gerry engaged in the same fiction that many, though certainly not all, colonial officials adopted: that America's complaint was with Parlia-

Engraving of King George III by Robert Pollard, 1778.

ment and, more specifically, the administration of Prime Minister Lord North, who was driving Britain toward war—and not with the British people or with King George, who was still viewed in the colonies as a benevolent ruler who desired reconciliation. Gerry's preamble stated that it was North's majority in Parliament, "being divested of justice and humanity," that had "been endeavoring, through a series of years," to establish "a system of despotism over the American colonies" through "their venal and corrupt measures." As a result, the administration had become "a political engine of slavery." The preamble also argued that since the commencement of hostilities, the Royal Navy, at Parliament's direction, had been "infesting the sea coasts [of the colonies] with armed vessels, and daily endeavoring to distress the inhabitants, by burning their towns, and destroying their dwellings . . . plundering livestock, and making captures of provision and other vessels, being the property of said inhabitants." Furthermore, Gerry claimed that the Massachusetts Charter compelled the colony to defend itself against external enemies, the enemy in this case being Parliament itself. In relying on the charter for guidance, Gerry conveniently ignored the fact that the Massachusetts

Prime Minister Lord North, circa 1780.

Government Act, one of the Intolerable Acts, had abrogated the charter in 1774.

As Gerry later explained, "I grounded [the preamble] on the royal charter of the province, which authorized us to levy war against the common enemy of both countries. Such we considered the British nation, with the ships of war and armies employed against us; and we, accordingly, as loyal subjects, used all the power given us by the charter to capture and destroy them." In other words, Massachusetts was fighting on behalf of itself *and* Great Britain *against* Parliament. It was a highly creative, though dubious, argument. When the act was printed in a London magazine, it was labeled a "political curiosity."

It was also effective. The Massachusetts act granted letters of marque to individuals to fit out and operate privateers at their own expense. They were limited to attacking British vessels that assaulted American ships or invaded any part of America, or that were supplying the British fleet or army. To guarantee that privateers would stay within the law, shipowners were required to post a $5,000 bond (later $4,000), which would be forfeited if the privateer violated the restrictions. Finally, the law estab-

lished vice admiralty courts at various ports throughout the colony that
would have the responsibility of determining whether vessels brought in
by privateers were valid prizes. If a prize were deemed valid, the judge
would condemn the vessel and cargo and arrange for them to be sold at a
public auction. After deducting the costs of the trial and auction, the judge
handed over the rest of the proceeds to the privateer's owners to distrib-
ute according to the arrangement they had agreed upon among themselves
and the vessel's officers and crew.

America's first official privateer force was authorized, and nobody was
happier than John Adams. Four days after the November 1 law passed,
Adams wrote to James Warren, speaker of the House of Representatives
of the Massachusetts General Court: "I want to know what is become of
the whalemen, codfishers and other seamen belonging to our province,
and what number of them you imagine might be enlisted into the service
of the continent, or of the province, for private adventures, in case a taste
of privateering and maritime warfare should prevail." Warren responded
enthusiastically: "What numbers might be enlisted in that service I can't
readily compute, but I have no difficulty in supposing, that at least three
battalions might be raised in this colony. The taste for it runs high here."

The first letter of marque was granted on December 7, when the *Boston
Revenge* officially became a privateer. Others followed, although initially
not in the overwhelming numbers that Warren had predicted, no doubt
because cold weather was fast approaching and because it took time for
merchants to finance and outfit vessels. Through early 1776, perhaps a
dozen Massachusetts privateers went out. Among them was the *Washington*, a schooner out of Newburyport, which received its commission just a
few days after the *Boston Revenge*.

THE *WASHINGTON* WAS a relatively small privateer of forty tons, crewed
by forty men, and armed with nine cannons and ten smaller swivel guns.
Its captain was twenty-eight-year-old Offin Boardman, born and bred in
the waterside part of Newbury (which became Newburyport in 1764), and
a descendant of a long line of mariners. The *Washington* left port in late
December for a cruise along the coast. It was a dull cruise, until January 15.

That morning, off Plum Island, just a few miles from central Newburyport, Boardman spied a vessel in the distance. After a short chase,

the brig *Sukey* surrendered without a shot being fired and was taken into Newburyport, which sits on the banks of the Merrimack River. Ten weeks out of Cork, Ireland, the *Sukey* was laden with supplies for British troops, including 18,000 pounds of the "best beef," 18,000 pounds of butter, and 700 gallons of claret.

Later that day, a ship flying British colors appeared just beyond the bar at the mouth of the river, tacking back and forth. Some men in town surmised that the vessel must have been lost and was trying to get its bearings. A plan was soon devised, and seventeen men, led by Boardman, all hiding weapons under their coats, piled into three whaleboats and began rowing toward the mystery vessel. Upon arrival, Boardman hailed the ship, inquiring where it came from and where it was heading. It was the *Friends*, sailing from London to Boston, came the reply from Captain Archibald Bowie. He asked what land was nearby and where the whaleboats had come from. Boardman responded, "We are from Boston, do you want a pilot?"*

Bowie, eager for the assistance, and seemingly unconcerned about the large number of men in the whaleboats, assented and welcomed Boardman onto the ship. The two men shook hands and shared recent news about London and Boston, while the Americans on the whaleboats casually ascended the gangway and a few came onto the main deck. Satisfied that all was in place, Boardmen abandoned the ruse and demanded that Bowie strike his colors immediately. Thunderstruck, Bowie complied.

Like the *Sukey*, the *Friends* was brought into Newburyport. It represented another impressive haul. Its cargo, destined for British forces in Boston, included roughly 160,000 pounds of coal, 12,000 gallons of beer, and twenty-three live hogs. The *Friends* had another surprise as well: military documents hidden in a secret compartment, which, along with a British lieutenant on board, were promptly turned over to George Washington at his headquarters in Cambridge.

NOT ONLY WAS Massachusetts the first colony to officially sanction and promote privateering, its actions also prompted other colonies to take

---

* A master mariner who guides vessels through congested waters and keeps them away from waterborne hazards.

similar ones. As early as December 1775, Joseph Ward, aide-de-camp to his distant cousin Major General Artemis Ward, predicted that the privateering impulse would spread beyond Massachusetts. "The good success of our privateers . . . is very encouraging," Joseph Ward wrote to John Adams, "and I hope it will stimulate the seafaring gentlemen to greater exertions in that way." In due course, where Massachusetts went, New Hampshire and Rhode Island soon followed, enacting their own privateering legislation in January and early March 1776, respectively.

The importance of the Massachusetts act of November 1, 1775, in unleashing privateering in the colonies became even clearer in hindsight. Some forty years later, Adams would write that the passage of the privateering act "is one of the most important documents in history. The declaration of independence is a *brimborion** in comparison with it." But privateers were hardly the only American vessels looking to capture British ships. Colonial (later state) navies were also on the hunt.

---

* Archaic French word meaning a trifle or thing of little value.

Expanding the Fight at Sea

Burning of the *Gaspee*, by
Howard Pyle, circa 1901.

I N AN EFFORT TO BOLSTER COLONIAL DEFENSES, ON JULY 18, 1775, the Continental Congress recommended that each colony fund and send out vessels to protect "their harbors and navigation on their sea coasts, against all unlawful invasions, attacks, and depredations, from [British] cutters and ships of war." Rhode Island, for its part, had already established its own state navy, an action propelled by a deep-seated anger at British imperiousness along the coast. That anger had roots in numerous prior events but primarily in what was known as the *Gaspee* affair and its aftermath.

Rhode Island had a long history of smuggling to avoid paying customs duties. The British government, furious about the practice, sent multiple armed ships to the colony in the years leading up to the Revolution to enforce the Navigation Acts. These acts required European goods coming into the colonies to be transported on English ships manned predominantly by Englishmen. Further, the goods had to be transshipped through England, where steep customs duties had to be paid.

One such armed ship was the *Gaspee*, a schooner that arrived in the spring of 1772. The *Gaspee*'s commander, William Dudingston, whom the *Providence Gazette* characterized as "haughty, insolent, and intolerable," took his job quite seriously, to the indignation of colonial merchants and sailors who didn't like having their ships aggressively searched and called to account. The situation grew increasingly tense until, on June 9, Rhode Islanders decided that they had had enough.

Early that day, the packet ship *Hannah*, captained by Thomas Lindsey, left Newport for a short run to Providence, with the *Gaspee* in hot pursuit. Lindsey had no interest in being questioned about his cargo, so instead of heaving to and waiting for Dudingston to board, he continued sailing up Narragansett Bay and into the mouth of the Providence River. As the river narrowed and became shallower, the *Gaspee* shadowed *Hannah*'s every move. Lindsey, who was familiar with the river's hazards, expertly maneuvered around Namquid Point, knowing that a sand spit would be just under the surface when the tide ebbed. Dudingston was unaware of this danger, and the *Gaspee* shuddered to a stop, grounded in the sand.

The *Hannah* docked at Providence's bustling wharves as the sun was setting. Lindsey immediately informed John Brown, one of the city's leading citizens and foremost merchants, what had happened, and told him that the *Gaspee* would likely be unable to get off the spit for many hours. Brown, whose ships had often been boarded by Dudingston and his men, seized on the "opportunity offered of putting an end to the trouble and vexation she [the *Gaspee*] daily caused."

Brown called for eight longboats to be tied up at a wharf right across from Sabin's Tavern, a popular Providence inn. He also sent a boy through the streets, beating a drum, shouting that the *Gaspee* was run aground, and inviting any "persons who felt a disposition to go and destroy that troublesome vessel" to assemble at the tavern and to bring weapons. In short order, dozens of men piled into the boats and began rowing down-river. To make the approach as stealthy as possible, the boats' wooden oar-locks were wrapped in cloth so as to muffle the sound of the oars rubbing against them. Leading the operation was thirty-nine-year-old Abraham Whipple, who had gained fame as a captain of more than one highly suc-cessful privateer in the Seven Years' War.

When the flotilla was within about sixty yards of the *Gaspee*, a Brit-ish sentinel shouted, "Who comes there?" Receiving no answer, he hailed again but still was met with silence. At that point, Dudingston, who had been below sleeping, came rushing up to the main deck in his nightshirt, clutching a sword and pistol. He called out twice before Whipple replied, "I am the sheriff of the county of Kent—I have got a warrant to apprehend you, so surrender."

No sooner had Dudingston declined this request than Whipple yelled, "Men, spring to your oars," and the longboats surged ahead toward the *Gaspee*'s bow. Most of the Rhode Islanders began climbing ropes hanging down from the ship; reaching the top, they jumped over the rails, bran-dishing guns, staves, and stones. Dudingston rallied his men to repel the attackers, wildly slashing at them as they attempted to board.

On one of the longboats, nineteen-year-old Ephraim Bowen cradled a loaded gun and watched the action. Joseph Bucklin, on the same boat, said to him, "Ephe, reach me your gun, and I can kill that fellow," refer-ring to Dudingston. Bucklin steadied himself and fired. Dudingston fell to the deck, whereupon Bucklin yelled, "I have killed the rascal!" But Dud-ingston was not dead. The bullet went through his left arm and groin, and as he lay bleeding, seeing so many of his crew already knocked down or subdued, he surrendered. Dudingston would survive his wounds. He and all of his men were taken off the *Gaspee*, which was promptly burned to the waterline.

Enraged British authorities wanted desperately to punish those responsible, but Rhode Islanders refused to inform on their countrymen, and all legal efforts to investigate the matter came to nothing. Two years later, in November 1774, the HMS *Rose*, a far more powerful ship than the *Gaspee*, was stationed in Rhode Island to enforce the Navigation Acts. The *Rose's* captain, James Wallace, quickly won the enmity of Rhode Islanders by effectively shutting down their maritime trade.

It was in response to the arrival of the *Rose* that Rhode Island launched its own navy in mid-June 1775, fitting out two small sloops, the *Katy* and the *Washington*. Although they were no match for the *Rose*, they did set a precedent. Within the coming year, eleven of the thirteen colonies established navies (Delaware and New Jersey being the lone holdouts). Most of these fleets were fairly small, and at no time during the Revolution were

The Massachusetts state navy's twenty-gun frigate *Protector* battling the British letter of marque *Admiral Duff* off Newfoundland on June 9, 1780. The action lasted about one and a half hours, at which point the fire on the *Admiral Duff*, which had first consumed some sails, rapidly spread through the ship, ultimately reaching the powder magazine. The entire stern of the ship was blown apart, releasing all its valuable cargo into the sea. While the *Admiral Duff* sank, the Americans were able to save fifty-five British sailors.

there more than forty state naval vessels in total. They generally protected the coast and coastal shipping, but in some instances they went much farther afield, bringing home valuable British prizes.

THE STATE NAVIES WERE an example of a broader trend in the maritime war. While today the United States, like other nations, has a single, unified navy, during the Revolution the war at sea was waged by numerous types of vessels under the command of different officers. In 1775, in fact, George Washington himself was pursuing his own maritime ambitions.

Washington's entire military career up until the outbreak of the Revolution had taken place on land. His only maritime experience came in late 1751, when he visited Barbados, accompanying his elder half brother Lawrence, who had hoped that the island's salubrious weather would lessen the effects of tuberculosis.* Because of Washington's lack of experience, some historians have assumed that Washington was utterly ignorant of maritime affairs, but that was not the case. As a rich landowner and farmer whose fortune depended largely upon maritime trade, he grasped the importance of the oceans and clearly understood the basics of naval power. Still, upon taking command of the Continental army on July 5, 1775, Washington had no interest in engaging the British on the water. He was focused on creating an effective land fighting force out of a ragtag collection of militias so dreadfully low on gunpowder that each soldier only had enough to fire his musket nine times.

In early August, when the Massachusetts General Court approached him with a plan to create a state navy, Washington dismissed it. He wrote to the court: "As to the furnishing vessels of force, you, gentlemen, will anticipate me, in pointing out our weakness and the enemy's strength at sea. There would be great danger, that, with the best preparations we could make, they would fall an easy prey" to the British. Washington also told the court that because his army had so little gunpowder, he couldn't spare any for maritime adventures.

Before long, however, Washington's attitude on the viability of naval

---

* George contracted smallpox on the island and then quickly recovered before his return voyage, without Lawrence, early the following year. As for Lawrence, he continued to deteriorate, and died in July 1752, just a short time after returning to Virginia.

operations shifted. It is not exactly clear what changed his mind, but among the factors was surely an increase in powder on hand, the continued stalemate on land, and the advice of some of his officers who were more sanguine about American prospects in naval warfare.

The question was by what authority he could begin naval operations. While Congress had given Washington broad powers as commander in chief of the Continental army, his instructions said nothing about maritime warfare. He took that omission as an opportunity. Without asking for permission from Congress or even informing it of his actions, he ordered that Colonel John Glover's Marblehead schooner *Hannah* be fitted out as an armed vessel under the authority of the Continental army. On September 7, the *Hannah* set sail.* Washington had launched his own navy.

In his instructions to the *Hannah*'s captain, Marbleheader Nicholson Broughton, Washington told him to seek out and seize vessels with soldiers, munitions, and provisions intended for the British army. The *Hannah*'s crew was in Continental employ and received their army pay in addition to splitting one-third of the value of any cargo they took, with the exception of any military or naval stores, which were to be reserved for the army.

Washington finally informed Congress about his bold action in early October. By that time he was already in the process of adding two more vessels to his infant fleet. Congress blessed his actions, because it saw the obvious value in harassing and capturing British supply ships, even though it was then exploring the possibility of establishing a navy itself.

---

* The *Hannah* inaugurated an ongoing argument about which town or city can claim to be the "birthplace of the American navy." Two of the main contenders are Marblehead and Beverly. The *Hannah* was owned and manned by Marbleheaders, giving that town standing. However, the *Hannah* was outfitted for its mission in and sailed from Beverly, which is the basis for its claim to the title. But Providence also has a claim, given its launch of the *Katy* and the *Washington*, and so too does Machias, Maine, from which Jeremiah O'Brien and Benjamin Foster left to battle the *Margaretta*. But as will become clear later on in this book, Philadelphia has, arguably, the strongest claim, because that is where the Continental Congress was when it decided to officially launch the first phase of the true "Continental navy," on October 13, 1775. This debate won't be settled here, because there really is no way to settle it once and for all, since historians use different criteria to support their preferred candidate. So the best thing is for all of these locales to be justifiably proud of their contributions to the revolutionary cause, regardless of whether any of them is in fact "*the*" birthplace."

Independent of Congress's actions on that front, Washington continued to enlarge his fleet over the next six months, ultimately commissioning eight vessels. Those ships have generated a great deal of confusion among historians. Washington almost always referred to them as privateers, as did his contemporaries. Many historians have followed suit. But Washington's squadron were not privateers. Even though the men on board the ships received a cut of the prize money, the ships were not issued letters of marque and the men were employed by the army.

Washington's little navy captured fifty-five prizes between 1775 and 1777, seventeen of which were recaptured by the British, leaving a net gain of thirty-eight. Many were relatively inconsequential, but a few were of great importance. Foremost among those were the *Nancy* and the *Hope*.

THE *LEE*, A VESSEL in Washington's fleet, was cruising the coast of Massachusetts in late November 1775 when its captain, John Manley, spied a large brig heading toward Boston Harbor. While Manley was deciding whether or not this was a potential prize, the brig laid its sails aback and signaled for a pilot to take it into port. Manley couldn't have been happier with this action, and he dispatched eight of his best men, hiding arms under their coats, to the brig to lend a hand.

The 250-ton *Nancy* had been battling rough weather for weeks, trying desperately to get into port. Captain Robert Hunter warmly welcomed Manley's men, believing that they were his salvation. But as soon as they boarded, they drew their cutlasses and pistols. The brig was theirs, without a shot having been fired. In the *Nancy*'s hold was a Midas treasure's worth of munitions. There were 2,000 muskets with bayonets, 53 kegs of flints for the muskets' firing mechanisms, 7,000 cannonballs of varying poundage, 30 tons of shot, 2,000 cartridge boxes with belts, and a great variety of other military stores. The item that received the most attention was a thirteen-inch brass cohorn, or mortar—an artillery piece that fires explosive shells—which "was pronounced to be the noblest piece of ordnance ever landed in America."

Manley took the *Nancy* into Gloucester, where all the munitions were unloaded and transported to army headquarters in Cambridge. Washington was thrilled by the capture, calling the event an "instance of divine favor; for nothing, surely, ever came more apropos." Everyone under his command was equally moved. Muster-Master General Stephen Moylan wrote, "Such universal joy ran through the whole camp as if each grasped victory in his hand."

Throughout his career in Washington's navy, Manley captured numerous other prizes and became one of the first heroes of the Revolution. In 1776, "Manley, a Favorite New Song" trumpeted his success; it was addressed to "JOLLY TARS [sailors] who are fighting for the RIGHTS and LIBERTIES of AMERICA." Two of its stanzas follow; they perpetuate the mistaken assumption that Manley was a privateersman and emphasize how important money was in luring men to sign up for the naval war.

> *BRAVE MANLEY he is stout, and his Men have proved true,*
> *By taking of those English ships, he makes their Jacks to rue;*
> *To our Ports he sends their Ships and Men, let's give a hearty*
> *   Cheer*
> *To Him and all those valiant Souls who go in Privateers.*
> *And a Privateering we will go, my boys, my Boys,*
> *And a Privateering we will go.*

> . . .

> *I pray you Landsmen enter, you'll find such charming fun,*
> *When to our ports by dozens their largest ships they come;*
> *Then make your fortunes now, my lads, before it is too late,*
> *Defend, defend, I say defend an INDEPENDENT STATE.*
> *And a Privateering we will go, my boys, my Boys,*
> *And a Privateering we will go.*

About five months after Manley seized the *Nancy*, Marblehead's James Mugford Jr. achieved another triumph for Washington's navy. By this time, the siege of Boston was over. British troops and the Royal Navy, finding themselves in an indefensible position after the sudden appearance of patriot cannons on Dorchester Heights, retreated and sailed to Halifax, Nova Scotia, on March 17—a date still celebrated by Bostonians as Evacuation Day. A few warships, however, remained in the vicinity of the Boston

Woodcut of John Manley that accompanied "Manley, a Favorite New Song," circa 1776. Manley did in fact captain privateers later in the Revolution. One of those, the *Jason*, out of Boston, was captured by the British frigate *Surprise* on September 30, 1779. In the battle's aftermath, Joshua Davis, a crewman on the *Jason*, "went on deck, and found the ship reeling one way and the other. The man at the wheel was killed, and no one to take the helm. The rigging, sails, yards, &c. were spread all over the deck—the wounded men were carried to the cockpit; the dead men lying on deck, and no one to throw them overboard." Eighteen on the *Jason* were killed and twelve wounded, while the *Surprise* had seven dead.

Lighthouse, at the mouth of the harbor, to warn other ships coming from Britain that the army had departed.

The ordnance ship *Hope* left from Cork, Ireland, on April 10, 1776, heading for Boston unaware that the British no longer controlled the city. In heavy fog and rough weather, the *Hope* became separated from the convoy it had been traveling with and, alone at sea, continued on its original course right into Mugford's path.

On Friday, May 17, Mugford, captain of the schooner *Franklin*, saw the heavily laden *Hope* laboring in swells about twenty-four miles east of the Boston Lighthouse. He shadowed the *Hope* until both were almost at the

James Mugford Jr. mez-
zotint, probably by Samuel
Blyth, circa 1780.

lighthouse. If he was going to act, he had to do it now, since His Majesty's warships *Renown* and *Experiment* were in sight, just within the harbor's mouth though unable to sail out to aid the *Hope* due to strong easterly winds.

The *Franklin* closed in quickly and grappled onto the *Hope*'s stern. Mugford and his men rushed onto the deck, cannons at the ready. The captain of the *Hope* and his crew of eighteen surrendered without firing a shot. Mugford sailed the *Hope* into the harbor through a shallow channel well out of range of the *Renown*'s and the *Experiment*'s cannons. But the tide was ebbing and the ship grounded in the mud in Pulling Point Gut* close to shore. Word spread along the coast that a wonderful prize had been taken, rivaling the *Nancy*. On board were 1,000 carbines, 10,000 sand bags, and, most importantly, 1,500 barrels of precious gunpowder.

When John Glover learned of the capture, he raced with his men from Marblehead to Boston to offload most of the gunpowder, using small boats to ferry the barrels ashore. He then arranged for guards to watch the ship overnight lest the British try to reclaim it. On Saturday, when the *Hope* floated free, it was brought to Boston and anchored safely near the wharf.

---

* The town of Winthrop, adjoining Boston, used to be called Pulling Point and Pulling Point Gut, and later Shirley Gut; it is gone, filled in by the causeway to the Deer Island Wastewater Treatment Plant.

Late the following day, Mugford, in the company of the privateer *Lady Washington*, attempted to sail out of the harbor, but the *Franklin* grounded and the *Lady Washington* anchored nearby. Mugford expected the British to attack, and they did, the *Renown* and *Experiment* sending five boats filled with armed soldiers and marines. Cannon and musket fire rained down on the British, but three of the boats managed to pull alongside the *Franklin*, while the other two were kept at bay by the *Lady Washington*. Mugford and his men fought valiantly as the British attempted to climb aboard. According to one account, "The brave Captain Mugford making a blow at the people in the boats with a cutlass, received a wound in the breast, on which he called his lieutenant, and said, 'I am a dead man; don't give up the vessel;* you will be able to beat them' . . . and then expired in a few minutes."

The battle lasted about a half hour before the British retreated, with one British longboat capsized and seven men killed. On the American side, only one other man besides Mugford lost his life. A few days later, the *New-England Chronicle*, commenting on Mugford's burial in Marblehead, wrote that he had "left this honor to embalm his memory, that he made as brave and vigorous a stand in defense of American Liberty as any among the living can boast of."

WASHINGTON'S NAVY WAS more of an ad hoc creation than a true Continental navy. Congress had first considered the possibility of a Continental navy over the summer of 1775, but rather than move ahead, it had decided to urge the colonies to send out armed vessels themselves. Yet the calculus soon changed. The Royal Navy had continued harassing and seizing colonial vessels, the British army's grip on Boston showed no sign of loosening, and any hope of reconciliation with the mother country was receding.

Two other developments contributed to the momentum for a Continental navy: a request from Rhode Island and a delivery from one John Barry. Although Rhode Island's new, two-vessel navy managed to capture the HMS *Rose*'s tender, it didn't stand a chance against the warship itself,

---

* During the War of 1812, Captain James Lawrence of the United States Navy, in an engagement between his ship, *Chesapeake*, and the HMS *Shannon*, found himself on the losing side. Just before dying from a sharpshooter's bullet, his last command to his crew was reportedly, "Don't give up the ship." It appears that Mugford beat him to the rhetorical punch, although "ship" does sound better than "vessel." The phrase "Don't give up the ship" later became the unofficial motto of the navy.

which was blockading Narragansett Bay, sending the local economy into free fall. On August 26 the Rhode Island General Assembly resolved "that the building and equipping an American fleet, as soon as possible, would greatly and essentially conduce to the preservation of the lives, liberty and property of the good people of these colonies." The assembly instructed its delegates "to use their whole influence" to convince Congress to build "at Continental expense a fleet of sufficient force, for the protection" of the colonies and to "annoy our enemies." The Rhode Island delegates waited until October 3 to raise the issue in Congress, and it was quickly tabled and scheduled for later debate. But then Barry, captain of the merchant-man *Black Prince*, sailed into Philadelphia with valuable intelligence.

On October 5, Barry delivered to Congress letters from London that told of two British brigs sailing from London to Quebec with military sup-plies and no convoy to protect them. Congress appointed a committee to decide what to do. The committee reported back at lightning speed the same day recommending that Washington ask the Massachusetts General Court for two armed vessels to capture the British brigs so that the army could secure the desperately needed munitions. Committee member John Adams noted that the opposition to the recommended action was "very loud and vehement," arguing that sending out armed ships against Britain was "the most wild, visionary, mad project that ever had been imagined. It was an infant, taking a mad bull by his horns."

The opposition had a point. It was a bold move for the rebellious Ameri-cans to even consider confronting the Royal Navy on the open sea. As James Thomson's 1736 poem *Liberty* proclaimed, "The winds and seas are Brit-ain's wide domain; and not a sail, but by permission, spreads." The British *Seaman's Vade-Mecum*, published in 1744, stated with considerable justi-fication "that the monarchs of Great Britain have a peculiar and sovereign authority upon the ocean." Nothing had changed by the outbreak of the Revolution. With 270 warships, 131 of which were ships of the line carrying 60 or more cannons apiece, the British could back up their arrogance. Even though many of those warships were not in the best condition due to neglect since the end of the Seven Years' War—quite a few were unfit for duty—it was an accepted truth that there was no naval force in the world that could take on Britain. Certainly, most observers believed, the upstart Americans with no naval force at all at the war's beginning didn't stand a chance.

Despite the serious opposition to the committee's proposal, Congress passed a resolution adopting its recommendations, adding that any commissioned vessels would be "on the continental risk and pay," and that their crews would be entitled to one-half of the value of any prizes taken. In the end, the expedition to capture the British brigs came up empty, but it did have the effect of prompting Congress to think more seriously about establishing a navy. The day after the resolution passed, the same committee came out with another report, this one encouraging Congress to outfit two armed vessels to prowl the eastern Atlantic to capture any ships supplying British forces in Boston. This, plus Rhode Island's resolution asking Congress to build an "American fleet," ignited a more heated debate over the need for a Continental navy.

Proponents said it was high time that Congress establish a navy, while the opposition continued to think it was an unwise if not insane notion. Samuel Chase, a delegate from Maryland, contended that "it is the maddest idea in the world, to think of building an American fleet. Its latitude is wonderful. We should mortgage the whole continent." Then, on October 13, a letter from Washington arrived that changed everything.

The letter revealed to Congress the existence of the general's private navy. Congress was quite surprised, but because Washington had already plunged ahead on his own initiative, it decided to follow his lead. That same day, it adopted the committee's latest recommendation and authorized the fitting out of two armed vessels, with eighty men each, to seize ships transporting military and other supplies to the British. Congress established another committee to prepare an estimate of the cost of purchasing and supplying the vessels. Since this was the first time that Congress had approved the fitting out of armed vessels to confront the enemy, October 13, 1775, is considered the official birth date of the American Navy.

The second committee's report on costs landed on October 30, and that day Congress voted to move ahead with the purchasing and fitting out of four armed vessels (the two original and two more). Over the next few months, the Continental navy expanded and was more formally organized. Congress authorized the construction of thirteen frigates,* at the staggering and unusually specific cost of $866,666.66, designated committees to oversee construction of the frigates and the operation of the

---

* Five were to be outfitted with thirty-two guns apiece, five with twenty-eight, and three with twenty-four.

navy, and established regulations for naval operations. Those regulations initially restricted naval captures to British vessels of war and transports— British commercial vessels were not fair game—and authorized vice admiralty courts to adjudicate the disposition of prizes. The regulations also set the pay rates for naval personnel and gave them a stake in the action, much like that given to privateers, though the cut was smaller. Whereas the owners and the officers and crews of privateers shared 100 percent of the proceeds of prizes, the officers and crews of naval vessels shared one-half of all warships captured, and one-third of transport vessels, with the rest going to Congress, for the use of the United Colonies, which was what Congress called the emerging nation before independence was declared. In October 1776, the split for naval vessels was changed to make Continental service more lucrative. From that point forward, the officers and crews would receive 100 percent for warships and British privateers, and one-half of all other prizes. It was hoped that the enhanced financial rewards would not only encourage more men to enlist in the navy but also increase

Model of the Continental frigate *Raleigh*, thirty-two guns, one of the vessels that the Continental Congress had built for the navy. It was launched in May 1776.

the chances that naval ships would actually attack heavily armed British warships and privateers.

Well aware that many in the colonies still hoped for reconciliation with Britain, Congress presented the new navy as a defensive measure that was amply justified by British aggression. Even as they were creating a navy together, the colonies received news that made it clear that such aggression would worsen. On November 9, word arrived in America that King George had not only rejected the Olive Branch Petition but refused to receive it. About the same time, Congress learned of the king's Proclamation for Suppressing Rebellion and Sedition, issued August 23, 1775, in which he said that the colonies were in "open and avowed rebellion, by arraying themselves in hostile manner to withstand the execution of the law, and traitorously preparing, ordering, and levying war against us." Furthermore, the king urged his officers, civil and military, "to exert their utmost endeavors to suppress such rebellion, and to bring the traitors to justice."

BY EARLY 1776, the upstart Americans had made considerable progress in taking the fight to sea. Between state navies, Washington's navy, privateers from some individual colonies, and the nascent Continental navy, the colonies were demonstrating their maritime creativity and potency. But one major feature of their maritime strategy was conspicuous in its absence: privateers commissioned by Congress.

Delegates had received many entreaties urging them to pursue this course. In late November 1775, for example, Simeon Deane, a Connecticut merchant, wrote to Silas, his brother and a congressional delegate, "I am desired by a number of gentlemen here, to ask, through your influence, whether the Congress will grant commission to private adventurers to fit out a privateer or privateers to take British property on this coast, or in the West Indies." Just over a week later, William Cooper, a member of the Sons of Liberty* and the town clerk for Boston, wrote to John Adams to complain about Congress's inaction. "Is a sea coast of above 2,000 Miles extent from whence two hundred sail of privateers might this winter . . .

---

* A grassroots group that employed civil disobedience and, at times, violence to assert/defend/advance American rights and attack/defy/resist British policies/rule, especially the imposition of tax policies, most notably the Stamp Act.

be launched out upon the British trade, still [to] be held in a state of neu-
trality under a notion that we are opposing [the North] Ministry & not the
people of Britain, while our enemies are employing the whole force of the
Nation to plunder and ruin us?" By failing to use all of the maritime tools
available to it, Congress was, in Cooper's eyes, hobbling the American
cause. "I some time ago ventured a prophesy," Cooper told Adams, "that it
would not be long before we realized our importance as a maritime power,
and the success attending our first naval enterprises, are very encouraging
presages of what is yet to come, but if weak nerves and large estates should
operate to the preventing the whole force of the colonies being exerted
against the common enemy, the issue of so unequal and unheard of a war,
may be easily augured."

Fortunately for Cooper and many others who held similar views, Congress did not remain silent on the subject of privateering for very long.

All In

Letter of marque issued on October 24, 1776, to
James Powell, commander of the thirty-ton schooner
Northampton, signed by John Hancock.

NEWS OF THE LATEST SALVO FROM PARLIAMENT REACHED AMERICA
in February 1776, sending shock waves throughout the colonies. This was
the Prohibitory Act, passed in late December. John Adams called it "a
complete dismemberment of the British Empire. It throws thirteen colonies out of the royal protection, levels all distinctions, and makes us independent in spite of our supplications and entreaties. It may be fortunate
that the Act of Independency [as it was called by many] should come from

the British Parliament, rather than the American Congress; but it is very odd that Americans should hesitate at accepting such a gift from them."

The Prohibitory Act completely cut off trade between the American colonies and Britain and its other colonies, left all colonial vessels vulnerable to seizure by British ships, and made it lawful for British naval officers to impress American sailors onto their ships. In effect a blockade of American shipping, the act was nothing less than a declaration of economic warfare intended to hobble the colonies amid the expanding conflict.

As Adams feared, Congress hesitated in reaction to the act. But while independence would have to wait, privateering wouldn't. When the merchants and other leading citizens of Philadelphia sent a petition to Congress in late February, asking for permission to "fit out privateers, and make reprisals on all British vessels," Congress was now receptive to the idea.* Reflecting on the petition's merits, New Hampshire delegate Josiah Bartlett opined, "It seems very hard that Britain is seizing all American vessels and the Americans are not permitted to return the compliment." He also noted that the Prohibitory Act "had altered the minds of" those in Congress who had come to view privateering in a very favorable light. Oliver Wolcott, a delegate from Connecticut, was more succinct. Since the act had effectively cast the colonies out of the paternal embrace of empire, Wolcott said, "it behooves us therefore to take care of ourselves."

The privateering debate soon commenced. Although a few delegates were wary of its authorization, the vast majority were strongly in favor of it. The only real sticking point concerned the language in the preamble of the resulting resolution, as the issue of privateering had raised a much larger problem. On March 22, an amendment was offered "wherein the King was made the author of our miseries instead of the ministry." While Adams and many other of the more radical delegates had long believed that the king, along with the ministry, was culpable, blaming the monarchy for the colonies' woes remained an explosive move. More than a few of the moderate delegates still clung fiercely to the idea that the colonies were fighting Parliament and not the king.

For four hours the delegates argued over the amendment. Opponents claimed that the language "was effectually severing the King from us for-

---

* Unfortunately, the actual petition itself has been lost, and what we know about it comes from those who made reference to it in their letters.

Detail of an engraving entitled *An east prospect of the city of Philadelphia*, by Thomas Jefferys, 1771.

ever," which was, as they saw it, tantamount to a declaration of independence. Congress, however, was not ready to take such a bold stance, so the amendment to the preamble was vetoed. The very next day, March 23, 1776, Congress passed the privateering resolution into law.

THE PREAMBLE IN the final resolution blamed the British fleets and armies for prosecuting "an unjust war . . . in a cruel manner," and it singled out the Prohibitory Act as being particularly injurious. Congress concluded that it was "manifest that the iniquitous scheme, concerted to deprive" the colonies "of the liberty they have a right to by the laws of nature and the English Constitution, will be pertinaciously pursued." Congress had no alternative but to "provide for their defense and security" by authorizing the colonies to fit out privateers to cruise against the enemy.

The Prohibitory Act had declared all colonial vessels fair game; Congress now returned the favor. Privateers were free to capture any British vessel, not just those that were delivering supplies to British forces in America. (Later, neutral ships carrying goods bound for British use were also deemed acceptable targets). About the same time, Congress also unleashed Continental navy ships, allowing them to attack all British vessels as well as neutral ships carrying British supplies.

Privateers were required to bring their captures before courts of vice admiralty established in various ports, where the vessels and their cargo would be libeled, or have a suit brought against them, to determine whether they were lawful prizes. If the capture was not a lawful prize, it would be

In CONGRESS,

WEDNESDAY, April 3, 1776.

INSTRUCTIONS *to the* COMMANDERS *of Private Ships or Vessels of War, which shall have Commissions or Letters of Marque and Reprisal, authorising them to make Captures of British Vessels and Cargoes.*

I.

YOU may, by Force of Arms, attack, subdue, and take all Ships and other Vessels belonging to the Inhabitants of Great Britain, on the High Seas, or between high-water and low-water Marks, except Ships and Vessels bringing Persons who intend to settle and reside in the United Colonies, or bringing Arms, Ammunition or Warlike Stores to the said Colonies, for the Use of such Inhabitants thereof as are Friends to the American Cause, which you shall suffer to pass unmolested, the Commanders thereof permitting a peaceable Search, and giving satisfactory Information of the Contents of the Ladings, and Destinations of the Voyages.

II.

You may, by Force of Arms, attack, subdue, and take all Ships and other Vessels whatsoever carrying Soldiers, Arms, Gun powder, Ammunition, Provisions, or any other contraband Goods, to any of the British Armies or Ships of War employed against these Colonies.

III.

You shall bring such Ships and Vessels as you shall take, with their Guns, Rigging, Tackle, Apparel, Furniture and Ladings, to some convenient Port or Ports of the United Colonies, that Proceedings may thereupon be had in due Form before the Courts which are or shall be there appointed to hear and determine Causes civil and maritime.

IV.

You or one of your Chief Officers shall bring or send the Master and Pilot and one or more principal Person or Persons of the Company of every Ship or Vessel by you taken, as soon after the Capture as may be, to the Judge or Judges of such Court as aforesaid, to be examined upon Oath, and make Answer to the Interrogatories which may be propounded touching the Interest or Property of the Ship or Vessel and her Lading ; and at the same Time you shall deliver or cause to be delivered to the Judge or Judges, all Passes, Sea-Briefs, Charter Parties, Bills of Lading, Cockets, Letters, and other Documents and Writings found on Board, proving the said Papers by the Affidavit of yourself, or of some other Person present at the Capture, to be produced as they were received, without Fraud, Addition, Subduction, or Embezzlement.

V.

You shall keep and preserve every Ship or Vessel and Cargo by you taken, until they shall by Sentence of a Court properly authorised be adjudged lawful Prize, not selling, spoiling, wasting, or diminishing the same or breaking the Bulk thereof, nor suffering any such Thing to be done.

VI.

If you, or any of your Officers or Crew shall, in cold Blood, kill or maim, or by Torture or otherwise, cruelly, inhumanly, and contrary to common Usage and the Practice of civilized Nations in War, treat any Person or Persons surprized in the Ship or Vessel you shall take, the Offender shall be severely punished.

VII.

You shall, by all convenient Opportunities, send to Congress written Accounts of the Captures you shall make, with the Number and Names of the Captives, Copies of your Journal from Time to Time, and Intelligence of what may occur or be discovered concerning the Designs of the Enemy, and the Destinations, Motions, and Operations of their Fleets and Armies.

VIII.

One Third, at the least, of your whole Company shall be Land Men.

IX.

You shall not ransome any Prisoners or Captives, but shall dispose of them in such Manner as the Congress, or if that be not sitting in the Colony whither they shall be brought, as the General Assembly, Convention, or Council or Committee of Safety of such Colony shall direct.

X.

You shall observe all such further Instructions as Congress shall hereafter give in the Premises, when you shall have Notice thereof.

XI.

If you shall do any Thing contrary to these Instructions, or to others hereafter to be given, or willingly suffer such Thing to be done, you shall not only forfeit your Commission, and be liable to an Action for Breach of the Condition of your Bond, but be responsible to the Party grieved for Damages sustained by such Mal-versation.

By Order of CONGRESS.

JOHN HANCOCK, *President.*

Instructions to privateers issued on April 3, 1776, "By Order of Congress," and signed "John Hancock, President."

returned to its owners. If it was a lawful prize, the privateer owners and the privateersmen split all of the prize money, minus the cost of the trial.

Adams rejoiced over the privateering resolution. On the day it passed, he wrote to Brigadier General Horatio Gates, who served as the adjutant general of the Continental army, with the good news. "We have hitherto conducted half a war. . . . But you will see by tomorrow's paper that, for the future, we are likely to wage three-quarters of a war. The Continental ships-of-war, and the Provincial ships-of-war [the state navies], and letters of marque and privateers, are permitted to cruise on British property, wherever found on the ocean." However, before the law could go into effect, Congress needed to spell out the regulations governing privateers. It did so on April 3.

Although the privateering system was authorized by Congress, it would be implemented by the colonies. The colonies that had passed their own privateering laws—Massachusetts, Rhode Island, and New Hampshire— updated them to reflect the congressional terms. Even though the colonial laws remained on the books, virtually all privateering commissions in America were Continental from this point forward. Congress would supply the colonies with privateering commissions that were to be filled out by those applying for letters of marque. The commissions had blank spaces for the name and tonnage of the vessel as well as the number of cannons and officers and crew on board, among other items. The applicants would also usually indicate whether the vessel would act solely as a privateer or as a letter of marque engaging both in trade and capturing prizes. The owner or commander was required to post a bond of $5,000 for vessels under 100 tons and $10,000 for larger vessels, payable to the president of the Congress. That bond was intended to ensure that the commander and his crew would not violate the terms of the commission, which detailed what actions privateers could take and what actions were prohibited. In May 1780, the bond amount was raised to $20,000 for all privateers.

If privateersmen killed, maimed, tortured, or in any other manner treated the officers or crew of captured ships cruelly or inhumanely—or in a way that was contrary to the "practices of civilized nations in war"—the offenders would be severely punished. Also, one-third of the crew had to be landsmen, or non-mariners. The goal was to limit the number of sailors who decided to become privateers, given that it potentially paid better than serving on Continental navy ships. That way, the thinking went, the chances of navy ships filling out their crews with seasoned mariners improved.

In his letter to the colonies announcing the law and the regulations, John Hancock, president of the Continental Congress, said: "It is necessary in conducting the warlike operations on the part of America, to meet our enemy on every ground, and to defend ourselves in the best manner we can against all attempts, in whatever shape, to deprive us of either liberty or property." Privateers were now to be a major part of the colonial war effort.

JOHN ADAMS HAD BEEN yearning for the colonies to formally break free of Britain since the middle of 1775, but he knew that the privateering law, no matter how revolutionary it was, did not go that far. "This is not Independency," he said in his letter to Gates, "you know nothing like it." Nevertheless, the privateering law did push the colonies more in that direction. It was yet another tear in the gossamer fabric holding the colonies and Britain together.

The slow lurch toward independence was sped along by the thunderclap of a pamphlet written by Thomas Paine, titled *Common Sense*, first published on January 10, 1776. Born in England, Paine had failed his way through a number of professions, including corset maker and tobacconist, before emigrating to Philadelphia in late 1774 with a letter of recommendation in his pocket from Benjamin Franklin. That entrée helped him obtain citizenship in Pennsylvania and win a job as editor of the *Pennsylvania Magazine*, where he honed his writing skills and became swept up in the political currents roiling the colonies.

Privateering might have ended Paine's writing career well before it started. In 1756, at the beginning the Seven Years' War, he had joined the crew of the *Terrible*, a British privateer captained by William Death. Paine's father, a Quaker committed to pacifism, protested his son's decision and convinced him to leave the ship. That was a providential turn of events. Not long after the *Terrible* sailed, typhus fever raced through the ranks, incapacitating and killing many. Shorthanded, the *Terrible* managed to take a prize, sustaining casualties in the process, before tangling with a much more powerful French privateer, the *Vengeance*. In the ensuing battle, Captain Death lived up to his name. He was hit with two lead musket balls, and after he had surrendered, a Frenchman shot him in the back of his head. Most of the *Terrible*'s crew were also killed during the fight. The survivors were placed in the overcrowded hold of the French ship, where another twenty-seven of them "were smothered to death." The few who were still alive at that point were then thrown into prison at Saint-Malo.

Paine soon discounted his father's concerns and, knowing nothing about the bloodbath on the *Terrible*, signed on to another privateer. Fortunately, for him, the *King of Prussia*'s relatively short cruise was much less eventful, and it returned to London with a few prizes in tow. How much Paine earned from this adventure is unknown, but he did return with his life, and he soon continued his winding path toward becoming one of the most influential proponents of the revolutionary cause.

Engraving from 1797 showing the deadly battle between the British privateer *Terrible* and the French privateer *Vengeance*.

In *Common Sense*, Paine argued that, given all the blood that had been spilled already, "reconciliation is . . . a fallacious dream," and that the time for independence from Britain was now. "Everything short of that is mere patchwork, that it can afford no lasting felicity,—that it is leaving the sword to our children, and shrinking back at a time, when, a little more, a little farther, would have rendered this continent the glory of the earth." Paine derided the unwritten British constitution as the "base remains of two ancient tyrannies"—monarchy and aristocracy. "Government by kings" fared no better: he called it "the most prosperous invention the Devil ever set on foot for the promotion of idolatry," and he labeled King George "the Royal Brute." As Paine proclaimed of the rebellion: "The sun never shined on a cause of greater worth. 'Tis not the affair of a city, a county, a province, or a kingdom; but of a continent. . . . We have it in our power to begin the world over again. A situation, similar to the present, hath not happened since the days of Noah until now. The birthday of a new world is at hand."

Paine's timing couldn't have been better. January 10 was the same day that the text of King George's speech opening Parliament on October 26, 1775, arrived in America. In his oration the king made clear that he was going to pursue war against the colonies, which "now openly avow their revolt, hostility, and rebellion," with renewed vigor, including by sending more naval and land forces to America. The king's goal was "to put a speedy end to these disorders by the most decisive exertions." "The Royal Brute" could hardly have done more to corroborate Paine's argument that independence was an idea whose time had come.

Many of the arguments in *Common Sense* had been bandied about in the colonies for months, if not years, but Paine's synthesis, written for common people and leavened with his own powerful insights, caused a sensation. In 1776 alone, twenty-five editions of *Common* Sense were published, and within a few months of its first appearance it had sold roughly 100,000 copies, an astonishing number considering that the entire population of the colonies was only 2.5 million, and more than 500,000 of those were enslaved persons. (During the course of the Revolution, roughly half a million copies of *Common Sense* were sold, including unauthorized editions.) *Common Sense* became the intellectual and emotional backdrop to all subsequent debates about the future of the colonies.

After the privateering law passed, those debates took on even greater urgency. On April 6, in another reaction to the Prohibitory Act, Congress opened colonial ports to trade with all nations' ships except those from Britain and its other colonies. By early June, the majority of the thirteen colonies had instructed their delegates to support independence. On June 7, Virginia's Richard Henry Lee presented a resolution in Congress declaring "that these United Colonies are, and of right ought to be, free and independent states, that they are absolved from all allegiance to the British Crown, and that all political connection between them and the State of Great Britain is, and ought to be, totally dissolved."

Such actions and words were like a tonic to Adams. On June 9, he told William Cushing, a fellow lawyer and later one of the original justices of the United States Supreme Court, that "objects of the most stupendous magnitude, measures in which the lives and liberties of millions, born and unborn are most essentially interested, are now before us. We are in the very midst of a revolution, the most complete, unexpected, and remarkable of any in the history of nations."

A few days later, Congress appointed a committee of five to draft a document justifying independence from Britain in the event that Lee's resolution was approved. Among the committee members were Benjamin Franklin, John Adams, and Thomas Jefferson, the last of whom wrote most of the document, which was presented to Congress on June 28.

Still hesitant to make a clean break, Congress waited until July 2 to adopt Lee's resolution. Adams was thrilled, writing to his wife, Abigail, that "the second day of July 1776, will be the most memorable epocha [sic], in the history of America.—I am apt to believe that it will be celebrated, by succeeding generations, as the great anniversary festival." In this instance, Adams proved to be a poor prophet. It wasn't until July 4 that the delegates, after making a number of revisions to the committee of five's document, formally approved what thereafter became known as the Declaration of Independence.*

The declaration described the many oppressive, punitive, and harmful actions that compelled the colonies to break free. Among these were taxation without representation, cutting off colonial trade with the world,

---

* While July 4, 1776, is the date that the colonies declared their independence from Great Britain, Rhode Island had made a similar declaration two months earlier. Greatly angered by both the mother country's restrictions on the colony's commerce and its harassment of colonists and colonial vessels (including the *Gaspee* affair), the Rhode Island General Assembly voted on May 4, 1776, to renounce its allegiance to King George III and sever ties with Great Britain.

Engraving titled *The manner in which the American colonies*
declared themselves independent of the King of England, throughout
the different provinces, on July 4, 1776, circa 1783.

impressing sailors, restricting fishing in colonial seas, burning towns,
and destroying "the lives of our people." There would be no more giving the monarchy the benefit of the doubt. "The history of the present
King of Great Britain," the declaration claimed, "is a history of repeated
injuries and usurpations, all having in direct object the establishment of
an absolute tyranny over these states." As a nation of "free and independent states," the colonies asserted their right to "levy war, conclude peace,

contract alliances, establish commerce, and to do all other acts and things which independent states may of right do."

BY THIS POINT, the pace of privateering activity had picked up. On April 11, the first vessels obtained Continental commissions. Philadelphia's *Chance* and *Congress* had formerly earned their keep as pilot boats in New York. They were diminutive sloops, with four and six cannons, respectively, and around forty to fifty crewmen each. While preparing to head out on their first privateering cruise, the sloops received assistance from Congress. With gunpowder in short supply in Pennsylvania, a representative of the shipowners asked Congress for permission to buy four hundred pounds of it, and Congress agreed. Armed and ready, the two sloops slipped down the Delaware River and into the Atlantic in mid-April.

They sailed in tandem to the West Indies, hunting for prizes. It was a good choice. As the influential Caribbean historian and politician Eric Williams noted, "The West Indian islands became the hub of the British Empire . . . [and] the most precious colonies ever recorded in the whole annals of imperialism." Their great wealth was based on sugarcane cultivation and a brutal slave regime. With this came a corresponding flood of maritime traffic between the islands and Britain, which the sloops began picking off.

In less than a month, the *Chance* and *Congress* captured four British merchant ships that were transiting from Jamaica to London. It was a spectacular haul. The ships' cargoes included more than 1,000 hogsheads of sugar, 25 tons of cocoa, nearly 22,000 gallons of rum, and, of greatest value, 22,420 Spanish silver dollars as well as 200 gold Spanish "half joes," each of which was worth around 8 Spanish silver dollars.

The four prizes, with skeleton prize crews on board, were sent into various colonial ports to be libeled. But before setting out, the merchantmen were stripped of their silver and gold, which was placed on the *Chance* and *Congress*. Concerned about a British warship that had been lurking at the mouth of the Delaware and the potential loss of their treasure, the sloops' captains sailed to the more secluded Little Egg Harbor in New Jersey rather than their home port. They arrived in early June and offloaded the silver and gold, placing it on wagons to be transported overland to Philadelphia. Then the *Chance* and *Congress* made a mad dash up the Delaware, evading the HMS *Liverpool* and reaching Philadelphia on June 5.

The same day that the *Chance* and *Congress* arrived in Philadelphia, Robert Morris, a wealthy merchant and congressional delegate, wrote to Silas Deane, then the colonies' secret envoy to France, recounting the privateers' great success and predicting that it was only a beginning. "I fancy many more West Indiamen will be taken this summer and probably Great Britain may have cause to repent the Prohibitory Act, especially as they have much more property to lose than we have."

As someone who cared deeply about the colonies' fiscal health, and who would in 1781 become the superintendent of finance, Morris was particularly excited, as were his fellow delegates, about the Spanish silver dollars. Such coins were the "first truly global currency," welcomed everywhere. In contrast, the paper currency issued by Congress, known as Continental bills, or more commonly continentals, was of dubious worth and depreciated quickly. As a result, it was difficult to use it in both colonial and international transactions, the latter of which were critical to America's hope of purchasing military supplies from overseas. As John Hancock put it, Congress had "great occasion for the hard money," and the legislature asked the privateers' owners to hand over their 22,420 silver dollars. The owners "very generously furnished it, which Congress looked upon as of essential service." In exchange for the "hard money," Congress gave the owners an equivalent amount in continentals.

When the value of the silver and gold was added to the money generated by the sale of four British prizes and their cargo, the two owners and a few other main investors in the *Chance* and *Congress* walked away with the princely sum of at least £5,000 each. The crew of the two privateers had quite a payday as well, with the common seaman earning as much as £500. To put such numbers in perspective, at this time a prosperous merchant might have a net worth of around £6,000, while a typical carpenter in Rhode Island earned about £82 per year, and common laborers pulled in a little more than half of that. As for mariners, the captain of a merchantman earned around £10 per month, whereas a common sailor earned £3. By one calculation, £5,000 in 1776 would be worth around £650,000, or roughly $900,000, today.

NEWS OF THE *Chance*'s and the *Congress*'s success raced through the colonies, spurring other privateering ventures. By the end of June, Adams was predicting that "privateers will swarm in great numbers." A little more than a month later, after the colonies had declared their independence, he wrote to Abigail, "Thousands of schemes for privateering are afloat in American imaginations. . . . Out of these speculations many fruitless and some profitable projects will grow." Abigail's response was equally optimistic. "The rage for privateering is as great here as anywhere and I believe the success has been as great." Around the same time, James Warren, president of the Massachusetts Provincial Congress, wrote to Samuel Adams: "The spirit of privateering prevails here greatly. The success of those that have before engaged in that business has been sufficient to the make the whole country privateering mad."

That madness persisted for most of the Revolution, and many shared Warren's astonishment. At the end of 1776, Robert Morris observed, "In the eastern states, they are so intent on privateering that they mind little else." Two years later, an unidentified author from Boston noted that "privateering was never more in vogue than at the present—two or three privateers sail every week from this port, and men seem as plenty as grasshoppers in the field; no vessel being detained an hour for want of them." That same year, merchant William Pickman of Salem wrote to Timothy Pickering, adjutant general of the Continental army: "Privateering still flourishes, and although some individuals are losers yet the bulk are great gainers and may make amazing fortunes." The demand for privateering commissions was so great that many colonies repeatedly ran out of the pre-printed letters of marque, and colonial officials begged Congress to send more. In the summer of 1779, Virginia's second governor, Thomas Jefferson, claimed that "for want of [such letters] our people have long and exceedingly suffered" because they had not been able to send forth privateers.

Before continuing with the narrative and telling the tale of how the explosion of American privateering shaped the war, let's consider what type of men launched privateering cruises, what type of men signed on to crew privateers, why they did so given the risks involved, and how privateers and their crews went about their thrilling, lucrative, and dangerous business.

A Privateersman's Life

Model of the sixteen-gun American privateer
Rattlesnake, 1781, by Raymond W. Stone.

═══

WHILE IN PHILADELPHIA ATTENDING THE CONTINENTAL CON-
gress, John Adams frequently wrote to Abigail, who was living in their
family home in Braintree, Massachusetts. In these letters he expressed his
love for her and shared observations on life and politics. On the morning of April 23, 1777, he chose to tell her about a conversation he'd had
with his barber, John Byrne, "during the gay moments of shaving." Adams

inquired, "Well, Byrne, what is the lye of the day?" The "sprightly" barber replied that he had just been told "that a privateer from Baltimore has taken two valuable prizes, with sixteen cannons each. I can scarcely believe it." Adams did him one better. "Have you heard of the success of the *Rattlesnake* of Philadelphia, and the *Sturdy Beggar* of Maryland, Mr. Byrne? These two privateers have taken eleven prizes, and sent them into the West India Islands, nine transports and two Guinea men" (common slang for slave ships from Africa). Clearly annoyed at hearing this, Byrne proceeded to tell a tale of misfortune.

> Confound the ill luck, sir, I was going to sea myself on board the *Rattlesnake* and my wife fell a yelping. These wives are queer things. I told her I wondered she had no more ambition. Now, says I, when you walk the street, and anybody asks who that is? The answer is "Byrne the Barber's wife." Should you not be better pleased to hear it said, "That is Captain Byrne's lady, the Captain of marines on board the *Rattlesnake?*"
>
> Oh! says she, I had rather be called Byrne the barber's wife, than Captain Byrne's Widow. I don't desire to live better, than you maintain me, my dear.
>
> So it is, sir, by this sweet, honey language I am choused [cheated] out of my prizes, and must go on, with my soap and razors and pinchers and combs. I wish she had more ambition.

After relaying this melancholy account to his wife, Adams added, "If this letter should be intercepted by the Tories, they will get a booty—let them enjoy it."

Byrne's story contained more than an element of truth. Throughout the colonies, the draw of privateering was strong, as shown by the tens of thousands of men who enthusiastically signed on to cruises. Although privateering depended on the skill and brawn of officers and crews, it was shipowners and investors who got individual ventures off the ground.

The Boston Port Act and the Restraining Act, on a limited basis, and then the Prohibitory Act, covering all the colonies, nearly shut down American maritime commerce. Sailors and fishermen were out of work, and the vessels they had sailed on were idled. With their capital tied up at the docks or moored in the harbors, shipowners eagerly pursued pri-

Nathaniel Shaw's granite mansion in New London, now home
to the New London County Historical Society. Shaw and
two of his sons, Nathaniel Shaw Jr. and Thomas Shaw, were
leading merchants of the day, and this house served as the
headquarters for the Connecticut navy. Nearly fifty privateers
sailed from New London during the war; many were fully or
partly owned by the Shaws. Photograph taken in the 1930s.

vateering as a means of reinvigorating their business or to avoid bank-
ruptcy. Prizes brought in by privateers provided goods and ships they
could sell, and dual-purpose letters of marque held out the opportunity
of profiting from cargoes transported and prizes captured along the way.
As a group of Bostonians concluded at a town meeting in 1781, "The stagnation of the fishery furnished us with the means of cruising against the
enemy's property, and 'tis to the astonishing successes that have hitherto
attended to that kind of enterprise, that we owe the principal part of our
present trade."

Merchants were also motivated by anger. This can be seen in the trans-
formation of Robert Morris. In September 1776 he wrote to Silas Deane
that even though "those who have engaged in privateering are making
large fortunes in a most rapid manner, I have not meddled in this business which I confess does not square with my principles for I have long
had extensive connections and dealings with many worthy men in Eng-

land and could not consent to take any part of their property because the government have seized mine, which is the case in several instances." By December, Morris had changed his mind. "You must know," he wrote to a business associate, "I had determined not to be concerned in privateering but having had several vessels taken from me and otherways lost a great deal of my property by this war, I conceive myself perfectly justifiable in the eyes of god or man to seek what I have lost, from those that have plundered me." Morris proceeded to make his first investment in a privateer, and when that privateer captured thirteen prizes, he let go of any remaining reservations. "My scruples about privateering are all done away" with, he wrote to that same associate in April 1777. "I have seen such rapine, plunder & destruction denounced against and executed on the Americans that I join you in thinking it a duty to oppose and distress so merciless an enemy in every shape we can[.]" Fueled by a desire to strike back—and

Early twentieth-century picture of a painting of
Robert Morris by Charles Willson Peale.

surely by the immense returns as well—Morris spearheaded multiple privateering ventures.

One of the most active merchant-privateers was Elias Hasket Derby, of Salem, Massachusetts. A bustling seaport town of roughly five thousand on the eve of the Revolution, Salem saw its sizable commercial fleet idled by the war and punitive British actions. Many of Salem's leading merchants transitioned to privateering, none more successfully than Derby, whose family had been engaged in maritime trade since the late 1600s. Of the 158 privateers Salem launched during the war, 39 of them were either owned or partially owned by Derby.

Another privateering baron was Philadelphia's Blair McClenachan. After serving in the Continental army and seeing action at the Battles of Trenton and Princeton, this Scottish immigrant set his sights on the sea. From 1777 through the end of the war, McClenachan owned or had a major stake in fifty-five privateers. Many of them were extremely successful, their profits leading Americans to call him the "Midas" of the Revolution. Some of the men on his privateers even took to affectionately calling him "The Millionaire Maker."

Shipowners such as Morris, Derby, and McClenachan often invested in privateering ventures involving other men's vessels. But there was another class of men who were not shipowners themselves but crucial to privateering solely as investors. Privateering spurred a speculative frenzy across

A view of the Salem waterfront, circa 1770s.

the colonies. Among the more illustrious speculators was General George Washington, who invested in at least one privateer (appropriately enough, the *General Washington*). Generals Nathanael Greene and Henry Knox, as well as Elbridge Gerry, each invested in multiple ventures. Other noted personages who gambled on privateering included Samuel A. Otis, a Boston merchant who served in the Massachusetts House of Representatives and was a purchasing agent for the army's quartermaster general, Greene; Isaac Sears, an early leader of New York's Sons of Liberty and a man who was ironically dubbed "King Sears" for his role in fomenting anti-British demonstrations in the years leading up to the Revolution; John Winthrop, Hollis Professor of Mathematics and Natural Philosophy at Harvard, and former acting president of the university; and Paul Revere, the Boston silversmith whose midnight ride on April 18, 1775, warning the countryside that the British regulars were coming was immortalized in Henry Wadsworth Longfellow's largely inaccurate 1860 poem "Paul Revere's Ride."

Beyond owning or investing in a privateer, there was yet another method of profiting from privateering. One could bet on the outcome of a cruise by paying a crewman for the rights to a portion of his future prize earnings. Such transactions benefited the privateers by giving them ready cash that could help them support their families while they were away. But the purchaser only gained if the cruise was a success, and that was by no means assured. More than a few privateering ventures went bust, meaning that there were no profits to share. When Andrew Sherburne, a New Hampshire boy of fifteen, sailed with the privateer *Alexander*, he granted power of attorney to his mother, giving her free rein to sell interest in his prize share while he was away. She exercised that option by selling one-quarter of his share for seventy dollars. While the purchaser lost his entire investment when the *Alexander* came back empty-handed, the seventy dollars was a boon to Sherburne's mother, enabling her to buy firewood, fodder for her only cow, and other essentials.

Whether as owners, investors, or purchasers of future earnings, wiser speculators factored in the fluctuations of the privateering enterprise and spread their money across many ventures. As Morris observed, "It is well worth risking largely, for one arrival will pay for two, three, or four losses, therefore it is best to keep doing something constantly."

Just as the prospect of making money motivated privateer owners and investors, so too did it motivate the crews. Captains and officers were typi-

The swift-sailing Sloop H O P E.

On Thurſday next will ſail (comꞏ pleatly fitted for a ſhort Cruize of Fifty Days) the ſwift-ſailing Priꞏ vateer Sloop H O P E, mounting 10 Carriage Guns, C H R I S ꞏ T O P H E R   S M I T H, Comꞏ mander.   All Gentlemen Seaꞏ men, and able-bodied Landſmen, who wiſh to try their Fortunes, may have an Opportunity, by applyꞏ ing at the Rendezvous, at Mr. Joſhua Hacker's, or to the Commander on board, at Clark and Nightinꞏ gale's Wharff.

Advertisement in the *Providence Gazette and Country Journal*, August 4, 1781, encouraging men to join the privateer sloop *Hope*.

cally men known to the owners by virtue of past service or reputation, and would usually be hired directly and offered the largest number of shares of any prizes taken. While crewmen were sometimes known by the owners prior to being hired, in most cases they were not, and had to be found and enticed.

It was common to see advertisements in colonial newspapers encouraging men to sign on for a cruise. One that ran in the *Boston Gazette* on November 13, 1780, was headlined "An Invitation to all brave Seamen and Marines, who have an inclination to serve their country and make their fortunes." It continued:

The grand privateer Ship *Deane*, commanded by Elisha Hinman, esquire, will sail on a cruise against the enemies of the United States of America, by the 20th instant. The *Deane* [has] 30 carriage guns,* and is excellently well calculated for attacks, defenses, and pursuit. This therefore is to invite all those jolly fellows, who love their country, and want to make their fortune at one stroke, to repair immediately to the rendezvous at the head of his excellency's, Governor Hancock's Wharf, where they will be received with a hearty

---

* In the literature and in accounts from the late 1700s, cannons were typically referred to as guns.

welcome by a number of brave fellows there assembled, and treated with that excellent liquor called GROG,* which is allowed by all true seamen, to be the LIQUOR OF LIFE.

The "hearty welcome" was a common tactic that privateer owners employed to get men to join the crew. Those who responded to a privateer recruiting ad in Salem in the summer of 1781 were feted at raucous multi-day gatherings at a local pub where the owners racked up a healthy bill supplying sixty-seven and a half bowls of punch, nine and a half bowls of grog, and thirty-six bowls of cherry toddy.

For many young men, joining a privateer represented an opportunity for adventure and fortune and also, perhaps, a chance to escape stultifying manual labor. As one New Hampshire mariner who would serve on a navy ship and a privateer related, "At this period it was not an uncommon thing for lads to come out of the country, step on board a privateer, make a cruise and return home, their friends remaining in entire ignorance of their fate until they heard it from themselves. . . . There was a disposition in commanders of privateers and recruiting officers to encourage this spirit of enterprise in young men and boys. Though these rash young adventurers did not count the cost, or think of looking at the dark side of the picture, yet this spirit, amidst the despondency of many, enabled our country to maintain a successful struggle and finally achieve her independence."

Once lured in, the men had to sign the ship's articles—the agreement between the captain and the crew laying out the owner's and captain's responsibilities, the duties of the crew while on board, rewards and punishments for certain behaviors, and the share distribution. The agreement for the privateer sloop *Hibernia*, which sailed from New London on October 10, 1780, included twelve articles. Under Article I, the owners agreed to fit out the *Hibernia* at their own expense and provide arms and food sufficient to last for a two-month cruise. In return, they would receive half of all prizes taken during the cruise. Additional articles spelled out incentives and disincentives for various actions. The first man to sight a valid prize was awarded a finder's fee of £100, and the first to board the enemy's ship after orders for boarding were issued would receive £300 "as recom-

---

* Grog was a term use for a variety of alcoholic beverages, but was most often a mixture of water and rum, served warm.

pence for his valor." If an officer or crewman shirked his duty or, worse, was found guilty of cowardice, mutiny, theft, embezzlement, concealment of any goods, or "any violence to a male or indecency to a female prisoner," he would forfeit his share(s) and "suffer such other punishment as the crime may deserve."

There was also a form of workmen's compensation. Should anyone, during an engagement with the enemy, lose a leg or arm, or otherwise be "so disabled as not to earn his bread," he was entitled to £1,000 from the profits generated by the first prize. Each person on board was allotted a specific number of shares, deducted from the 50 percent of the prize money due the ship's company. The captain received the most, eight shares, while boys under the age of sixteen were at the bottom of the scale, with half a share each. Other payouts included the surgeon, who received four shares, the carpenter, cook, and sailmaker, who each received two, and the gunner's mate and boatswain, who were given one and a half apiece. The articles set aside seven "dead shares" to be distributed at the end of the cruise to those men who had contributed most to making it a success. The *Hibernia*'s articles of agreement were typical, and many others had similar provisions, although the particulars might vary from venture to venture.

WHO SIGNED ON? Privateersmen are invariably described as being men because virtually all of them were. But there was at least one potential exception. According to early nineteenth-century historian Edgar Stanton Maclay, when the American privateer *Revenge* was captured by the British privateer *Belle Poole*, one of the men on board the *Revenge* stepped forward and announced that he was a she. "Her love for adventure had induced her to don male attire, and she had been serving many months without her sex having been known." Unfortunately, Maclay doesn't cite his sources, and a diligent search by this author failed to uncover any primary documents that would further illuminate this story. But, even if true, this female privateer stands alone in the known annals of the Revolution. There are, however, verified examples of women dressing as men and serving on whaling ships, in the Continental army, and on pirate ships, so the notion that some women joined privateers is possible.

While the sex of privateersmen is quite clear, identifying other common characteristics is more difficult.* There is no single source recording the ages or backgrounds of the many tens of thousands who became privateersmen. A sample of a few privateersmen would not necessarily reflect the whole. Nevertheless, there are some worthwhile generalizations that can be made. The average age of men serving in the Continental army was in the low to mid-twenties, and it is likely that the same was true on board privateers, since the average age of colonists hovered around sixteen, and going to sea, even for short periods of time, was not something for the faint of heart or weak in constitution. Lending further support to this range is the fact that the average age of professional seamen at this time was around twenty-five.

Many privateers had maritime backgrounds, something that roughly one in ten colonists could boast of. Privateering regulations set down by Congress, however, required that one-third of the crew be landsmen. Although there is little evidence that this was enforced, a significant number of privateersmen were landsmen, especially toward the end of the war, when many mariners had either been killed at sea or placed in prison. These landsmen, or green hands, had to learn on the job, likely experiencing bouts of seasickness and days or weeks of being thoroughly confused about a vessel's rigging and operation.

Privateer crews were frequently comprised of men and boys who knew each other. In fishing towns such as Marblehead, it was common for friends as well as multiple members of extended families to sign up for the same privateer. An extreme example was the privateer *Thorn*, which sailed out of Newburyport in early 1781. Captain Samuel Tucker and virtually all of the men in the 124-member crew hailed from Marblehead. Thirty-three were related.

---

* The most fanciful description of a privateer comes from Gomer Williams, who wrote a book on the history of privateers from Liverpool, England, during the American Revolution. "Your true privateersman was a sort of half-horse, half-alligator, with a streak of lightning in his composition—something like a man-of-war's man, but much more like a pirate—generally with a superabundance of whisker, as if he held with Sampson that his strength was in the quantity of his hair." A bit silly, not to mention derivative. The American folk hero frontiersman David Crockett (1786–1836) often referred to himself as "half-horse, half-alligator." And many people also used the same phrase to describe famed keelboatman and brawler Mike Fink (circa 1770/1780–1823). See Gomer Williams, *History of the Liverpool Privateers and Letters of Marque* (London: William Heinemann, 1897), 6.

After relinquishing com-
mand of the Continental
navy ship *Lexington*, John
Barry looked for another
navy post, but there were
too many commanders
and too few ships. So he
became captain of the
Philadelphia privateer
Delaware, which he took
on two successful cruises.
Engraving of John Barry,
by J. B. Longacre, after the
painting by Gilbert Stuart,
circa 1859.

Many privateersmen also served on Continental navy vessels. They
transitioned between the various forms of maritime service depending on
a range of factors, including the desire to earn more money, and limitations on the number of available berths on naval ships. By one account,
sixty men who captained privateers had also commanded or served as
officers on Continental navy ships during the war. Many would go on
to great fame after the war, establishing naval careers based in part on
skills acquired during their privateering past. These men include Silas
Talbot, future commander of the USS *Constitution*; Thomas Truxtun,
who would be one of the original six commanders appointed by George
Washington to the first permanent navy in the United States, established
in 1794; and John Barry, often called the father of the U.S. Navy, who had
an illustrious naval career during the Revolution and would rekindle his
fame during the Quasi-War with France (1798–1800) as commander of the
fleet.

Privateers also pulled men from the army, again for a variety of reasons, among them the prospect of striking it rich and the opportunity to
serve the revolutionary cause by other means. The latter is what compelled
James Campbell, a lieutenant in the eighth company of Maryland's forces,
to submit his resignation on May 1, 1776. In the letter announcing his decision to join the Baltimore privateer *Enterprize*, he assured his superiors

Thomas Truxtun, circa 1799. Truxtun captained or served on a number of privateers and letters of marque during the Revolution, including the privateer *Congress*, which, along with the *Chance*, were the first to obtain Continental commissions from Congress.

that "no consideration would induce me to leave the service but the hopes of being more useful in another department." His superior echoed this justification, informing the Maryland Council of Safety that Campbell was leaving the company "in order to be of more essential service to his country by distressing the trade of our enemies in a privateer."

Black men served on many privateers. Some were freemen who joined of their own volition. Others were enslaved persons who signed on after running away from their owners. Slave owners seeking to reclaim "property" who had fled to join a privateer would run advertisements in colonial papers. At the same time, many slaveholders rented out their enslaved persons to privateers as a moneymaking scheme. An ad in the *New-Hampshire Gazette* in 1776 adopted a light and airy tone for what was grim business: "To be SOLD for a CERTAIN TIME, or let by the month, a genteel sprightly NEGRO FELLOW, in fine health, about eighteen years of age, he can be recommended for many good qualities, has served at sea and land, waits on company well, and is extreme[ly] desirous of belonging to a captain of a privateer, or going in one, as may be agreed."

Then there were those Black men who were treated as transient property by the privateers themselves. When privateers captured British slavers, their human cargo was viewed as just another commodity and sold at slave auctions in the French West Indies or the American states—in effect,

Joshua Barney (*right*, circa 1805) captained privateers and Continental navy and Pennsylvania state navy ships during the Revolution. In early April 1782, as captain of the *Hyder Ally* and acting as a privateersman, he won a dramatic battle against the British sloop of war *General Monk* and the British privateer *Fair American*. (The bottom image, circa 1802, by Louis-Philippe Crépin, is titled *"Hyder Ally" Captures "General Monk," April 8, 1782*.) Although Barney had a privateering commission, that was only because Pennsylvania couldn't act fast enough to get legislation in place to purchase and commission the *Hyder Ally* as a state navy vessel. A consortium of merchants, fully expecting the legislation to ultimately pass (and it did, a few days after the April battle) stepped in and bought the *Hyder Ally* on behalf of the state, outfitted it, and put up a bond for the privateering commission. This enabled the *Hyder Ally* to go down the Delaware River and the Delaware Bay in convoy with merchant ships to protect them from British warships and privateers. While Barney was

technically a privateersmen, he was also a captain in the Pennsylvania state navy, and it seems more accurate to view the *Hyder Ally* as a state vessel, not a privateer, despite the commission. That is how Barney himself and contemporaries characterized the *Hyder Ally*.

transforming privateers into slave traders. American privateers captured more than forty British slave ships sailing from Africa to British-controlled Caribbean islands, with more than ten thousand enslaved persons on board in total, who were treated in this manner. While these actions should not surprise, they represent the greatest blemish on the privateering record.

But privateers may have had a related, and more positive, effect. According to historian Christian McBurney, who studied the role of privateers in the slave trade, "The unintended consequence of the American privateers' success against British slave ships was that British investors from Liverpool, Bristol and London" for most of the war "invested in many fewer African slave trading voyages. This development, in turn, resulted in tens of thousands of Africans not being involuntarily forced on board slave ships, forced to endure the horrors of the Middle Passage, and forced to spend their remaining days in enslavement."

Providence merchant John Brown, who had a stake in two slave trading ships prior to the Revolution, decided to capitalize on this potentially lucrative opening by dispatching the 250-ton, 20-gun privateer brig *Marlborough*, captained by George Waite Babcock, to the west coast of Africa

John Brown, circa 1794. On May 17, 1781, Brown placed an ad in the *Providence Gazette*, imploring men to sign on to his privateer, "the very likely and fast-sailing ship *Marquis de Lafayette*," which was "now fitting for a cruise, with all possible dispatch, against the common enemy." The banner across the top of the ad read, "The Best Encouragement! Good Living, and a Fortune."

in late 1777 with specific instructions to attack British slave trading interests. Babcock met with spectacular success. He ransacked a major slave
trading post and captured more than twenty prizes involved in the slave
trade, one of which, the *Fancy*, had 310 enslaved persons on board. He
placed a prize crew on board the *Fancy* and ordered them to sail it back
across the Atlantic to Charleston, South Carolina, home to the largest
slave market on mainland North American in colonial times. Whether it
made it to Charleston or another safe port or was captured by an enemy
vessel or sank at sea is not known. If it did ultimately make it to port, its
human cargo would have been sold to the highest bidder, with some portion of the profits ending up in Brown's pockets.

Privateers sometimes brought captured enslaved persons back to their
home ports and put them up for sale in the public auctions where the prize
ship and its contents were on the block. In Cape May, New Jersey, the number of enslaved persons owned by white households spiked—in some areas
tripling—during the war. From contemporary newspaper accounts and
legal notices, it is clear that much of that increase came from the sale of privateers' human cargo. As one study of the treatment of Africans seized by
privateers concluded, the prize system "presumed that blackness equaled
enslavement." The Northern states were complicit in slavery, and as so many
others have pointed out, the existence and pervasiveness of Black enslavement in the new nation contradicted its most fundamental principles.

At least one enslaved person, Titus, capitalized on privateering by serving as an agent for shipowners—finding men to sign on and receiving a fee
for each new recruit. Titus worked for the Cabot family of Salem, which
became wealthy through its ownership of numerous privateers. In the summer of 1781, Elizabeth Cabot was preparing her will. In it, she gave Titus
£40 and his freedom, provided he stay by her side until her demise. According to prolific diarist and Salem lawyer William Pynchon, "Titus cares not
[about such an inducement], as he gets money apace, being one of the agents
for some of the privateersmen, and wears cloth shoes, ruffled shirts, silk
breeches and stockings, and dances minuets at [Harvard] commencement."
Nevertheless, Titus remained with Mrs. Cabot until her death, in 1785.

MONEY WAS obviously a key factor in the dynamics of privateering, but
just how important was it? For the owners of privateers, it was the major

draw. They transformed their vessels in the hope of profiting handsomely from successful cruises, through their 50 percent of the haul. Privateersmen, too, were drawn in by money, but their calculations were often quite nuanced.

The financial reward for service on a privateer or a navy ship depended on the type of prize. If a naval ship captured a British warship, the officers and crew split 100 percent of the prize money, whereas if a privateer captured a British warship, the privateersmen only got 50 percent of the prize money, after the owners' cut. This would seem to be a clear incentive to join the navy rather than signing on to a privateer, but in reality it wasn't. Capturing a British warship was an exceedingly rare event, and not something to be expected. But capturing a merchantman was far more common—and the basis of the entire privateering enterprise.

After seizing a merchantman, naval officers and crew received 50 percent of the prize's value, the same percentage that went to privateersmen. But there were other factors at play. Naval ships were in the public service, and as such they could not exclusively pursue rich merchant prizes. Instead, much of their time was devoted to ferrying diplomats and dispatches across the Atlantic, convoying merchant ships, and protecting American ports from British attacks. These duties meant that naval ships were not free to cruise waters where the prospect for capturing prizes was greatest. In contrast, since privateers' sole purpose was to capture prizes, they could sail where they wanted and attack any legitimate target, thereby greatly increasing their chances of success and profits.

Privateers offered better financial prospects through the disposition of prizes as well. When naval ships brought in a prize loaded with supplies that would benefit the navy or army, Continental purchasing agents sometimes appealed to the patriotism of other bidders to persuade them to refrain from bidding at the prize auction, allowing Congress to obtain the munitions or other goods at a cheaper cost. Officers and crew of the naval ship would receive less money for their portion of the prize than they otherwise would have, had the auction been an open contest among all comers.

The reality that privateering was more financially attractive than naval service created a major problem for both the Continental and state navies. Because many potential recruits chose to join privateers rather than naval vessels, the latter often had a difficult time filling their rosters. The role of money in the American maritime war launched a debate that continues to this day. Were privateer owners and privateersmen motivated by greed, patriotism, or some combination of the two?

Famed naval officer John Paul Jones believed it was nothing but greed. Early on in the war, he wrote to Robert Morris, complaining that "the common class of mankind are actuated by no nobler principle than that of self-interest; this, and this alone determines all adventurers in privateers; the owners, as well as those whom they employ." A less cynical assessment comes from the late nineteenth-century historian Francis Raymond Stark, who agreed that while money was a key driver, privateersmen in the Revolution "were unlike any which the world had ever seen before. It would be idle, of course, to pretend that they were all inspired by patriotic motives only; but it is certain that the patriotism of most of them was of a purer character than that of their English and French predecessors. For the first time in its history the privateer-system assumed approximately the shape of a marine militia or volunteer navy."

Only a small number of privateers, owners, and investors ever wrote or spoke about their true motivations, leaving later generations to speculate about what was in the hearts and souls of so many people, an impossible task. As historian Paul A. Gilje observed, "Thousands of men sailed under the American flag during the war and each came from his own particular background and had his own special reasons. There was no single Jack Tar." Nevertheless, given what we do know, Stark's perspective seems closer to the truth.

Part of the reason privateering was scorned was that many believed the practice undermined the republican ideals of the Revolution, which called for the sacrifice of private interests in the pursuit of liberty. According to Mercy Otis Warren, author of one of the earliest histories of the Revolution, privateering "had a tendency to contract the mind, and led it to shrink into selfish views and indulgencies, totally inconsistent with genuine republicanism. The coffers of the rich were not unlocked for the public benefit, but their contents were liberally squandered in pursuit of frivolous enjoyments, to which most of them had heretofore been strangers." Many of the Founding Fathers (and Mothers) and other elites would have agreed, in theory. To them, the Revolution was not to be driven by the pursuit of profit but rather by the pursuit of the public good and America's right to self-determination and control over its own destiny. By the same token, the men who fought in the Revolution, from top to bottom, should be mainly propelled by the same forces.

In practice, however, many of the Founding Fathers and other elites had a more complex view of patriotism, one that wasn't based on hewing to republican ideals above all else. The majority of the delegates to Congress clearly believed that privateering was a patriotic endeavor that served the public good; they made it a major part of America's war strategy, fully aware that it was making some—themselves included—rich, or at least better off. Had Congress deemed that privateering worked against the public good, or that it wasn't a net benefit to the war effort, it could have ended the practice, but it never entertained that thought after the passage of the privateering resolution in March 1776.* John Adams, Elbridge Gerry, and Robert Morris, as well as the other delegates who voted enthusiastically for privateering, were all passionately committed to republican ideals, yet clear-eyed enough to realize that privateering, however ignoble it might be, would help the United States reach the ultimate goal of gaining independence from Britain. In short, the delegates, and many other political and civic leaders, didn't view patriotism and the pursuit of profit as mutually exclusive.

The argument that privateers were only in it for the money implies that others engaged in the fight weren't. But that was not true. While the men who rose up after the Battle of Bunker Hill were burning with patriotic fervor, that fire was difficult to maintain for many soldiers by the later years of the war. In 1780, Brigadier General John Paterson wrote to Major General William Heath complaining about the ragged and discontented state of the men under his command. "It really gives me pain to think of our public affairs, where is the public spirit of the Year 1775? Where are those flaming patriots who were ready to sacrifice their lives, their fortunes, their all for the public[?]" The only way that Congress could keep some semblance of a strong fighting force was to use cash bonuses and the promise of land to induce men to enlist for three-year stints or the duration of the conflict.

---

* Congress's support for privateering, despite grumblings from some, brings to mind an observation made by the Welsh jurist and politician Sir Leoline Jenkins in the late 1600s. "Privateers are like the astrologers of ancient Rome," he said. "Everyone condemns them, but whenever occasion offers, everyone makes use of them." See Frederick J. Jacobsen, *Laws of the Sea, with Reference to Maritime Commerce, During Peace and War*, trans. William Frick (Baltimore: Edward J. Coale, 1818), 385.

Some colonies offered similar inducements to fulfill their troop quotas. The resulting army was largely composed of men from the bottom of the social hierarchy, the poorest and most desperate, while men of means shied away from serving because they could afford to. As John Adams observed, why would "men who could get at home better living, more comfortable lodgings, more than double the wages, in safety, not exposed to the sicknesses of the camp . . . bind themselves [to the military] during the war?" Without bonus payments in cash or land for soldiers on top of their salaries, the ranks of the army would have been much thinner than they were.

The navy was no different. The mariners who joined Washington's navy, as well as those who signed up for state navies and the Continental navy, were all partially motivated by money. Each of the naval services offered officers and crew a cut of the profits in addition to their base salaries, because few would have joined otherwise, as those who created the navy knew full well. Virtually all the world's navies—including the Royal Navy— at the time used prize money on top of base pay to entice recruits, since life at sea was so difficult and unprofitable that it would be impossible to find enough men to crew the ships. John Paul Jones understood this dynamic. When he was in Portsmouth, New Hampshire, in July 1777, hoping to rally a crew for the Continental navy ship *Ranger*, he posted an advertisement that could have just as easily been a recruiting poster for a privateer. Under the heading "Great Encouragement for Seamen," it read, in part:

ALL GENTLEMEN SEAMEN and able-bodied LANDSMEN who have a mind to distinguish themselves in the GLORIOUS CAUSE of their country, and make their fortunes, an opportunity now offers on board the ship RANGER, of twenty guns . . . now laying in Portsmouth . . . commanded by JOHN PAUL JONES Esq; let them repair to the ship's rendezvous in Portsmouth, or at the sign of Commodore Manley, in Salem, where they will be kindly entertained, and receive the greatest encouragement.—The Ship *Ranger*, in the opinion of every person who has seen her is looked upon to be one of the best cruisers in America.—She . . . was ever calculated for sailing faster, and making good weather.

Any gentlemen volunteers who have a mind to take an agreeable voyage in this pleasant season of the year, may, by entering on board the above ship *Ranger*, meet with every civility they can possibly

expect, and for a further encouragement depend on the first opportunity being embraced to reward each one agreeable to his merit.

In addition to the prospect of fast sailing and being "entertained," the
poster added yet another enticement, stating that by order of the Congress,
every able seaman who answered this call or any other call to sign on to a
Continental navy vessel would receive an advance of $40, while every ordi-
nary seaman or landsman would get $20.

George Washington, that paragon of Republican virtue, understood
the mixed motivations of men all too well, having had to deal with numerous soldiers and sailors disgruntled over their pay, or lack thereof. On April
21, 1778, he wrote from Valley Forge to John Banister, his friend and officer
in the Virginia militia, demonstrating keen insight into human nature.

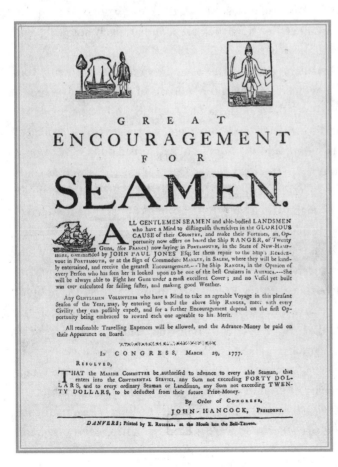

Broadside
published in
July 1777.

Men may speculate as they will—they may talk of patriotism—they may draw a few examples from ancient story of great achievements performed by its influence; but whoever builds upon it, as a sufficient basis, for conducting a long and bloody war, will find themselves deceived in the end. We must take the passions of men, as nature has given them, and those principles as a guide, which are generally the rule of action. I do not mean to exclude altogether the idea of patriotism. I know it exists, and I know it has done much in the present contest. But I will venture to assert, that a great and lasting war can never be supported on this principle alone—It must be aided by a prospect of interest or some reward. For a time it may, of itself, push men to action—to bear much—to encounter difficulties; but it will not endure unassisted by interest.

At another time, Washington observed that the men "who act upon principles of disinterestedness [civic virtue], are, comparatively speaking—no more than a drop in the ocean."

Taking this broader view, privateersmen weren't so different from their peers. If one wants to impugn the motives of the former, one must also be ready to impugn those of the latter. A kinder and, arguably, fairer way to understand what drove men to engage in privateering is to accept that the pursuit of money and the pursuit of patriotism don't have to be at odds with one another. Yes, it is true that all privateers, as well as owners and those who invested in them, were driven by money; and certainly many of them had that as their sole motivation. After all, the merchants who sponsored privateering vessels were businessmen, and privateering definitely was a business venture. The men who sailed on privateers had the welfare of themselves and often their families to consider, and that made it imperative that they try to generate income as best they could. Although many cruises came up empty, enough succeeded to keep the promise of profit alive. But it is equally true that many privateer owners, investors, officers, and crew also believed in the revolutionary cause and were indeed patriots who had the public interest in mind—or at least their interest in being part of an independent country no longer shackled by the constraints of a distant controlling power. Who knows how many privateer owners and privateersmen were moved by patriotic impulses, but that percentage was surely in line with the levels of patriotism prevalent in the society at large.

Without question, Lieutenant Campbell, the Maryland man who left the army to sign up with privateers, believed his commitment to privateering was rooted, in part, in patriotism. Others shared his perspective. As privateersman and soldier Christopher Prince said, looking back on his revolutionary career, "Through the whole course of the war I have had two motives in view, one was the freedom of my country, and the other was the luxuries of life." Rhode Islander Samuel Phillips, who like Campbell left soldiering to become a privateersman, serving on or captaining five cruises, commented on his motivation for joining the fray: "I have ever strove hard and suffered much to help to gain the independence of my country, which I ever held near and dear to me." Privateersman Charles Herbert expressed his devotion to the glorious cause of revolution while in the bowels of Mill Prison, in Plymouth, England, where he had ended up after the Newburyport privateer he was serving on, the *Dalton*, was captured by the HMS *Raisonnable*. In March 1778, having been in prison for nearly nine months, Herbert was visited by a minister and merchant sympathetic to the American cause who told him that the war was going well for his side. Herbert was elated by the news, writing in his diary, "I hope our long wished for prize is just at hand—a prize that is preferable to any other earthly enjoyment. I hope our days of trouble are nearly at an end, and after we have borne them with a spirit of manly fortitude, we shall be returned to a free country to enjoy our just rights and privileges, for which we have been so long contending. This will make ample satisfaction for all our sufferings." Herbert's words were clearly those of a patriot, albeit one who had hoped to make some money as a result of his actions.

The question of patriotism versus greed is complicated by the risks privateers were taking. Benjamin Franklin reportedly said, upon signing the Declaration of Independence, "We must all hang together gentlemen, or, most assuredly, we shall all hang separately." The comment may be apocryphal, but even if Franklin never uttered these words, they ring true. Patriots' lives were in the balance, whether they were captured by the British during the war or seized after, should they lose. Privateersmen faced an additional danger. The British government viewed them as pirates, and, as such, they could legally be hanged. Although they were often threatened with such treatment, those threats were not carried out. Nevertheless, the British government despised privateersmen and threw them into prisons where horrific conditions killed many thousands. Thus capture could be a death sentence. And if the war had been lost, privateersmen and shipowners might have been pursued and jailed, or worse, because of their traitorous behavior. Of course, privateersmen put their lives at risk every time they set sail. Engagements with the enemy were often deadly, and there was also the inherent uncertainty of being on the ocean; more than a few privateers foundered or were lost without a trace. Given all of the hazards involved, it is hard to imagine that money alone could have been reason enough for every privateersman to take up the fight. Some, and most likely a considerable number, must have been moved to action by patriotism as well.

If privateersmen faced particular risks that men in the navy or army did not, many, if not most, nevertheless would have shared a fundamental worldview with their countrymen and countrywomen. On the eve of the Revolution, Americans were arguably among the richest people in the Western world on a per capita basis, and they had one of the highest standards of living. It is no surprise, therefore, that the pursuit of money was seen as a noble calling in the colonies. While much of the strife and anger in the run-up to the Revolution had to do with rights and representation, it also centered on pounds, shillings, and pence. The colonists wanted to be left alone to pursue lucrative commerce without being told what to do. They did not want to be forced to pay taxes when they had no say in the levying of those taxes. During the Revolution, money was an even more pressing concern; without it, there would be no means of paying for the war, and it would have been over quickly. After the Revolution, and up through the present, money has powered American society. To truly understand United States history, therefore, one must follow the money trail, and take notice of who is benefiting or being hurt financially. This is not to say that there aren't many other factors that played a role in determining the course of colonial, revolutionary, or more recent history. Of course, issues of morality, democracy, and justice are also key, and they should be more important than they typically are in practice. But money, and the desire for it, is central as well. Given this, it seems odd and unfair to fault privateersmen for their interest in money, when that same interest has been so tightly woven into the fabric of American society from the very beginning.

REGARDLESS OF THEIR MOTIVATIONS, privateersmen needed a vessel. In practice, most privateers were former merchantmen or fishing vessels, and the most common types were sloops, schooners, brigs, and brigantines, with a smaller number of ships, boats, galleys, and even diminutive whaleboats, which were just twenty to thirty feet long. Later in the war, an increasing number of privateers were built to order, one of the most impressive being Derby's *Grand Turk*, a 300-ton ship pierced for 28 cannons that was launched in May 1781. The key characteristic of privateers, other than basic seaworthiness, was swiftness, which proved critical both to chasing vessels and fleeing a superior foe. As ship historian Howard I. Chappelle correctly noted, "The great American deity, 'Speed,' had no more devout worshipers than the designers and builders of privateers."

Successful privateers also needed to be able to fight, and that meant being well armed. For new vessels such as the *Grand Turk*, the design took into account the need for armaments. Merchantmen and fishing vessels, however, had to be transformed. While they typically had a few small

During the American Revolution, the *Grand Turk* captured sixteen valuable prizes. By the end of the war, the merchant Elias Hasket Derby had built two more 300-ton privateers. This Chinese punch bowl, circa 1786, depicts the *Grand Turk*, one of the first American ships to visit China after America gained its independence.

weapons already on board, such as sidearms and pikes, they needed much more robust offensive and defensive capability. This usually required the addition of cannons or swivel guns, or both.* To accommodate the former, the hull or the bulwarks were pierced, while the latter were bolted to the rail. Cannons added to privateers tended to be on the smaller side, three- and six-pounders the most commonly used. For cannon rounds, privateers secured balls, bar shot, chain shot, and grapeshot, the last of which consisted of canvas bags filled with small iron pellets; grapeshot was intended to kill men, not damage an opposing ship. Swivel guns were much smaller, with each ball about half a pound. In addition to artillery, privateers relied on a range of smaller guns, such as muskets, blunderbusses, and pistols, as well as cutlasses.

Privateers had much larger crews than merchantmen or fishing vessels, often heading out for a cruise with more than fifty men, and sometimes well over one hundred. The large crews were needed to fight and to man prizes. The more prizes taken, the smaller the crew became, and the greater the number of prisoners on board. At some point, it would be either foolhardy or impossible to continue the cruise, forcing the privateer to return home with its now skeleton crew.

Early in the war, most privateers didn't venture too far from their home ports, and cruises lasted only a few days or weeks, or at most a little longer than a month. Later on, as privateers ranged farther out into the Atlantic to the coasts of Europe and Africa, cruises of two or three months or even longer were not uncommon. The combination of large crews and long cruises demanded well-stocked holds. When the New London privateer *American Revenue* left on a relatively short cruise of just over a month, in the summer of 1776, its hold included 23 barrels of salted beef, 28.5 barrels of salted pork, 3,370 pounds of bread or hardtack,† and 7 bushels of corn, with each bushel weighing 65 pounds. There was, of course, plenty of rum loaded as

---

* When privateers couldn't afford or obtain enough cannons and wanted to appear more powerful than they were, they used Quaker guns—wooden dummies that looked like the real thing and often fooled the enemy.

† Hardtack is a rock-hard biscuit made by repeatedly baking bread to remove as much moisture as possible. It could remain "fresh" for months, if not years, withstanding rough handling and varying temperatures. The biscuits could not be eaten directly, so sailors soaked them in water, brine, or coffee to soften them up to the point that they wouldn't crack a tooth. Hardtack could also be cooked as an ingredient in a dish that included meat and vegetables.

Late eighteenth-
century six-
pounder Saker
bronze cannon
with oak naval
carriage.

A three-quarter-pound swivel gun taken from the wreck of either the
HMS *Cerberus* or the HMS *Orpheus*, which were sunk in Narragansett Bay
in the summer of 1778. Swivel guns were small cannons on a swiveling
stand or fork that in turn was mounted on the vessel's rails. Charged
with grapeshot or small balls, they could be pointed in any direction
that fell within the swivel's arc. They were not powerful enough to sink
or even heavily damage a ship but instead were used as an anti-personnel
weapon. The large ball in the lower right-hand corner is a twelve-pound
cannonball, while the smaller ball in the back is a grenade.

well, although the amount was not recorded. No self-respecting privateersmen or any sailor, for that matter, would think about going to sea without
liquor to lubricate the cruise and also provide a tastier and often healthier
alternative to the water on board, which not uncommonly putrefied due to
contamination after long periods of being stored in wooden casks.

The names of privateers offer insight into what the owners loved, valued, admired, or deemed to be worth fighting for. Many were christened after wives, mothers, and daughters. There were at least twenty-five *Betseys*, fifteen *Nancys*, thirteen *Dianas*, twelve *Pattys*, and eleven *Sallys*. Others honored the leaders and heroes of the Revolution. Along with at least eight *Washingtons* and four *General Washingtons*, there were nine *Marquis de Lafayettes*, nine *General Greenes*, six *Count de Grasses*, and five *Franklins*. Some names reflected the tenor of the times, including seventeen *Revenges*, twelve *Libertys*, ten *Unions*, nine *Retaliations*, and six *Independences*. There were twenty-three *Hopes*, but it is unclear if their owners were hoping for riches, or freedom from Britain, or perhaps both. Speed and cunning were other themes, with twenty-five *Dolphins*, twenty-three ships named *Fox*, ten *Swifts*, and seven *Greyhounds*. Other names were literary or philosophical allusions, among them one *Romeo*, one *Tristram Shandy*, and nine *Catos*, after Roman philosopher Cato the Younger (95–46 BC), a determined foe of power-hungry Julius Caesar and a revered figure for the colonists, chiefly elites, who believed he stood against tyranny and for liberty. Then there were privateer names that defied categorization, including two *Additions*, and one each of *Black Sloven* and *Impromptu*.

Once a privateer was christened or rechristened, fitted out, and manned, the cruise could begin. Sometimes, however, extra seasoning was required. With so many non-mariners on board many privateers, it could take a few days or weeks to get the crews in sailing and fighting form. This on-the-job training typically occurred close to the port of departure, because most captains wanted to avoid engaging the enemy with an inexperienced crew.

In the summer of 1778, Captain Charles Biddle of the *Cornelia* was so concerned with the maritime timber of his men that he moored the privateer near the mouth of North Carolina's Neuse River for three weeks to exercise them "in the working of the ship, sending them down the yards and topmasts, and doing everything I could to make them useful and prepare them for action." He deemed this preparation particularly valuable because just past the river's bar were several British cruisers looking to capture American ships. Biddle ultimately ran the gauntlet past the cruisers, and the training continued at sea. To make his men more comfortable with climbing the masts while the ship was in motion, he lashed the hand pump for the ship's water supply to the main topmast. If his men wanted to drink, they had to climb. Biddle later wrote that, for a few days, "many of them would come upon deck, look up wistfully at the pump, but rather than go aloft would go down again." Soon, however, the reluctant crewmen were scampering up the mast with ease. Biddle's confidence in his crew rose, and he felt they "would fight well if brought to action."

Privateering cruises were characterized by lengthy periods of relative inactivity, punctuated by brief moments of intense action. To locate British ships, privateers patrolled areas where they were most likely to be found. Favorite hunting grounds included the vicinity of Britain's sugar colonies in the Caribbean, such as Jamaica and Barbados, off the coast of New York, and as far afield as along western Europe and Africa.

Most of the time, privateers hunted alone, but often enough they sailed in small packs. The increased firepower made them more intimidating, but it came at a cost, given that the proceeds from prizes jointly captured were divided, with the vice admiralty court deciding which of the privateers involved in the action had made the most significant contribution.

Many packs of privateers were successful, but a few were absolute failures. In the late spring of 1780, the New London privateer sloop *Hancock*, captained by Peter Richards, had only recently left port when it fell in with another New London privateer, the schooner *Minerva*—the captain was Nicoll Fosdick—and one from Salem, a brig, captained by a man named Welden. They decided to sail together and, upon sighting a powerful British ship with twenty-four cannons, agreed on a plan of attack. The *Hancock* would go in first and engage the British vessel, whereupon the two other privateers would swoop in and get under its stern to compel its surrender with raking fire.

The *Hancock* did its part, yet when the shooting began, the schooner and the brig were where the *Hancock* had left them, six miles off. For an hour, the *Hancock* and the British ship fought at close quarters. Much of the *Hancock*'s rigging was cut away, and two men were killed. Finally, the schooner and the brig started sailing toward the action, but very slowly. While they were still a good distance off, a twelve-pound cannonball ripped through the *Hancock*'s mainmast about fourteen feet from the deck, nearly toppling it. According to one of the *Hancock*'s officers, the sloop was in "a perilous situation, for all our stays and many of our shrouds were cut away and nothing to secure the mast, which must be done immediately or we should become a wreck."

A short while later, more than two hours after the battle had begun, the Salem brig was within fifty feet of the *Hancock*. In a fit of anger, one of the *Hancock*'s gunners fired on the brig, almost hitting the man at the helm and damaging the main boom. Welden yelled across the water demanding to know why the *Hancock* had fired on them, to which Richards responded that he hadn't ordered the firing, and that he would brook no more questions on the subject. Perhaps chastised, Welden maneuvered into position behind the British ship's stern and fired, prompting it to disengage from the fight and sail away.

The men on the *Hancock* cleared the decks, tended to the injured, and consigned seven of their brethren to the deep. Then they began repairing the rigging and shoring up the mainmast. While the work was underway, the *Minerva* came up alongside and Fosdick asked a few questions of the *Hancock*'s crew but was ignored. When Welden offered his assistance, the men on the *Hancock* responded with derision. "We told him we despised his conduct, for if he and Fosdick had come as they ought to have done, we should have that ship now in possession." As for Fosdick, the *Hancock*'s crew branded him a "coward." The owner of the *Minerva* agreed, and when his schooner returned to New London, he barred Fosdick from ever commanding another of his privateers. Despite Fosdick's well-earned reputation as a coward, he was later hired as captain of the New London privateer *Randolph*, which went on to compile a respectable record of captures.

LIFE ON BOARD a privateer was fairly monotonous most of the time, and the work was relatively light because of the many hands. Watches scanned the horizon for vessels, while other crew prepared the ship for an engagement by practicing the manning of battle stations and checking that all armaments were in good working order. Given the relatively large crews, sleeping arrangements were tight, especially for winter cruises in the northern latitudes when the men had no alternative but to sleep belowdecks.

The food was not particularly tasty, but it served its main purpose of supplying enough calories for the men to perform their jobs. On the privateer *Porus*, sailing from Salem in 1781, the bill of fare ran as follows: Sunday, beef and pudding;* Monday, pork and peas; Wednesday, beef; Thursday, beef; Friday, pork and beans; and Saturday, salted fish. What the men ate on Tuesday is not clear, since the captain's clerk failed to record that day's repast, although it surely wasn't any more inspired than the meals on the other days. There were occasional treats, often served on Sundays, such as lobscouse, a mixture of chopped meat, vegetables, and biscuits boiled with grease and spices. And depending on the initiative and skill of those on board, fresh fish, caught off the side of the vessel, could be added to the diet. Such was the case on the Providence privateer *Hope*, which was off the coast of Virginia when one of the men caught a herring-hog, or harbor porpoise, that made "a fine breakfast, and dinner for the whole crew."

The limited variety of food was not the only downside to the gustatory options available to privateers. The longer the cruise, the greater the likelihood that stores would spoil—if the food wasn't already spoiled when loaded in the first place, given that provisioners were not always the most honest individuals. Rotten meat and vegetables, as well as bread riddled with weevils, were relatively common.

THE CAPTAIN WAS the ultimate authority on a privateer. This was no pirate ship where the crewmen voted their leader in or out. When a vessel was sighted, the captain had to decide whether or not to pursue it. The decision was easy to make when a large British warship was in view. The only rational thing to do in this instance was flee, because even a large privateer would not have a chance against such a ship. There were, however, a few smaller British warships that American privateers did engage and capture. Nevertheless, the main targets of privateers were merchantmen and military supply ships. Deciding whether to attack those sorts of vessels was often a harder decision, requiring skill at reading the signs.

The first task was to size up the potential prize. Merchantmen and supply ships were often formidable, bristling with cannons. If the vessel looked too imposing, the privateer would give it a pass. But if it was a manageable size, the next step was making sure it was a British ship, or a ship

---

* Pudding described a variety of concoctions, but a typical one included flour, lard, and yeast mixed with equal parts fresh and salt water. Sometimes raisins were added, transforming the mix into what was rather oddly called plum pudding.

from a neutral country that was supplying the British, which was also an allowable target. This was not always straightforward. Many ships carried multiple flags from different nations, using them to throw off potential enemies—the *ruse de guerre*, or flying of false flags. American privateers relied on the same tactic, often raising the British colors to lure ships in and then, when in firing range, hauling down the Union Jack and replacing it with an American flag—required before engaging with the enemy, according to international law, so as to leave no doubt about the vessel's true identity.* On more than one occasion, two American privateers, both engaging in such deception, began firing on each other before realizing their mistake.

The best means of determining if a vessel was a potential prize was to get close enough to ask for identification, typically using a speaking trumpet. If the answer raised suspicions, the privateer would likely ask the captain or crew to take down the vessel's colors and then prepare for boarding so the truth could be discerned. By the same token, if the answer made clear that the vessel was fair game, the privateer would order those on board to surrender. If the Americans were lucky, they would immediately do so. If there was any hesitation or aggressive action, the fight was on.

Privateers often tried to pound the enemy into submission through repeated broadsides. Sometimes sharpshooters on the masts or in the rigging picked off officers and crewmen on the other ship. Another tactic was to bring the privateer alongside the potential prize for boarding. Scores of privateersmen jumping over the rails, waving cutlasses and leveling pistols, frequently overwhelmed the enemy in short order, especially when they were boarding a merchantman with a small crew.

---

* There was no single flag that privateers used during the Revolution, because many still identified themselves by colony first. In trying to explain to the ambassador of Naples the different flags that American vessels might fly, Benjamin Franklin and John Adams said, "It is with pleasure that we acquaint your excellency that the flag of the United States of America consists of thirteen stripes, alternately red, white, and blue; a small square in the upper angle, next the flagstaff, is a blue field, with thirteen white stars, denoting a new constellation. Some of the States have vessels of war distinct from those of the United States. For example, the vessels of war of the State of Massachusetts Bay have sometimes a pine tree [with the words "Appeal the Heaven" beneath]; and those of South Carolina a rattlesnake, in the middle of the thirteen stripes. Merchant ships have often only thirteen stripes, but the flag of the United States, ordained by Congress, is the thirteen stripes and thirteen stars above described." See Franklin and Adams to the ambassador of Naples, October 9, 1778, *The Revolutionary Diplomatic Correspondence of the United States*, vol. 2, ed. Francis Wharton (Washington, DC: Government Printing Office, 1889), 759–60.

These drawings of the Philadelphia privateer sloop *Comet* (left), and the privateer schooner *Mars*, whose owners hailed from Cape May, Cape Henlopen, and Philadelphia, were made by a Hessian soldier, Andreas Wiederholdt. He was one of more than two hundred Hessians on board the British transport ship *Triton*, which was virtually wrecked by a major storm and then captured as a prize by the *Comet* and the *Mars* and brought into Little Egg Harbor, New Jersey. Note that these two vessels show variations on the American flag during the Revolution. The flags have thirteen stripes but no stars. The *Comet* has five red, four blue, and four white stripes, while the *Mars* has seven red stripes and six white.

Relatively large privateers with multiple cannons were not the only type of vessel that had any chance of success in a fight. The New Jersey privateer *Skunk*, an open boat with only two cannons and twelve men, captured nineteen prizes in 1779. But this feisty little vessel had obvious limitations. When it was off Egg Harbor, captain John Goldin spied through the fog what he thought was a very large merchantman in the distance, and warily approached it. Getting near, he spun the *Skunk* around, so that its stern gun was facing the looming ship, and let a single shot fly. Soon enough, Goldin realized his mistake. "A momentary pause ensued," wrote the *New Jersey State Gazette*. "All at once, the merchantman was transformed into a British 74,* and in another moment she gave the *Skunk* such a broadside that, as Goldin expressed it, 'the water flew around them like ten thousand whale-spouts.'" The *Skunk* was still afloat, but its sails and rigging were severely damaged. Goldin ordered his crew to man the oars, exhorting them to "lay low, boys! lay low for your lives!"

Some privateering captains relied on cunning rather than arms. In the summer of 1776, the Philadelphia privateer *Hancock* was cruising the tropics when it encountered the British merchantman *Reward*, which had just left Tortola and was bound for London. The 115-ton *Hancock* was dwarfed by the 600-ton *Reward*, and with only 12 cannons on board, the former had two fewer than the latter. But the *Hancock*'s captain, Wingate Newman, wasn't interested in a fight. Instead, he hoped to deceive. He had a British flag fluttering atop the mainmast and, to further allay the British captain's concerns, put out a light indicating that he was in need of a pilot.

It worked. As the *New-England Chronicle* later reported, "the captain of the [British ship] . . . taking the *Hancock* to be one of the Tyrant's pilferers was very much rejoiced to fall in with her." Since dusk was fast approaching, however, the British captain decided to wait until morning to lend a hand. When morning came, he invited Newman to come on board the *Reward* and share breakfast with him. Newman demurred, claiming that his hands were too few and most of them sick, making it difficult even to man a boat to take him over. In a courteous move, Newman invited the British captain and some of his crew to join him on the *Hancock* for a friendly repast. The British captain and twelve of his men climbed aboard the American privateer and were subdued in short order. Not a shot was fired. Newman sent twelve of his own men to the *Reward*,

---

* A 74 was a British warship with two gun decks and seventy-four guns. It was classified as a third-rate ship of the line by the British navy. It is likely that Goldin exaggerated its firepower; regardless, it was no lightly defended merchantman.

Schematic of a British third-rate ship of the line
from 1728. This is the size of the ship that the
Skunk encountered (see pages 77–78).

and the ruse was complete. The *Reward* was now Newman's prize, and it was quite a catch, carrying in its hold roughly a thousand hogsheads of sugar, a considerable amount of cotton, and a few cannons. But the most interesting items in the cargo were the large turtles intended for Prime Minister Lord North. So that there would be no mistake as to the intended recipient of these chelonian gifts, each turtle's shell had been inscribed with the minister's name.

DESPITE THE EVIDENCE to the contrary, many authors and historians over the years have claimed that privateers rarely fought, and in fact shied away from fighting. While capturing a prize in a bloodless manner was the preferred and most prudent course, it is not true that privateers were averse to fighting or that fights were rare. There are many accounts of privateers battling heroically, their crews sustaining numerous wounded and dead. Jonathan Haraden's career offers a series of examples, and another is provided by Wingate Newman during a cruise of the Newburyport privateer *Vengeance*.

A 400-ton brig with 20 cannons and 120 men, the *Vengeance* left Newburyport, captained by Newman, on August 16, 1778. One morning a little over a month later, Newman saw an enemy sailing in the distance and the chase commenced. Once the *Vengeance* was within firing range, a brief battle ensued, with the privateer using both bow chasers* and broadsides, after which the British packet *Harriot* struck its colors. While none were injured on the *Vengeance*, the *Harriot* had one killed and six wounded. Four days later, there was another firefight with the British packet *Eagle*, which the *Vengeance* quickly took. Again the men of the *Vengeance* were unscathed, except that Newman received a musket ball in the thigh. According to the *Vengeance*'s surgeon, Samuel Nye, the *Eagle* had "two of her people killed, and four or five wounded; one of them so badly I was obliged to amputate his leg." Unfortunately for the *Vengeance*, its luck didn't hold. In October it engaged in a vicious fight with the British brig *Defiance*, which had a crew of seventy-two and fourteen cannons. When the smoke cleared and the *Defiance* surrendered, eight British were dead or wounded. On the victorious *Vengeance*, the corresponding number was fifteen.

Losing battles could be ruinous for privateers. On June 7, 1776, the privateer brig *Yankee Hero*, 120 tons and 14 cannons, sailed out of Newburyport with only 26 men, not the 140 that would make up a full complement. Captain James Tracy planned to stop in Boston to fill out his roster before setting out on a six-month cruise. Soon after the *Yankee Hero* left Newburyport, two small boats filled with armed colonials came alongside informing Tracy that a number of British transports had been spotted in Massachusetts Bay that day, prime candidates for capture. Imagining that a fat prize would soon be theirs, fourteen of the men in the boats chose to join Tracy, bringing his crew to forty.

A short while later, a large vessel appeared on the horizon. Thinking it might be one of the British transports, full of army supplies, Tracy sailed for it. When he came within six miles of his prey, however, he realized it was a British warship. Since the *Yankee Hero*, with a reduced crew, was

---

* A cannon placed on the bow of the ship so that it can fire forward at a ship being chased.

no match for such a powerful adversary, Tracy headed for shore, assuming that the warship could not catch up before the privateer reached a nearby harbor on Cape Ann. But the warship, which turned out to be the frigate *Milford*—nearly 600 tons, with 28 cannons and 280 men—was a fast sailer. Benefiting from favorable wind, it came within half a mile of the *Yankee Hero* in an hour's time and fired its bow chasers, to which Tracy responded with swivel guns, reserving his big cannons for the contest to come.

As the *Milford* closed to within fifty yards, it let go with a deafening broadside, and its marines, standing on a main deck that towered over the relatively diminutive *Yankee Hero*, rained down musket and swivel gun fire. According to a report from the American crew, for an hour and twenty minutes the two vessels "lay not a hundred feet from each other, yawing to and fro . . . the privateer's men valiantly maintaining their quarters against such a superior force." To avoid the *Milford*'s big cannons, Tracy maneuvered the *Yankee Hero* under the warship's stern. As the smoke cleared, he could see "his rigging to be most shockingly cut, yards flying about without braces, some of his principal sails shot to rags and half his men to appearance dying, and wounded."

The *Milford* sheared off, and Tracy and his men used the reprieve to try to repair the rigging, yards, and sails. But before they made much headway, the *Milford* came in for another round. The *Yankee Hero* got off two broadsides, which were returned, but Tracy went down, shot through his right thigh. Still eager to continue the fight, he draped himself over a nearby arms chest and continued to bark orders, yet the excruciating pain and loss of blood made him faint. He was brought to his cabin, where he lay unconscious for a few minutes. When he awoke and found that the privateer had stopped firing, and that many "people round him [were] wounded, and . . . in a most distressed situation, most of them groaning, some expiring," Tracy ordered his men "to take him up in a chair upon the quarterdeck, and [he] resolved again to attack the ship, which was all this time keeping up her fire."

It was not to be. On the verge of fainting again, and seeing his brig crippled and so few men able to fight, Tracy surrendered. Four Americans were dead and thirteen wounded. There were casualties on the *Milford* as well, though how many is not known. Tracy and the other wounded privateersmen were sent to a jail in Halifax, from which Tracy and his fellow officers were paroled in the fall. The rest of the crew was impressed into service on the *Milford* and the *Renown*. As for the *Yankee Hero*, it was repaired and transformed into the HMS *Postillion*, and sent to serve off Newfoundland.

Then there were those battles that the combatants neither won nor lost but rather fought to a debilitating draw. The privateer *Hampden*'s engagement in March 1779 was just such an encounter. While cruising in the Bay of Fundy late in the morning on March 7, the *Hampden* spied a large ship in the distance and began the chase. Seven hours later, the ship hoisted the Union Jack, to which the *Hampden* responded by firing a shot, hoping to get the ship to heave to. But it continued on, and as darkness fell, the *Hampden* lost sight of it.

That night, the Americans "were in complete readiness for action," and as dawn broke, the ship was just a few miles distant: close enough for the Americans to see that it was a "beautiful" 800-ton East Indiaman "of much superior force," with 32 large cannons, "two tier of cabin windows, and a stern galley." Its name was *Bridgewater*. Despite being outgunned, the *Hampden*'s captain, Thomas Pickering, assumed that the *Bridgewater*, not being a warship, was "badly manned," and therefore he "determined to fight" it "as long as we could."

An hour later, the battle started when the *Hampden* "came up under his lee quarter within hail, hoisted Continental colors, and gave him a broadside." For the next three hours the two ships pummeled each other with cannon and small arms fire. By the time the shooting tailed off, the *Hampden*'s main deck was awash in blood and covered with splintered wood. Its three masts and the bowsprit were gravely damaged, the rigging and sails shredded, with four men dead and sixteen wounded. Pickering was among those killed. A crewman who had both of his lower legs shot off would manage to hang on for nine agonizing days before dying. Another crewman had "his mouth shot to pieces." The *Bridgewater* was devastated as well, though its casualty figure was unknown.

The shattered *Hampden*, with only its foresail intact, was in no position to take the *Bridgewater* as a prize. Instead, its surviving men let out a defiant cheer, and the American privateer limped away. A month later, the frigate arrived back in Portsmouth, New Hampshire, its flag at half-mast, lucky to have made it without being overtaken and captured by the British. As for the *Bridgewater*, it ultimately returned to England. James Fenimore Cooper, in his history of the navy, wrote that "this [fight] was one of the most closely contested actions of the war, both sides appearing to have fought with perseverance and gallantry."

A FEW PRIVATEERS simply disappeared, along with their crews. On the night of May 3, 1780, a somber scene unfolded at the home of William Pynchon, a prominent Salem lawyer. His son William Jr., called Billy, was having dinner with his parents before heading out that evening on the privateer *Fame* for a voyage to Europe in search of prizes. According to William's diary, Billy "looks sober, eats but little, seems to have no appetite." As Billy said goodbye, his mother and brother cried and his sister made "a long face; grief is contagious."

The *Fame* was in Amsterdam five weeks later, having captured a few prizes on its sail across the Atlantic. It soon headed for home. On the Grand Banks of Newfoundland, it snared another prize, which arrived in Salem on September 20. Upon stepping ashore, a member of the prize crew crowed that the *Fame* "sailed finely and chased all she saw."

The prize's arrival caused the Pynchon family considerable worry, since it had been captured twelve days earlier, plenty of time for the *Fame* to have sailed back to port from the banks. That night, Pynchon vented in his diary: "Now who tells us where she is? At Halifax, New York, or was she chased in her turn, and gone into some harbor?" The next day he cried out for his son, writing "No news of the *Fame*; William! William! *Animum rege*."* On October 6, Pynchon wrote that his wife "is greatly dejected, having no news of the *Fame*. She has neither sleep nor rest." Two days later, he reported that a neighbor "prophesies that the *Fame* and crew are gone to [the] bottom; it at present seems to be the language of fear; they may, for any one circumstance to the contrary, be either at New York, Newfoundland, Charleston, Quebec, or Europe, as well as foundered. Why then need they be given up for lost? God forbid!" The Pynchons' suffering would continue, and over the next ten months, William often repeated the

---

* Latin for "temper," or "rule thy mind."

same refrains—exclaiming that there was no news of the *Fame* or recording still more rumors of the lost ship. Then his entries stopped. Billy and
the *Fame* had vanished.

As DANGEROUS AS battles at sea and sailing in perilous waters could be,
getting prizes back to port was also a fraught and sometimes deadly task.
Prizes were necessarily shorthanded, given that privateers, seeking to continue their cruises, could not afford to place too many crew members on
board. Most of the time, the prize's relatively small crew was not a liability,
and the journey to port was uneventful. But there were many instances of
prizes being recaptured by a British vessel. Even worse were those cases in
which the prisoners retook their own ship.

The British privateer sloop *Tartar* was captured by three American
privateers off the Capes of Delaware in early June 1779. A prize crew was
placed on the sloop, and all of the men on board the *Tartar* were taken
onto the American vessels as prisoners, save for the captain, a Mr. Downe,
and three other men, two of whom were handcuffed. The three American privateers continued to the West Indies, while the *Tartar* was sent
to Philadelphia. It never appeared. A few days after the capture, Downe
managed to slip into the main cabin unnoticed, where he took the priming
powder out of the pans of some pistols located there and also grabbed a
cutlass. Rushing onto the main deck, Downe slashed violently at his captors and was soon joined in the attack by the *Tartar* crewman who had
been given the liberty to walk the deck. Hearing the commotion, the two
handcuffed prisoners stormed out of the hold and knocked down those
Americans who were still standing. Two of the prize crew were killed, the
rest injured or otherwise subdued. Captain again, Downe sailed the *Tartar* into British-held New York City, where the surviving Americans were
thrown in jail.

Privateers that were too successful could be vulnerable to the prisoners
on board as well. The sloop *Eagle*, a New London privateer with a crew
of thirty and six cannons, had an enviable run in the spring of 1779 cruising Long Island Sound and Block Island Sound, capturing seven British
vessels. Manning them as prizes stripped the *Eagle* of half of its crew and
created an imbalance on board the privateer, where there were now sixteen prisoners who immediately began plotting their revenge. When an

opportune moment presented itself, they rose up and slaughtered every American save for two boys. The victors then sailed the *Eagle* to British-controlled Newport.

ONCE A SHIP WAS CAPTURED, sent into port, adjudicated in the vice admiralty court, and found to be a lawful prize, a public auction was held by the court's marshal, the local sheriff, or an auction house to sell the ship and its contents. Anyone could bid, including quartermasters of the army and navy, as well as the owners of the privateers themselves. The proceeds were then distributed according to the privateer's articles of agreement. In the later years of the war, instead of selling the contents and doling out the shares in money, the cargo itself was dispensed because Continental currency depreciated so rapidly that its value declined almost the second it was paid—hence the phrase "not worth a continental," which was commonly used at the time.

When privateersmen returned from a successful cruise, like many sailors they often spent their money recklessly on drinks and entertainment, carnal and otherwise. Afterall, the sailor's creed was "what I had I got, what I spent I saved, and what I kept I lost." A British commander captured by a privateer and imprisoned in Boston in May 1777 observed that

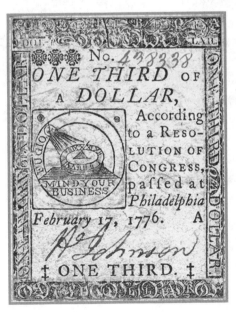

Continental bill
from 1776.

"Boston Harbor swarms with privateers and their prizes. This is a great place of rendezvous with them. The privateersmen come on shore here full of money, and enjoy themselves much after the same manner the English seamen at Portsmouth and Plymouth did in the late war."

A humorous account of what awaited a triumphant privateersman on his return home appeared in the January 4, 1779, issue of the *Boston Gazette*. "Well Jack! what think you of the times! Do you intend to sheath this trip? Did you see Mol last night? Why she is as fine as a fiddle, she's got all Dick's prize money . . . I see her there in that shop buying gauze and ribbons, *the trumpery of the times*—burn my old shoes if privateering hasn't made *some* of the girls look finer than their mistresses. . . . We must raise our wages or take more prizes, for my purse is going into a consumption fast."

The following month, the same newspaper ran a letter from another privateersman that was hardly funny at all. This man returned home from a cruise in February 1779 only to discover that his hard-earned savings had been depleted by his wife, and he let his feelings be known. "Whereas Elizabeth the wife of me the subscriber, has run me in debt while I was at sea, wasting my substance by riotous living, and as I am in danger of being further run in debt by the said Elizabeth, this is to warn all persons harboring or trusting her on my account for the future, as I will not pay one farthing from this date." Whether the marriage lasted is unknown.

Despite the vicissitudes of privateering, many men became serial privateersmen, signing on for multiple cruises. Few, if any, surpassed Philip Besom of Marblehead for sheer devotion to this kind of revolutionary career. By the end of the war, Besom had served on ten different privateers. And when the War of 1812 began, he took up privateering once again.

AMERICAN PRIVATEERSMEN SAILED throughout the Atlantic in search of prey, traveling from Nova Scotia to the West Indies, and from the North Sea to Africa. Their aims and exploits made them central to the American Revolution. And one of the most important roles they played in the conflict involved France.

The French Connection

Louis XVI, king of France, wearing his
grand royal costume in 1779. Oil painting
by Antoine-François Callet, 1789.

WILLIAM BINGHAM GREW UP IN A PROSPEROUS HOUSEHOLD IN PHIL-adelphia. A precocious student, he entered the College of Philadelphia (later University of Pennsylvania) in 1765 at the age of thirteen, graduating with honors three years later, and then spent another two years pursuing a masters of arts degree. After that, he worked for a Philadelphia merchant and also invested in a number of shipping ventures, before going abroad for a Grand Tour. In late 1775 Bingham was tapped to be secretary of the Continental Congress's Committee of Secret Correspondence,* whose purpose was in part to develop relationships with potential allies, especially France, and win their support for the revolutionary cause. Among the committee's more active members were Benjamin Franklin and Robert Morris.

Bingham's tenure as secretary was relatively brief, because it turned out that the committee needed him for an even more delicate job. He was to be the committee's man in the French colony of Martinique, where he was assigned multiple roles. He would present himself as an American merchant, in the employ of Robert Morris's firm—Willing, Morris, & Co.—conducting private business. At the same time, however, he would be working for the committee to obtain munitions and supplies, as well as intelligence about France's intentions regarding the Revolution and whether it would support the Americans. In the words of the committee, Bingham was "to feel the pulse of the French Government, to know whether it beat towards American independency."

In addition to intelligence gathering, Bingham was instructed to extend American privateering efforts. Specifically, the committee told him to "encourage as many private adventurers as you can," and to secure permission from the French to allow American privateers to enter the port of Saint-Pierre to sell their prizes. If Bingham were successful in these two tasks, the number of privateers harassing the British would increase, and it would be much easier for American privateers to operate in the Caribbean. They would no longer need to travel back to colonial ports to sell their prizes and get fitted out for their next cruises.

On July 3, 1776, Bingham sailed from Philadelphia to Martinique on board the Continental navy ship *Reprisal*, carrying with him a fistful of let-

---

* It was later renamed the Committee of Foreign Affairs.

William Bingham.

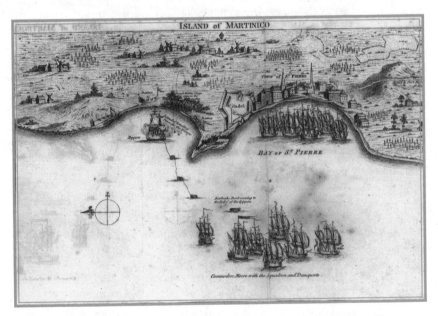

Island of Martinique, circa 1762, showing the port of Saint-Pierre
under attack during the Seven Years' War by a squadron of British
warships. During the Revolution, Saint-Pierre became a center
for American privateering. A massive eruption of Mount Pelée
in 1902 destroyed the town, killing roughly 28,000 people.

ters of marque. He arrived on July 27 to a notably warm welcome. France had already been clandestinely supplying the Americans with money and arms, and just a few days before Bingham set foot in Martinique, a French frigate had arrived with a message from the home government, ordering the colonial governor "to give all possible assistance and protection to the American vessels" and to allow American privateers to bring their prizes to Martinique and dispose of them "as they should think proper." Bingham, who was "treated with as much respect [by the island's governor] as the British ambassador at Paris," was delighted, as was the committee. Over the next year and a half, he carried out his duties with consistent effectiveness, acquiring or facilitating the transfer of arms and gaining valuable intelligence. But it was in the privateering arena that his impact was most significant.

Soon after he arrived in Martinique, Bingham's mission evolved. One of his main goals was now to create more friction between the British and the French, in the hope that a major rupture would result in France's formally allying with the Americans and declaring war on the British, thereby necessarily greatly improving America's chances of success in the contest. Britain and France had been intermittent enemies for centuries, and ever since the latter's ignominious defeat in the Seven Years' War, it had had sought revenge and to regain its position of preeminence in Europe and around the world. Bingham perceived that privateering could deepen British anger and further his broader aims. In his own words, he tried to provoke "the two powers to mutual depredations on each other, by sowing the seeds of jealousy and discord betwixt them, and by affording them matter for present resentment, and renewing in their minds the objects of their ancient animosity. . . . Hence, I took an early and active part in the arming of privateers out of this port, to annoy and cruise against British property." Bingham dispensed privateering commissions and helped American privateers auction their prizes in Saint-Pierre. He also invested in many privateers himself. The privateers he commissioned and invested in were of a different sort than those originating in the colonies. Instead of being manned mainly by Americans, Bingham's privateers were typically crewed mostly by Frenchmen but captained by Americans, and sometimes supplemented with a few American crew members to give the privateers the legal patina of American sponsorship.

Bingham's privateering activities infuriated Britain. After all, Britain's trade with its West Indian colonies was far more valuable than its trade with its American colonies. Europeans were addicted to sugar, now requir-

A Representation of the SUGAR-CANE and the Art of Making Sugar.

This 1749 engraving by John Hinton, titled *A representation of the sugar-cane and the art of making sugar*, shows a white overseer directing enslaved persons at a sugar plantation in the West Indies.

ing it for their tea, coffee, cocoa, jams, and cakes, and Britain's sugar colonies, including Jamaica and Barbados, helped them satisfy these cravings, all while filling Britain's coffers. On the eve of the American Revolution, Britain's sugar trade brought in £3 million, roughly twice the amount from American imports. To grow and process all that sugar, Britain's sugar colonies used huge numbers of enslaved people, most of whom were brought to the Caribbean by British slave traders at phenomenal profit. In promoting privateering and threatening Britain's lucrative West Indian trade, Bingham was aiming a dagger at the heart of Britain's Atlantic empire.*

---

* For an authoritative British perspective on the importance of the empire's West Indian colonies, consider King George's comments in early 1779, when Britain and France were at war. "Our islands must be defended, even at the risk of invasion of this island [England]. If we lose our sugar islands, it will be impossible to raise money to continue the war" (King George to Lord Sandwich, September 13, 1779, *The Correspondence of King George the Third from 1760 to December 1783, Printed from the Original Papers in the Royal Archives at Windsor Castle: 1778–1779*, vol. 4, ed. John Fortescue [London: Macmillan and Company, 1928], 433).

In January 1777, Thomas Shirley, the governor of the Bahamas, a British colony, sent a letter to the comte Robert d'Argout, French governor of Martinique, bemoaning d'Argout's support of privateering. As Shirley said, that stance "is a matter of great concern and alarm to His Majesty's loyal subjects here, looking upon this [as a] piratical kind of war." A few months later, a resident of British-controlled Grenada offered a glimpse of the damage those privateers had wrought. "Everything continues excessive dear here, and we are happy if we can get anything for money, by reason of the quantity of vessels that are taken by the American privateers. A fleet of vessels came from Ireland a few days ago; from sixty vessels that departed from Ireland not above twenty-five arrived in this and the neighboring islands; the others (as it is thought) being all taken by the American privateers. God knows, if this American war continues much longer, we shall all die with hunger." Around the same time, an Englishman in Jamaica complained that "within the space of one week upward of fourteen sail of our ships" had been carried into Martinique by American privateers. According to a British spy in Saint-Pierre, on a particularly busy day in 1777, there were eighty-two captured British ships in the harbor, all waiting to auctioned to the highest bidder.

Sugar ships from Barbados were often forced to delay their departures, waiting "for the arrival of men-of-war from England to convoy them home, they not daring to stir on account of the multitude of American privateers." But convoys worked only as long as the warships remained at the side of the merchant vessels. In one instance, nine ships from the sugar islands were convoyed for more than five hundred miles before the men-of-war left them, the assumption being that the merchant ships were no longer in danger. According to London's *Public Advertiser*, soon after the men-of-war departed, the American privateers *Revenge* and *Montgomery* picked off seven of the nine ships "with the greatest of ease," even though they only had twenty-two cannons between them.

Early in 1777, a group of London merchants sent a letter to the British Admiralty claiming that captures by American privateers and naval ships in the West Indies had cost them £1.8 million. A year later, the House of Lords was presented with statistics showing that American privateers— those commissioned by Bingham, as well as other coming from the American states—had captured roughly 250 British ships trading with the West

Indies since the commencement of hostilities. It was estimated that the volume of British trade with the West Indies had fallen 66 percent from prewar levels. These losses ruined many West Indian trading firms and forced the British government to divert more naval ships to convoy duties, leaving fewer available for military actions. Predictably, insurance rates rose. Before the war, the rate for merchantmen traveling to the West Indies was 2 percent. That figure doubled, provided that the ship was accompanied by a convoy. If there was no convoy, the rate jumped to 15 percent (some contemporary sources suggest that insurance rates rose to 30 and 50 percent, respectively, for ships with and without an armed escort). Seamen's wages spiked, in some cases almost tripling, as did the cost of sugar and other West Indian products. So alarming were these figures that the Earl of Suffolk urged Parliament to keep them from the public, pointing out the "impropriety of acknowledging what ought not to be acknowledged at so critical a period, the weakness of the nation."

Britain was irate over these losses, but its anger went beyond commercial concerns. In its eyes, the French were violating international law and their treaty obligations. Because the British viewed American privateers as pirates, France was guilty of promoting piracy. Worse, the French were disregarding the terms of the Treaty of Utrecht, signed between England and France in 1713 at the end of the War of the Spanish Succession. It specifically forbade either power from harboring or aiding privateers from other countries, especially if they had captured British or French vessels. The only exception was when a foreign privateer was in need of immediate assistance due to distress caused by severe weather or damage to the vessel. In that case, the privateer could enter a British or French port for protection or repairs, but it needed to be sent away as quickly as possible.

British ire was directed at the Dutch, Spanish, and Danish as well: although they didn't hand out privateering commissions to the Americans, they had, like the French, opened the ports of their Caribbean colonies to American vessels, including privateers, which were free to come and go and to sell their prizes. The Dutch island of St. Eustatius (today Sint Eustatius) was a particular problem, as the British saw it. On November 16, 1776, when the Continental naval brig *Andrew Doria* sailed into the island's main port, flying American colors, its cannons roared in a ritual salute, to which the guns of Fort Orange responded in kind. With that act

Etching, circa 1781, showing St. Eustatius being
attacked by British warships. The attack ended with
the British capture of the island from the Dutch.

of welcome, the Dutch became the first foreign power, in the wake of the
Declaration of Independence, to recognize American nationhood. In the
years that followed, the tiny volcanic island, which came to be known as
the "Golden Rock" for the flood of trade that it supported, angered Britain
even more by becoming a rendezvous point for American privateers.

AT ROUGHLY THE SAME TIME that Bingham was in Martinique, schem-
ing to support privateers and fuel animosity between France and England,
other American agents were involved in similar efforts across the Atlantic.
In March 1776 the Committee of Secret Correspondence appointed former
congressional delegate Silas Deane, a lawyer and merchant, as an envoy
to France. Like Bingham, he was to present himself as a merchant intent
on trade but was also instructed to provide intelligence to the committee,
and to cultivate a relationship with the French government with the goal of
convincing the country to aid the Americans. Also like Bingham, Deane
quickly discovered that the French were more than willing to help American privateers. By December Deane was writing to fellow committee member John Jay to tell him that "blank commissions are wanted here" to allow

Silas Deane,
circa 1783.

French sailors to cruise under the American flag: "This is a capital stroke and must bring on a war"—a war in which Deane expected that the French would ally themselves with America against their joint enemy, Britain.

In another letter to the committee, Deane made clear that outfitting American privateers in France was not only eminently feasible but could be done stealthily, and that it would redound greatly to America's advantage. "It is certainly . . . a very practicable and safe plan to arm a ship here as if [it were a merchantman heading] for the coast of Africa or the West Indies," and to have that ship stay in port until a valuable British ship leaves from England. At that point, the armed ship, or privateer, could leave the French port, capture the British ship, and bring it to America. When the British ship arrived, it could be added to the American navy, while its cargo could supply the country.

Deane was soon joined in France by Benjamin Franklin, who came over in late 1776. With Virginia doctor and lawyer Arthur Lee, they formed a three-man diplomatic mission intent on negotiating a formal alliance with France. Congress viewed the negotiations as critical. On December 21, 1776, the congressional Committee of Foreign Affairs wrote to the members of the mission clarifying how important it was that the French declare their support for the American cause. For France's own sake, or course. The military force that Britain had brought to bear in America, the likeli-

This engraving shows the Continental navy brig *Reprisal*, captained by Lambert Wickes, being chased by a British cruiser in late 1776. Benjamin Franklin was on board, along with two of his grandsons; Franklin was being taken to France to begin his tenure as one of the American commissioners. It was an eventful trip. Not only was the *Reprisal* chased by British cruisers, but it also captured two British prizes along the way. Since Wickes was under orders from Congress to keep his famous passenger out of danger, he asked Franklin's permission before engaging the first prize. Franklin assented, and Wickes followed up with the second capture a short while later. The *Reprisal* arrived in France's Quiberon Bay on November 29, 1776, the first Continental navy ship in European waters. Bad weather kept Franklin on board for a few days, and finally, on December 3, he and his grandsons were placed on a fishing boat and taken to shore at Auray, eventually making their way to Nantes.

hood of British reinforcements, and the perilous state of American finances "all conspire to prove, incontestably, that if France desires to preclude the possibility of North America being ever reunited with Great Britain, now is the favorable moment for establishing the glory, strength, and commercial greatness of the former kingdom, by the ruin of her ancient rival. A decided part now taken by the Court of Versailles, and a vigorous engagement in the war, in union with North America," would vanquish the British fleet and army, and run them from the continent.

In addition to seeking an alliance, the members of the diplomatic mission had also been tasked by Congress with persuading France to allow American privateers to sell their prizes in France at French ports (not just in Martinique), and to protect those privateers while that business was being conducted. There was yet another privateering initiative that Franklin wanted to pursue. Like Deane, he hoped to commission American privateers to sail from French ports—captained by Americans, manned by Frenchmen. Both men believed that privateering would make war between France and England more likely. Thus began an intricate diplomatic dance involving the French, the British, and the Americans.

DAVID MURRAY, 2nd Earl of Mansfield, or Lord Stormont, as he was more commonly known, was the British ambassador to France. Cultured, sociable, excitable, and paranoid, Stormont was to keep an eye on French activity, most notably any actions that might benefit the American colonies. He viewed Franklin's arrival with grave concern. "I have intelligence from America," he wrote to Lord Weymouth, secretary of state for the Southern Department (which included the American colonies). "Franklin is come with his pocket full of letters of marque, and . . . his intention is to engage French ships, fit those ships with men of this country, and by putting an American or two on board, and giving letters of marque, try to make these vessels pass for American Privateers."

Stormont demanded a meeting with the French foreign minister, Charles Gravier, comte de Vergennes, to see if the rumor was true and, more importantly, what France would do if it was. Stormont told Vergennes that it was "a wild, and extravagant idea, the execution of which, would never be suffered here." Vergennes replied, according to Stormont, "with great seeming openness, that what Franklin had, or had not brought,

David Murray, 2nd Earl of
Mansfield, known as Lord
Stormont. Painted by Sylves-
ter Harding, circa 1760–1809.

he could not pretend to say. *Je n'ai pas fouille dans ses portefeuilles* [I did not search through his papers], but this I can say, that if he has such letters, he never will make use of them here, upon a thing of this nature . . . I can answer you at once, and in the most positive manner, from what I know of His Majesty's fixed resolution, which is not to suffer, any armament, or enrollment whatever, to be made in his dominions, in favor of the Americans."

In early 1777, when the first few American privateers were allowed to enter French ports, Stormont rushed back to Vergennes's office in a rage to lodge a formal protest. He used the same arguments that Britain had employed to object to the open embrace of privateers in Martinique—namely, that the privateers were pirates, and welcoming them violated the Treaty of Utrecht. Vergennes, ever the nimble diplomat, reassured Stormont that France would most certainly uphold its treaty obligations. American privateers would not be allowed to use French ports, except in cases of distress, as the treaty allowed. Nor would France sanction the commissioning of privateers from French shores.

Vergennes was deceiving Stormont. He signaled to the Americans early on that their privateers would be allowed to dispose of their prizes as long as they did so in a manner that gave the appearance of complying with treaty restrictions. That led to some creative solutions, including privateers selling their prizes far away from French ports to Frenchmen who, in turn, brought the prizes in as their own vessels. Other times, privateers would remain offshore, where they would disguise their prize as something other than a British merchantman. A skeleton crew would then sail the prize into Dunkirk (Dunkerque) or other French ports where it would be sold, whereupon the crew would return to its privateer, flush with cash. American privateers also made liberal use of the "distress" clause in the treaty, claiming that their prizes were leaking, for instance, allowing the French to let them in. Once in port, the prize could quickly and quietly be sold. As one nineteenth-century historian observed, "Distress, of course, became a chronic condition of the American privateers in Euro-

Franklin's reception at the court of France, 1778, by Anton Hohenstein, circa 1860. Franklin was arguably the most famous American of the day, and certainly the most revered, not only for his scientific accomplishments and inventions but for his political, philosophical, and literary genius. It was his diplomatic skill, however, that proved most important to the American cause, playing a critical role in bringing the French into the war on the American side.

Charles Gravier, comte
de Vergennes, circa
1774–1789.

pean waters." Vergennes also let Franklin commission privateers, though
he had to do it secretly so as not to further arouse British suspicion.

Vergennes, and the French government he represented, wanted to aid
the Americans for selfish reasons. Not only would American privateers
inflict pain on their historic enemies,* but France feared that if it didn't aid
the Americans, the latter might make peace with Britain—the very thing
that the Committee of Foreign Affairs had warned might happen if France
didn't act. Peace would ruin France's chances of delivering a crushing blow
to the British Empire, and of dominating the trade that France believed
would result from an independent United States. Yet France also didn't
want to anger the British so much that the two empires would go to war
again—at least not yet. France was still rebuilding its military might and

---

* The depth of that animosity can be gleaned from written comments Vergennes made in the
spring of 1776 in a presentation to Louis XVI: "England is the natural enemy of France; and she is
an avid enemy, ambitious, unjust, brimming with bad faith; the permanent and cherished object
of her policy is the humiliation and ruin of France." See Walter Isaacson, *Benjamin Franklin: An
American Life* (New York: Simon & Schuster, 2003), 337.

wasn't ready to fight the British. And the French were not yet convinced that the Americans could beat Britain, with or without French help, so they wanted to bide their time until backing the Americans emerged as the obvious move. Thus Vergennes stuck with his privateering charade—telling Stormont one thing, but secretly doing another—walking a diplomatic tightrope.

His act didn't fool Stormont, who not only had plentiful evidence of privateers coming and going at French ports but also had a network of spies, including the American commission's private secretary, Edward Bancroft, who fed him information about Franklin's designs. Stormont knew exactly what was going on, and he was irate. As the number of American privateers frequenting French ports grew in 1777, and Franklin began handing out privateering commissions, Stormont repeatedly demanded that the French stop aiding the Americans and at one point threatened to immediately return to London unless France clamped down on privateering. Vergennes kept brushing aside Stormont's concerns, either claiming ignorance of American actions—asserting that the privateers were "leaking" and were let into French ports on compassionate grounds—or stating that France was giving American privateers no assistance whatsoever. Vergennes would promise to look into the matter, only to delay the response and come back claiming that nothing untoward was going on. He would also claim that "American" prizes that concerned Stormont actually had French or Dutch owners. Occasionally the French made moves to restrict privateering, arresting privateersmen or seizing a prize, but these were minor actions intended to assuage British concerns, and soon enough the French would revert to form, allowing privateering to proceed.

In early July 1777, Lord Weymouth wrote to Stormont to comment on American strategy for managing the two empires and on the centrality of privateering to that strategy. "The views of the rebels are evident. They know that the honor of this country, and the proper feelings of the people in general will not submit to such open violation of solemn treaties and established laws acknowledged by all nations. The necessary consequence must be a war, which is the object they have in view, and they are not delicate in the choice of means that may bring about an end so much desired by them." But Britain was preoccupied with the Americans and, like France, wanted to avoid another war with its imperial rival. So the British could do little but fume.

FRANKLIN AND HIS fellow American commissioners were convinced that privateering was helping their cause with the French while at the same time injuring Britain. "That which makes the greatest impression in our favor here," wrote the commissioners to Congress, "is the prodigious success of our armed ships and privateers. . . . This mode of exerting our force against them should be pushed with vigor. It is that in which we can most sensibly hurt" the British. Franklin was delighted with France's support of American privateers. "England is extremely exasperated [by] . . . the favor our armed vessels have met with here," he told Congress, in a letter in early September 1777.

Deane, too, was thrilled with France's double game. In a letter to Morris in late August 1777, he told of the many American privateers putting in at French ports to dispose of prizes they had captured in the waters around Great Britain. Such actions had, he gleefully noted, "been of infinite prejudice to our enemies, both to their commerce and reputation—nothing can be more humiliating to these once proud lords of the ocean then the insults they receive on their own coasts and from those they so lately despised."

At about the same time, William Carmichael, secretary to the commissioners, boasted to C. W. F. Dumas, a Swiss national who acted as secret agent for the Continental Congress in Holland, about a Maryland ferryboat turned privateer that had captured five British ships in the English Channel. Carmichael knew the diminutive twenty-ton ferryboat well, having crossed Chesapeake Bay on it on more than one occasion. He was proud of its privateering success against much larger vessels, and he shared with Dumas a recent conversation he had had with a high-ranking British official. The haughty Briton had told him, Carmichael wrote, "that resistance was a chimera in us, since their armed vessels would swarm so much in our rivers as even to intercept the ferryboats." As Carmichael put it, "His assertions are verified vice versa; our ferryboats ruin their commerce." Carmichael added in a postscript that when the captain of the Maryland privateer boarded a British transport and told its captain that he was a prisoner, the astonished man "very insolently asked where his ship was, not conceiving that any person would have crossed the ocean in so small a boat."

And Carmichael, like the commissioners he served, hoped that privateers would help spark war between France and Britain. "It is our business," he wrote to Bingham in July 1777, "to force on a war in spite of their inclinations to the contrary, for which purpose I see nothing so likely as fitting out privateers from the ports and islands of France."

THE SITUATION WAS CHANGING, however. From the end of 1776 through the summer of 1777, British commerce in its home waters had faced constant harassment. The *London Annual Register* ruefully noted "that the coasts of Great Britain and Ireland were insulted by the American privateers in a manner which our hardiest enemies had never ventured on in our most arduous contentions with foreigners. Thus were the inmost and most domestic recesses of our trade rendered insecure; and a convoy for the protection of the linen ships from Dublin and Newry was now for the first time seen."

London's *Public Advertiser* bemoaned the fact "that the greatest encouragement is given not only . . . [at Dunkirk] but all over France, to the fitting out of privateers against the English; that no less than thirty are now equipping in different ports of that Kingdom, and that they want only a sufficient number of American captains to send them all out. . . . Franklin is permitted to grant letters of marque to every ship that is commanded by a native of his own continent." Another day, the same paper asserted that if France continued to allow American privateers to sally forth from French ports to attack British ships, "an immediate war between France and this country will be the inevitable consequence."

One of the most spectacular examples of an American privateer benefiting from French hospitality concerned the Massachusetts privateer *General Mifflin*, captained by William Day. On a cruise off the coast of England in the summer of 1777, the privateer captured twelve British vessels. In honor of their success, the men on board composed a song, one stanza of which went as follows:

> *Let England's boasted Navy,*
> *Return to guard their coast;*
> *For while they war in foreign climes,*
> *Their native wealth is lost.*

But they (once conquering tars) no more laurel'd wreath shall
    wear;
We'll rend them from their vanquished brows to grace our
    privateer.

Day sailed to the French port city of Brest with a few of his prizes in tow. As he entered the harbor, he found a French squadron anchored there, under the command of Admiral Louis Charles du Chaffault de Besné. Day gave the squadron a customary seven-gun salute. According to a contemporary account, this display of respect caused du Chaffault considerable consternation. "A council of war was held therefore immediately, when, after an hour and a half's consultation, it was agreed to return the salute, which was done in form, as to the vessel of a sovereign independent state." When Stormont learned of this, he was apoplectic, and demanded that the *General Mifflin* be sent from the port, which it was, eventually, but not before it sold some of its prizes and its crew was treated royally. As Day later recounted, "We were permitted to go into the King's dock at Brest, to clean (a privilege never granted to a Briton) and when there, received every assistance we could expect, both from the gentlemen of the navy and army, of his Most Christian Majesty."

Britain placed the blame for the maritime assaults in their home waters squarely on the American privateers' being aided and abetted by France. But this was only partially correct. While it is true that American privateers used French ports to dispose of their prizes, and many privateers received letters of marque from Franklin, more than a few of the American vessels attacking the British and selling their prizes in France were not privateers at all. Some were Continental navy ships, or ships hired by Franklin and his fellow commissioners and placed under the command of naval officers, making them, in effect, part of the official navy. The cruises of four naval ships, *Surprise*, *Reprisal*, *Lexington*, and *Dolphin*, captured twenty prizes combined. Additionally, some of the American vessels seizing British ships in the vicinity of Great Britain had no connection to France. These included privateers sailing from the American states that sent their prizes back home, and privateers as well as naval ships that sent their prizes to friendly ports in Spain and Holland. Nevertheless, the British government, British merchants, and the British press didn't make fine distinctions. To them, all the American ships attacking British merchantmen, both around Great Britain and in the Caribbean, were privateers, and most of those were being supported by France. By midsummer of 1777, Britain reached a breaking point over the issue.

Simply put, Britain could no longer ignore France's intentional failure to stop American privateering. Government officials, as well as King George, finally concluded that if France did not adhere to its treaty obligations, then Britain had no choice but to go to war. As Lord George Germain, British secretary of state for the colonies, wrote in a letter to Sir

Eighteenth-century engraving of Gustavus Conyngham. The British viewed him as a privateer and referred to him as the "Dunkirk Pirate." And yet his Continental navy lugger *Surprise* was not a privateer, and he was not engaged in privateering when he captained it—even though the commission he received from Franklin was a bit dodgy and caused problems later, when he tried to get compensation from Congress for his wartime activities. Further complicating the matter is the fact that Conyngham did captain a true privateer later in the war.

William Howe, commander in chief of British land forces in America, "We have lately had so many privateers upon our coasts and such encouragement given to them by the French, that I was apprehensive a few weeks ago that we should have been obliged to declare war." The gravity of Britain's view was made known to France through diplomatic channels, and France, not quite yet ready for open hostilities, buckled, informing the Americans that privateers were no longer welcome in France.

The Americans initially dismissed or misjudged the import of France's new position, assuming that it was just a continuation of the charade. But it wasn't, and the message finally got through. On November 30, 1777, the commissioners wrote to Congress that France was now sincere it its stated intent to stop privateering, and that it would be prudent "to forbear cruising on their coasts, and bringing prizes in here, till an open war takes place, which, though by no means certain, seems every now and then to be apprehended on both sides." Fortunately for the Americans, an open war soon began.

FOR THE MOST PART, 1776 (and most of 1777) was a terrible time for the Americans and their quest for independence. Though the Continental army successfully chased the British from Boston in March 1776 and won the Battles of Trenton and Princeton, it had been trounced by the British in the Battles of Long Island, White Plains, Brandywine, Germantown, and, in July 1777, Ticonderoga.* By the fall of 1777, the British controlled New York City and Philadelphia, and George Washington's army was poorly fed, poorly clothed, ill-equipped, and ravaged by sickness.

France, watching from afar, was dismayed. It was open to the idea of war against the British at this point, but it also wanted to back a likely winner, and the Americans just then appeared to be anything but. However, in early December, Jonathan Loring Austin, sent by the Massachusetts Board of War on a special mission, arrived at Franklin's door in Passy, then just outside Paris, with stupendous news.

Franklin and his fellow commissioners had already been alerted that a

---

* Upon hearing the outcome of the battle, in which British forces reclaimed Fort Ticonderoga, King George reportedly said, "I have beat them! I have beat all the Americans." How wrong he was. See John Fiske, "Ticonderoga, Bennington, and Oriskany," *Atlantic Monthly*, March 1889, 407.

messenger was in Paris, so they had assembled at the sumptuous Hôtel de Valentinois, where Franklin was staying. According to Austin's account, "Before he had time to alight, Dr. Franklin addressed him: 'Sir, is Philadelphia taken?' 'Yes, sir.' The old gentleman clasped his hands and returned to the hotel. 'But, sir, I have greater news than that; *General Burgoyne and his whole army are prisoners of war.*' The effect was electrical." The northern department of the Continental army, under the command of General Horatio Gates, had defeated British general John Burgoyne's army at Saratoga, New York, forcing him to surrender on October 17. Roughly 1,500 British officers and soldiers had been killed, and nearly 6,000 were captured, along with a considerable haul of artillery and other munitions. William Digby, a lieutenant under Burgoyne, said of the loss, "Thus ended all our hopes of victory, honor, glory, etc."

When news of the brilliant victory reached the French government, it moved quickly to formally recognize American independence and to negotiate an alliance. France knew it had to act fast: in the wake of the disastrous loss at Saratoga, England was sending out peace feelers to the Americans. As the comte de Vergennes observed, "The power that will first recognize the independence of the Americans will be the one that will reap the fruits of this war." To that end, the Treaty of Amity and Commerce and the Treaty of Alliance between France and America were signed on February 6, 1778. Samuel Cooper, a minister and friend of Franklin's, wrote from Boston to inform him how this turn of events was received back home. "You cannot conceive what joy the treaties with France have diffused among all true Americans." The Treaty of Amity and Commerce granted the colonies, among other things, most-favored-nation trading privileges and also officially opened French ports to American privateers, ending the need for elaborate pretenses. The Treaty of Alliance would only go into effect once war between France and England broke out, which happened in March. With that, the American Revolution became a world war. And when Spain declared war on Britain a year later, the scope of the Revolution expanded once again.

PRIVATEERING WAS instrumental in these momentous developments. The critical turning point in the Revolution was the defeat of Burgoyne's army at Saratoga, but privateering, while not causing a sharp turn in American fortunes on its own, helped create the situation in which a great American victory could prove decisive in bringing France into the conflict. With respect to American privateering in the Caribbean, historian Alan G. Jamieson presents a persuasive argument. The activities of those privateers "were not a major cause of the war between Britain and France in 1778, but it is clear that they played a part in sharpening the enmity between the two nations, as well as striking at the British merchant community in an area where it was particularly sensitive, the West India trade."

A similar case can be made for the importance of American privateering out of France. Taken as a whole, America's privateering success was, as historian Sam Willis has written, "part of a broader narrative of American successes in 1776 and 1777. Together, [all of these successes] demonstrated on an international stage that the Americans were committed to their revolution and that the British were vulnerable, and they heightened the tension between Britain and her traditional European enemies. In short, they created the opportunity for foreign intervention."

The entrance of France into the conflict had massive consequences. The most important was the French navy's crucial role in the Battle of the Chesapeake and in the ultimate American victory over the British in the Battle of Yorktown. When the British prime minister, the imperious Lord North, learned of Lord Charles Cornwallis's surrendered to George Washington at Yorktown on October 19, 1781, he wailed, "Oh God, it is all over!" He was almost correct. The surrender did lead to peace negotiations beginning in September 1782, resulting in the Treaty of Paris on September 3, 1783. But the surrender didn't end all fighting. There were continuing skirmishes on land and at sea during the negotiations, and even beyond.

The French alliance also reshaped American privateering. Now that there was no need to hide either intentions or actions, American privateers made full use of French ports to outfit vessels, hire crew, launch raids, and sell prizes. The French, too, got into the privateering game, often with an American twist. Between 1778 and the end of the war, at least 150 privateers were commissioned by the French, and of those, roughly 70 were commanded by American captains. These captains chose to fight for their new nation by leading French privateers displaying the French flag and almost entirely crewed by Frenchmen but still striking at the common enemy. A few of the American captains performed so brilliantly that the French government honored them with the rank of lieutenant of the king's frigates.

The French alliance also enabled American privateers to operate more freely throughout the Atlantic. When the French navy sent fleets to America, and battled the Royal Navy for control of colonies in the Caribbean, the Mediterranean, and the Indian Ocean, it stretched the mighty Royal Navy thin, reducing its ability to pursue American privateers. Seizing the opportunity, the number of American privateers surged. In 1776, 34 Continental letters of marque were issued, and the annual number grew sharply from there: to 69 (1777), 129 (1778), 209 (1779), 301 (1780), 550 (1781), and 383 (1782), before crashing down to 22 in 1783, the last year of the war.

Privateering Triumphs and Tragedies

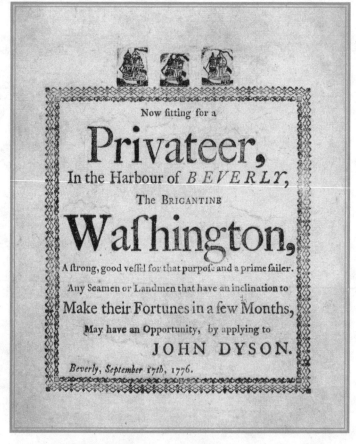

Broadside used to entice men to sign on to the privateer
brigantine *Washington*, out of Beverly, Massachusetts.

PRIVATEERS SAILED FROM MANY PORTS, INCLUDING ANNAPOLIS, Baltimore, Boston, Little Egg Harbor, Newburyport, New London, Newport, Philadelphia, Providence, Salem, Saint-Pierre, and Dunkirk. Of the tens of thousands of privateersmen who hunted the British from 1776 to the end of the Revolution, quite a few came back to their home ports with exciting tales to tell, of battles fought and riches taken. Others related accounts of woe, hardship, disaster, and death. And sometimes, the narratives contained elements of both success and failure. Here, then, are a few of their stories, which give a sense of the great range of the privateering experience.

THE TALE OF THE TWO
*GENERAL ARNOLD*S

Before he threw in his lot with the British in 1780 and his name became synonymous with treason, Benedict Arnold was a revered hero of the Revolution. He had helped take Fort Ticonderoga, conducted an incredible winter march through the wilderness of Maine and Canada to lay siege to Quebec, held off the British in the Battle of Valcour Island on Lake Champlain, and had his left leg shattered while leading American troops to victory in the decisive Saratoga campaign. Arnold was also part owner of at least one privateer, the *General McDougall*.

In a nod to Arnold's reputation and great courage, two privateer owners named their vessels after him, each christening his ship the *General Arnold* while the general was still on the American side. The two privateers had very different, almost opposite, careers. One, out of Newburyport, nabbed a few prizes and engaged in intense battles before being captured itself. The other, from Boston, came to a terrible end.

The Newburyport *General Arnold* was commissioned on April 16, 1778, and owned by Nathaniel Tracy, who amassed an impressive privateering record during the Revolution. Between 1775 and 1783, he was the principal owner of twenty-three letters of marque and twenty-four privateers, in addition to scores of other vessels engaged primarily in trade. His armed vessels captured 120 British ships, the cargoes of which sold for an astonishing $3,950,000.

Nathaniel Tracy,
painted by Mather
Brown, circa 1785.

In converting the *General Arnold*, a former 250-ton merchantman brig, Tracy had its upper deck taken off and added eighteen six-pounders, a process that took the better part of a winter to complete. Thirty-six-year-old Moses Brown was tapped as captain, and an excellent choice he was. Born in Salisbury, Massachusetts, on January 23, 1742, Brown was a man of the sea, having started his maritime life at the age of fifteen. It was said his career was "but a single, continuous, uninterrupted voyage." He was also noted for his probity and courage.

No sooner had Brown set out on his first cruise than he ordered a testing of the cannons, a prudent course given that all the cannons were new to him. As the powder in the touchhole was lit on the first gun, the men watched in keen anticipation. Seconds later the cannon exploded and, according to Brown, "killed or wounded all my officers." Out of this tragic event came a humorous story, likely apocryphal. An Irishman named Pat was severely wounded and taken belowdecks. Fearing the end was near, he asked Brown to come down. Pat pleaded with Brown that upon dying he not be "thrown overboard like a dog, but might have prayers read over him." Brown tried to comfort Pat, saying that he would survive, and that therefore prayers would not be needed. But Pat couldn't be dissuaded from focusing on his imminent end, and finally Brown consented, saying that "Mr. —— shall read prayers for you." This caused Pat, who apparently had a very low opinion of "Mr. ——," to cry out, "No, faith, thin I'll not die! Mr. —— shall never read prayers over *me*." When Brown agreed to read the prayers himself, Pat smiled and replied, "God bless ye Captain! *thin I'll die directly!*" Whether Pat perished or survived remains a mystery, assuming anything about this story is true.

After the explosion, Brown sailed the *General Arnold* back to Newburyport, where further testing of the cannons proved them all to be of inferior quality, with an additional four blowing up, though without casualties this time. Because of the heavy competition for cannons, it took more months to secure new ones. In August 1778, the *General Arnold* sailed out with around one hundred men on board. The first cruise was a bust; the *General Arnold* seized only one prize, and that prize was retaken by the British as the ship headed to port. Out again went Brown in February 1779, sailing across the Atlantic to the shipping lanes off the coasts of Spain and Portugal. Along the way, the *General Arnold* was plagued by further problems. The cook died about a week out, and the men's daily fare went from mediocre to worse. Then some of the brig's spars and, more concerning, its mainmast and foremast were sprung, developing cracks that threatened their integrity. This placed the vessel at a disadvantage while sailing unmolested, let alone in the heat of battle. Nevertheless, Brown continued on.

Early on the morning of March 28, near the Azorean island of St. Michael (today São Miguel), Brown saw a ship about ten miles away that was closing in. It proved to be the Liverpool privateer *Gregson*, with 20 twelve-pounders and 180 men. At 10:00 a.m., the *Gregson* hoisted its Union Jack, and the *General Arnold* replied with its colors. An hour later, the British fired bow chasers, and in short order a full-on battle commenced. It lasted for two hours, at which point the *Gregson* fled. Brown, who was convinced he had won the contest, tried to pursue and take his prize, but the *General Arnold*'s sailing disadvantages, combined with additional damage caused during the fight, rendered it a futile effort, and the *Gregson* escaped.

During the engagement, the *Gregson* had concentrated most of its fire on the *General Arnold*'s masts and sails, which explained why the American ship suffered almost no casualties. The *General Arnold*, in contrast, aimed for its opponent's hull and the main deck. Brown's sailing master, Thomas Greely, said that while they didn't know the number of men on the *Gregson* who were lost, judging "from appearance it must have been deplorable indeed." He was correct. An article in a British newspaper reported that the *Gregson*'s lieutenant and seventeen crewmen were killed, in addition to many wounded. The *Gregson*'s captain paid the *General Arnold* an unintentional compliment, or perhaps he wanted to make his losses more defensible: he told the newspaper that the American privateer was a frigate with thirty-two cannons. The captain also claimed that his ship had "beat off" the American, instead of the other way around.

Even in its damaged condition, the *General Arnold* captured a prize the following week. Soon after, Brown decided to travel to the friendly port of Coruña, Spain, for repairs and refitting. Returning to sea a month later, the *General Arnold* chased a British privateer off Cape Finisterre. It was the *Nanny*—Thomas Benyon, master—with sixteen six-pounders and fifty-seven men. As the *General Arnold* closed in, Brown tried to make the brig look more menacing by hanging ceramic firepots off the foreyards and the jibboom. The pots were filled with gunpowder that could be lit via a wick and thrown onto an enemy ship, where they would explode, sending out a flaming spray that would, it was hoped, ignite a conflagration. Once within trumpeting range, Brown called over to the *Nanny*, ordering its captain to haul down his colors. Benyon was not cowed. "I desired him to begin to blaze away," he later wrote to the *Nanny*'s owners, "for I was determined to know his force before I gave up to him."

After two hours of battling at close quarters, Benyon could have had no doubts about the *General Arnold*'s force. By that time the *Nanny*'s rigging and sails were destroyed, and its hull pierced below the waterline in many places. The pump couldn't keep up with the flood entering the hold, and when the water level reached seven feet and the *Nanny* was on the verge of sinking, Benyon surrendered. A few minutes after the last of the British crew had been evacuated, the *Nanny* disappeared under the waves.

Amazingly, given the damage to the *Nanny* and the fact that Brown's men, by their own admission, rained down more than seven hundred musket shots on the British vessel, only two of Benyon's men were injured, and by splinters, not lead balls (one does have to question either the quality of the muskets or the aim of the Americans, or both). The *Nanny*'s cook did drown during the encounter, and the only thing that the British saved from their ship was its ensign, which was riddled with holes. As for the *General Arnold*, its foreyard was cut away, its mainmast and rigging disabled, and six of its crew were wounded.

When Benyon came on board and relayed how few men were in his own crew, Brown was surprised. As Benyon recalled the conversation, Brown asked "what I meant by engaging him so long. I told him I was then his prisoner, and hoped he would not call me to any account for what I had done before the colors were hauled down. He said he approved of all I had done, and treated my officers and myself like gentlemen, and my people as his own."

Over the next few days, the *General Arnold* captured two more prizes and sent them to Coruña to be sold. But then Brown's luck ended. On June 4, the HMS *Experiment*, fifty cannons, captured the *General Arnold* after a brief firefight. When Brown was brought aboard the *Experiment*, Commander Sir James Wallace* asked him "if he was the captain of that rebel ship." Brown replied, "I was very lately," though "you are now," and presented his sword. "I never take a sword from a brave man!" Wallace said, and invited Brown into his cabin for drinks.

Conversation turned to the larger conflict. Wallace proposed a toast to "George the Third, and the Royal Family!" Although taken aback, Brown nevertheless didn't protest and took a draft of the wine. When Wallace invited Brown to deliver a toast of his own, the proud American did not hesitate: to "George Washington, the Commander-in-chief of the American forces!" What kind of toast Wallace expected Brown to utter is not clear, but this he perceived to be an act of defiance. Incensed, Wallace lowered his glass and said, "Do you mean to insult me, sir, in my own ship, by proposing the name of that arch-rebel?" "No," replied Brown, "if there was any insult, it was by your giving [a toast to] George the Third, which, however, I did not hesitate to drink, though you must have known it could not have been agreeable to me, who at this moment am a guest, though a prisoner." To his credit, Wallace realized that Brown was right and apologized. He then drank to General Washington, however bitterly.

---

* The same man who had captained the infamous HMS *Rose*, which shut down Rhode Island's maritime trade earlier in the war.

Wallace delivered Brown and his men to the Portuguese island of Madeira, and they were then shipped to Savannah, Georgia, and thrown on a prison ship. In November 1779, Brown was released in a prisoner exchange, but he had difficulty getting home. He traveled to Charleston and took passage on two different ships—one of which nearly foundered— whereupon he was dropped on Cape Ann and managed to acquire an old horse that took him back to Newburyport, but not before throwing him a few times. "I arrived home after fourteen months," Brown later wrote, "without money or goods; only one poor heart—and that was broken too."

THE OTHER *GENERAL ARNOLD* was a brand-new Massachusetts brig built for privateering, with 20 cannons and a crew of 105. It sailed out of Boston on Thursday, December 24, 1778, in the company of the privateer sloop *Revenge*, for a planned joint six-month cruise. At the helm was twenty-eight-year-old Captain James Magee, an experienced mariner who had commanded the privateer sloop *Independence* in 1777, capturing three prizes, including a British transport carrying military supplies. On Christmas morning a nor'easter blew in, separating the two vessels. While the *Revenge* made it around the tip of Cape Cod, ultimately arriving in the West Indies a few weeks later, the *General Arnold* was not so lucky. As the weather worsened and the privateer was driven toward the shallows, Magee decided to sail for Plymouth Harbor, where he hoped to find shelter from the storm.

By the time the *General Arnold* reached Plymouth late that afternoon, however, Magee felt it would be too dangerous to enter the harbor without a pilot. So he anchored just offshore, hopeful that the weather would clear. Instead, that night the storm intensified. As the wind strengthened and the seas mounted, Magee ordered his men to furl the sails and lower the sixteen main deck cannons into the hold to help stabilize the vessel, all the while praying that the anchors held. They didn't. On Saturday morning, the *General Arnold*, its anchors dragging behind, crashed into White Flats shoal near the harbor's mouth, puncturing its hull.

According to crewman Barnabas Downs, "The vessel began to leak very fast, and with every motion of the sea she struck the bottom as though she would split in pieces. We kept two pumps going, but could not gain upon the water. The storm now increased to a most prodigious degree: It

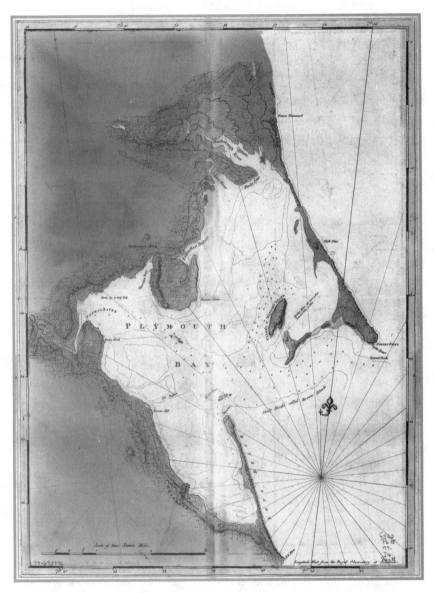

Circa 1770 map of Plymouth Harbor, which is part of Plymouth Bay. This is where the privateer *General Arnold* came to grief.

snowed so thick that we could see but a very little way from the brig, and the cold was extreme."

As the water rose, the brig shuddered with each passing wave, spraying the men and covering their clothes with ice. Panic and despair spread. The entire crew crowded onto the quarterdeck, where they were so tightly packed that one could "not stand up without treading upon one another." The conditions were ripe for conflict. Many of the men lashed out in anger, thrashing so violently that some of them lost their shoes, making their situation even more dire. To dull the pain and fear, some broke open the butts of rum on board and began drinking, while others let out "screeches, groans, and deep lamentations for themselves and their families, and earnest cries to GOD for mercy and relief!" The men found a sail and draped it over themselves for protection, but it was of little help. The first to die was thirty-one-year-old John Russell, of Barnstable, a big man who slipped on the slick deck and fell with such force that he never got up.

Late in the afternoon of December 26, the tide began receding, and by nine it was at its lowest ebb. The *General Arnold* lay motionless, wedged in the sand and mud, its decks no longer covered in water but a sheet of ice. Even though the storm had abated through the night, it got colder still. Death stalked the brig. "Fatigue and distress, added to the extreme cold and despair of relief, put a period to the lives of great numbers. Those who were able to stand were obliged to huddle up close together, and breathe in each other's faces to preserve them from freezing to death, while their comrades were dying around them all night." On Sunday morning, sixty men, contorted in gruesome poses, some embracing each other, were dead. The living stacked some of the corpses into a makeshift wall to shield them from the biting wind and make more room on the quarterdeck. Even so, in the coming hours more died.

Residents of Plymouth, watching the tragedy unfold within sight but unable to reach the *General Arnold* during the height of the storm, now ventured out to the stricken vessel, walking across the ice-choked harbor and using wood planks where necessary to connect the floes. They took the living and the dead ashore. Seventy-two frozen corpses were placed in the Mill River to thaw, and then transferred to the courthouse, where they were laid in coffins. Nine more crewman died in the coming week.

Barnabas Downs would have been counted among the dead had not one of his eyelids fluttered, alerting a rescuer that there was life left in him yet. He was taken to a local tavern, where his clothes were cut away and he was placed in cold water "to take out the frost" and then put in bed under heavy covers. His jaw had to be pried open at first to pour some "cordials" down his throat, but he slowly recovered. His feet, however, were beyond help and soon had to be amputated. Despite this, Downs went on to live

a full and productive life, marrying, siring five children, and working as
a cooper and metalsmith, before dying at age sixty. He maintained great
respect for his old captain, and even named one of his sons James Magee.

As for Captain Magee, he survived and thrived. He captained three
more privateers during the Revolution and later found significant success
in the China trade, commanding or investing in ships that sailed to the
Pacific Northwest to trade for furs with local Indians and then to China,
where the pelts were sold for enormous sums. In 1798 he bought a pala-
tial house in Boston once owned by Massachusetts colonial governor William Shirley, which today is known as the Shirley-Eustis House and is a
National Historic Landmark.

The storm that destroyed the *General Arnold* also caused a privateer to sink just off Martha's Vineyard, with the loss of seventeen men.
Yet the storm proved providential for the people of the island, who till
then had suffered during the Revolution . When the storm began to sub-
side, a resident walking along the northeastern end of the island noticed
something odd in a lagoon. The wind and the waves had cast an enormous number of striped bass into the shallows, and the frigid temperatures had frozen them solid, side by side as though in a tin holding very
large sardines. Word spread, and soon people from all over the island
came to hack out fish and take them home. The British had destroyed
the island's saltworks, and there was, as a result, very little salt for curing
fish. So the colonists packed the bass in snowbanks near their houses, to
keep through the winter, and whenever a hearty meal was desired, they
retrieved a fish.

WASHINGTON'S DENTIST

At the age of thirteen, in 1773, John Greenwood's parents sent him from
their home in Boston to Falmouth (now Portland), Maine, to live with an
uncle who was both a cabinetmaker and a lieutenant in the local militia.
Greenwood helped build cabinets by day and at night went to the militia's drill ground, where he was paid a small amount to play his fife while
the men perfected their marching. Over the next two years, Greenwood
watched from afar as the British moved to suppress the rebellious Bostonians, and as soon as he heard about the Battles of Lexington and Con-

John
Greenwood.

cord, he made up his mind to return to Boston and reunite with his family, fearing they would be killed by the British. He had asked his uncle on other occasions to be allowed to visit Boston, but the answer had always been no. This time, he didn't ask. Instead, early one Sunday at the beginning of May 1775, when he knew most people would be at home or in church, he strapped on his fife and sword, wrapped food and clothes in a handkerchief, and started walking.

Having never traveled on his own more than a few miles, he now walked more than one hundred, stopping occasionally in towns, where he told residents he was going to fight for his country and often struck up a tune on his fife for their entertainment. People warmly welcomed him and were "astonished such a little boy, and alone, should have such courage."

When Greenwood finally arrived in Charlestown, Boston was already under siege. Continental soldiers forbade him from crossing the Charles River to join his family. Even though he ultimately received a pass from army headquarters to enter the city, the soldiers in Charlestown still wouldn't let him through. Without other plans, and almost out of money, Greenwood enlisted in the army.

By the fall of 1776, Greenwood decided that he was finished with military life. He had served for eighteen months yet had only been paid for six. With his enlistment up, he went home to Boston. Over the next two years, he worked as a fisherman and served two brief stints back in the army before embarking on an unusual journey as a privateersman.

In late 1778, eighteen-year-old Greenwood signed on to the Boston privateer sloop *Cumberland* as the steward's mate and a midshipman. His captain was John Manley, who had become a celebrity of the Revolution for commanding the *Lee* as part of Washington's fleet and bringing in the British ship *Nancy* with a hold full of munitions. The *Cumberland* left Boston in early January, heading for Barbados, where it hoped to capture British merchantmen sailing back to Britain. On the morning of the twenty-sixth, not far from the island, the British frigate *Pomona*, with thirty-six cannons and three hundred men, bore down on the *Cumberland*. Manley tried to escape. For more than twelve hours, in squally weather and sometimes within musket range of the *Cumberland*, the *Pomona* continued its dogged pursuit.

During the chase, "one very singular circumstance happened," according to Greenwood. The captain of the maintop came down to the main deck for a drink, and before returning to his perch, he told all within earshot that he was certain he would "never come down again alive." Sure enough, a short while later, the *Pomona* fired a round of bar shot that literally cut the man in half.

That night, in an attempt to gain speed, Manley ordered his crew to throw eight cannons and some water barrels over the side. It was too late. Minutes later, the *Pomona* pounded the *Cumberland* with a booming broadside, sending multiple balls and bar shot through the rigging and sails and into the hull, causing the entire sloop to shudder. While the vessels were still moving ahead, the British captain called across the water, "Strike your d——d rebel colors."*

With no means of escape and no desire to surrender, Manley prepared

---

* As described by Greenwood, the *Cumberland*'s flag was white, with a green pine tree in the middle, below which was an image of a black snake with thirteen coils cut into thirteen pieces to represent the thirteen United States. Beneath the snake was a favorite American motto, Join or Die, in black letters.

to fight. Since the two vessels were parallel to each other, though with the *Cumberland* slightly ahead, Manley planned to turn his ship into the wind. This would swing the bow right into the path of the oncoming frigate, which would slam into the privateer amidships. Such a blow would no doubt sink the *Cumberland*. However, by that time Manley expected all his men to have boarded the *Pomona* for hand-to-hand combat, leading to victory, he hoped—and a new ship. His men were willing, but when they opened the arms chests, they found them almost empty, holding a mere thirty cutlasses and a few pikes. Now seeing no other choice, Manley ordered the colors struck, while many of his men raided the liquor in the storeroom "and became as drunk as so many devils."

Drunk or not, the Americans were hauled aboard the *Pomona*, stuffed in the fetid, steamy hold, and taken to the British jail in Bridgetown, Barbados. For five months, Greenwood languished there. At one point, he and fifty-nine other men were thrown into the dungeon and told that the next day they would be impressed into service on one of His Majesty's ships. So fearful of this prospect was Greenwood that the next morning he asked the *Cumberland*'s doctor, who still had access to his medicine chest, to give him an emetic. If he appeared sickly, Greenwood hoped, the British would not take him. When the first emetic didn't cause any change, Greenwood asked for another. The second dose worked, and when the British officers came to collect American sailors, Greenwood fell to vomiting so violently that he "thought I should have thrown up my entrails." Witnessing this, the officers left him behind.

In June, Greenwood was released as part of a prisoner exchange and was taken to Martinique. There he ran into an old schoolmate, who found him a spot on a brig that brought him to New Hampshire, where he caught a ship to Boston. Soon he signed on to another privateer, the *Tartar*, captained by David Porter, the father of Commodore David Porter. (Commodore Porter would distinguish himself during the War of 1812, and his son, Admiral David Dixon Porter, played a key role in the Civil War and served as superintendent of the U.S. Naval Academy.)

The *Tartar* was an "old, crazy, and leaky" ship, yet it still managed to sail to the West Indies and capture thirty prizes over a couple of months, sending all of them to French-controlled Port-au-Prince for sale. To keep from drawing the attention of British warships in the area, the *Tartar* would disguise itself, with its crew pulling the cannons in, repainting the sides, and striking the topgallant mast. These changes also made it look less threatening to merchantmen. Sometimes it even mimicked a vessel in distress.

In preparation for heading home, the *Tartar* headed to Port-au-Prince to stock up on supplies. As it approached its destination, three British warships appeared on the horizon. They had been sent from Jamaica to capture the *Tartar* and soon closed in. Realizing he would be intercepted before entering Port-au-Prince, Porter headed into a small embayment about thirty-five miles away called Petit-Goâve. Unfamiliar with this stretch of coast, he plowed into a submerged reef, piercing the vessel's hull and flooding the hold. Fortunately, there was a small French fort in the area, and it began firing on the British ships, which quickly departed. The *Tartar* was patched up and refloated, but when it finally arrived in Port-au-Prince, it sank to the bottom of the harbor, though none were lost from its crew.

Left to shift for himself in Martinique, Greenwood signed on to the *General Lincoln*, a letter of marque brig from Salem, captained by Jonathan Carnes, with six cannons and a crew of twenty-five. Off the Capes of Delaware, the HMS *Iris* captured the *General Lincoln* with only a few shots being fired. Typically, when a British ship captured an American prize, the American crew would be divided, with most forced onto the British vessel and the remainder confined on the prize, to be taken into port. The *Iris*'s captain, James Hawker, had a different idea. The Americans left on board the last privateer that the *Iris* had captured had blown up their own ship, killing themselves and the British prize crew, and Hawker wanted to avoid a reprise. He ordered that the entire crew of the *General Lincoln* be brought aboard the *Iris*. But before Greenwood could switch ships, the British captain, standing on the deck of the *General Lincoln*, called him forward. He had heard that Greenwood was a carpenter. Given that the *General Lincoln* was badly leaking, he ordered the young privateersman to stay on the brig, alone among the British prize crew, to repair the pumps and the hull.

A few days later, the *Iris* sailed into New York Harbor and up the East River with the *General Lincoln* in tow. They moored near the Fly Market, the busiest market in the city. While men on shore were grabbing ropes to haul the *General Lincoln* closer to the wharf, a large crowd gathered to see the rebels. With the brig about thirty feet off, an officer from the *Iris* came aboard and told Greenwood to "get your duds and jump into the boat alongside." Greenwood obligingly said yes, and the officer paid him no more attention and left for drinks in the captain's cabin.

In a bold move, Greenwood quickly gathered his clothes, his quadrant,* and his cotton-stuffed mattress and stood near the railing, "dallying a little." When the *General Lincoln* touched the wharf, he executed his plan. The two hundred or so spectators, eager to explore the prize, rushed onto the main deck. At the same time, Greenwood pushed through the crowd onto the open street beyond and briskly walked away.

He knew a loyalist in town who had been a friend of his father's, and he now walked to his house. "How do you do, Mr. Hill," Greenwood said when the man opened the door. Once he explained who he was, Hill replied, "Oho, you are my friend Greenwood's rebel son!" Greenwood said, "I am your friend's son John. Will you be so kind as to let me stay a few days in your house, as I have no home nor a farthing of money in my pocket?" Hill consented and asked Greenwood where he had come from and what had been doing, questions Greenwood parried without really answering, not revealing that he had recently been an American privateersmen.

In the coming days, though, Greenwood shared his story. Hill was alarmed at first, but friendship took precedence over loyalty to the British, and he decided to help Greenwood return home. In the end, Greenwood's host and another friend of his father's brought him to the head of British prisons in the city, one David Sproat, convincing the jailer to promise to include Greenwood in the next prisoner exchange, which was done. Deposited in New London, Greenwood sold his quadrant for $10, using the money to travel back to Boston.

Despite his checkered history at sea, in the final years of the Revolution Greenwood signed on to two more letters of marque, neither of which had a notable cruise. What Greenwood is remembered for, to the extent that anyone remembers him, is not his privateering but his efforts to help George Washington eat. After the war, he became a dentist, and Washington was his most famous client. From his inauguration as the country's first president in 1789 until his death in 1799, Washington wore four sets of

---

* A navigational tool that allows one to determine latitude by measuring the altitude of a heavenly body.

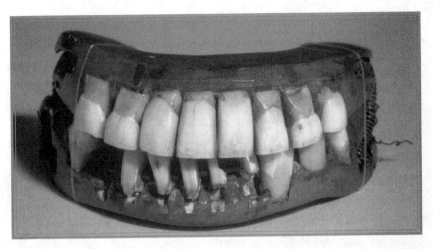

The only remaining complete set of George Washington's dentures, made by John Greenwood, circa 1790–1799, out of a variety of materials, including human teeth, lead, gold, and elephant, walrus, or hippopotamus ivory—as well as springs to help them open. The mistaken belief that they were made of wood arose because aged ivory and human teeth exhibit visible cracks and fractures and become stained brown over time if not cleaned properly. The dentures never fit quite right and were very uncomfortable—the cause, it is said, of Washington's reluctance to smile.

dentures, all of them manufactured and fitted by Greenwood, who later in his career publicized himself as "Washington's favorite dentist."

THE PENOBSCOT EXPEDITION

It was the largest American maritime force assembled during the Revolution: nineteen warships, including three Continental vessels, three Massachusetts state navy vessels, one New Hampshire state navy vessel, and twelve privateers, as well as twenty-five transport ships. Their mission was to dislodge British forces that were building a fort on Majabigwaduce, or more commonly Bagaduce, a peninsula in Maine's Penobscot Bay (in present-day Castine). It was an impressive show of force, at least by the numbers. Together, the vessels were bristling with 344 cannons and manned by nearly 2,000 sailors. Slightly more than 1,000 soldiers were on board the transport ships. As the fleet sailed from Boston on July 19, 1779, spirits were high. Everyone expected a splendid victory.

About a month before, three Royal Navy sloops of war with a total of fifty cannons sailed into Penobscot Bay, accompanied by transports. Soon after, seven hundred British regulars landed on Bagaduce and began building the fort—to be called Fort George. The British had a number of aims. First, Massachusetts privateers had for years been inflicting great damage on British shipping throughout the Atlantic, including along the Canadian coast. The fort would serve as a strategically located base that the Royal Navy could use to clamp down on the rebel raiders. Second, by establishing the fort and planting the flag, the British could lay claim to northeastern Maine. Such a claim would prove useful if they lost the war and were awarded the territory. Northern Maine would provide a valuable buffer between British Canada and the United States. Third, British officials were keen on creating a province in the region where loyalists could find refuge and support. Those loyalists would search the woods for towering pines that could be cut down and sent to Britain to supply the Royal Navy with the massive masts it needed to fit out its fleet. Finally, loyalists with holdings in northern Maine had long wanted Britain to establish control of the area and validate their tenuous claims to the land. If the hoped-for province were won, Britain already had a name picked out: New Ireland.

News of Britain's provocation reached Boston within days of its forces setting foot on Bagaduce. Alarmed and fearful that the colony's main timber supply would be cut off, the Massachusetts General Court issued a call to arms. Although this was to be a Massachusetts-led operation, the colony needed help, and it convinced the Continental Navy Board in Boston and the governor of New Hampshire to contribute forces. The court wanted the expedition to launch within six days, but there were great difficulties amassing ships, men, and supplies. To encourage privateer owners to participate, the court promised to indemnify them against any losses, pay for supplies, and give them 100 percent of any profits that might result from the endeavor. Despite these sweeteners, the court had to impress a few vessels, leading to anger among those ensnared in its net.

Recruiting soldiers proved similarly difficult. Fewer men turned out than hoped for, and those who did were of questionable use. As one officer noted, "Some part [of those who stepped forward] were old men, some boys, and some invalids. . . . they were soldiers, whether they could carry a gun, walk a mile without crutches, or only *compos mentis* [sane] sufficient to keep themselves out of fire and water." Meanwhile, the court's supplies agents went far afield to gather enough food, drink, tools, and munitions to enable three thousand men to survive and fight for a few weeks, perhaps more. A month passed before the expedition was ready to depart.

Forty-one-year-old Commodore Dudley Saltonstall was given command of the maritime forces, with the Continental frigate *Warren*, 32 cannons and 250 men, serving as his flagship. Hailing from Connecticut, Saltonstall was the only non-Massachusetts man chosen for a leadership position. Having obtained his naval commission due to the influence of Silas Deane, his brother-in-law, Saltonstall's reputation was mixed at best. While some viewed him as skilled in one-on-one battle, his suitability for fleet command was questioned. Many asked whether he had the right temperament. One detractor labeled him "willful & unaccommodating," while John Paul Jones, who served with Saltonstall earlier in the war, said that he "behaved towards inferiors indiscriminately as tho' they were of a lower species."

The colonial land forces were led by forty-seven-year-old Brigadier General Solomon Lovell, commander of the Suffolk County, Massachusetts, militia, and a farmer by profession. In contrast to Saltonstall, Lovell was a well-liked, highly respected military officer who had participated in numerous battles going back to 1776. One of his contemporaries called him "a true old Roman character, that would never flinch from danger."

Rather than give one of them overall control of the expedition, Massachusetts decided this would to be a joint operation. The General Court instructed the two men to consult and cooperate with each other in "endeavoring to capture, kill, or destroy the whole force of the enemy there by both sea & land."

As the expedition was going through its final preparations, Samuel Phillips Savage, president of the Massachusetts Board of War, expressed great optimism about the ultimate success of the venture. "We can't but flatter ourselves, that from the active zeal and spirited exertion of our worthy brethren in the eastern part of the state, the army will be raised and in such force as may effectually crush this daring attempt of the presumptuous foe, and render Majabigwaduce as brilliant in the annals of the United States as Saratoga or Charlestown." So certain were Bostonians and their neighbors that they would beat the British that they "bid high for their share of plunder they were to get," and some men who were part of the expedition were able to profit from such transactions.

BEFORE LANDING HIS troops on Bagaduce, Brigadier General Francis McLean, the leader of the British expedition, sent a proclamation to the American colonists ringing the bay and along the Penobscot River. Understandably, the locals were surprised and anxious about the arrival of such a large force, but McLean tried to put them at ease. He welcomed all colonists to "take oaths of allegiance and fidelity to his Majesty" within eight days. In return, British forces would protect them and allow them to fish coastal waters and, once a civil government was established, grant them rights to the land they had cultivated and improved. Ultimately, five hundred Mainers took the oath.

By the time the British heard that the American fleet had left Boston, they had been working on Fort George for a month. Yet it was still far from finished. McLean issued an urgent plea for help to the local population for aid with construction. One hundred men volunteered, but it was not enough. When the American fleet sailed into Penobscot Bay late in the afternoon on July 24, their masts creating a veritable forest of ships upon the ocean, the fort was not ready, and that made McLean very nervous.

Had the Americans used their overwhelming superiority in both men and firepower and attacked immediately and with determination, it is likely they would have defeated the British forces. In fact, the Massachusetts General Court had instructed Saltonstall and Lovell to do just that. Instead, what ensued was nearly three weeks of indecision, inexperience, half measures, and atrocious leadership. Rather than cooperate, Saltonstall and Lovell continually fought over what to do, with Saltonstall deserving most of the blame for the Americans failing to press their advantage. Most days, the American ships were content to lob desultory cannon fire at the fort and the British ships, doing little damage and allowing the enemy to dig in even further. The one time that American ground forces launched a major attack on the fort, on July 28, they stopped fighting right when they were on the precipice of overrunning the British. The sudden halt was due to a lack of professionalism and disorganization on the part of the militia and the inability of Lovell to rally his reluctant troops. This was a stroke of luck for the British: as McLean later commented, "I was in no situation to defend myself. I only meant to give them one or two guns, so as not to be called a coward, and then have struck my colors, which I stood for some time to do, as I did not wish to throw away the lives of my men for nothing."

With each passing day, American morale fell, and the fear that a British fleet would appear at the mouth of the bay increased. Lovell pleaded with Saltonstall to attack the existing British ships defending the half-built fort. His plea was echoed both by many of the men under Saltonstall's command and by the navy board, which sent dispatches expressing dismay that the attack hadn't already taken place. At one point, the board actively discussed replacing the commodore with a more competent leader, but nothing came of it. Finally, on August 12, Saltonstall and Lovell agreed to a massive coordinated assault, to begin the following day, targeting British ships and, over land, the fort. But soon after it was set in motion, a cloud of sails was spied on the horizon. The Royal Navy had arrived—seven warships with 1,000 men and 284 cannons. The flagship was the third-rate 64-gun ship of the line *Raisonnable*, carrying the commander of the force, Sir George Collier.

American forces on land were hastily called back to their transports, and Lovell proposed confronting the now enlarged British force. But Saltonstall offered no support, and by midday August 14 any resolve the Americans still possessed had vanished. What followed can only be described as a panicky retreat, with individual ships and men, too, fending for themselves. In the vanguard was Saltonstall, on the *Warren*, which sailed up the Penobscot River, leaving the other American vessels in its wake. Lovell could hardly believe the debacle as it unfolded:

> The transports then again weighed anchor, and to our great mortification were soon followed by our fleet of men of war, pursued by only four of the enemy's ships. The ships of war passed the transports, many of which got aground, and the British ships coming up the soldiers were obliged to take to the shore and set fire to their vessels. To attempt to give a description of this terrible day is out of my power. It would be a fit subject for some masterly hand to describe it in its true colors;—to see four ships pursuing seventeen

sail of armed vessels,* nine of which were stout ships—transports
on fire, men of war blowing up—provisions of all kinds, and every
kind of stores on shore (at least in small quantities) throwing about,
and as much confusion as can possibly be conceived.

That night the sky was illuminated by the glow of American ships set
afire by their own men to keep the vessels from falling into enemy hands.
Because the cannons had been primed for firing and the gunpowder magazine on each ship was full, most of the ships set ablaze soon blew up in a
final crescendo of defeat. In the end, sixteen American ships were burned,
and the rest captured or sunk. As for the men, soldiers and sailors alike
bolted into the woods and tried to find their way back to New Hampshire
and Massachusetts before starving. How many Americans died during
the siege of Penobscot and their precipitous flight is a matter of dispute,
with estimates ranging from as few as thirty-three to a high of nearly five
hundred.

Weeks later, the remnants of the expedition began straggling into
Boston, and the recriminations began. The General Court appointed a
committee comprised mainly of military leaders to determine why the
expedition had failed so miserably. Its report on October 7 concluded
that the principal reason for the failure was the "want of proper spirit and
energy on the part of the Commodore." More specifically, Saltonstall was
blamed for the destruction of the fleet due to his "not exerting himself at
all, in the time of the retreat, by opposing the enemy's foremost ships in
pursuit." This led to his dismissal from the Continental navy. Lovell, by
contrast, was exonerated. The report found that "Lovell throughout the
expedition and retreat, acted with proper courage and spirit," and it was
the court's opinion that "had he been furnished with all the men ordered
for the service, or been properly supported by the Commodore, he would
probably have reduced the enemy." Some have argued that Saltonstall was
made a scapegoat by the committee because he was from Connecticut,
and not a Massachusetts man. Yet actions or lack thereof during the siege
suggest that the committee got it mostly right. Some portion of the blame
should have accrued to Lovell, in view of his failure to take the fort during

---

* One of the American vessels was captured, and another was sunk lower down on the bay while
trying to outrun the British.

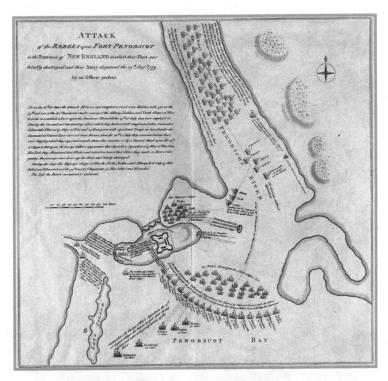

Drawing of British naval attack on American forces in Penobscot Bay by an officer present at the battle, circa 1785. It shows
the arrival of the British fleet, its initial confrontation with the
Americans, and then most of the American ships fleeing up the
Penobscot River with the British in pursuit.

the critical charge. In the pell-mell retreat up the river, he abandoned his
men and, like them, disappeared into the woods—not exactly a profile in
courage.

Colonel John Allan of the Massachusetts militia wrote that "the dishonorable flight" of the Americans at Penobscot Bay left him with a "feeling of mortification for the disgrace brought on the arms of our country."
The early nineteenth-century historian William D. Williamson was more
expansive in his condemnation. "A prodigious wreck of property—a dire
eclipse of reputation—and universal chagrin—were the fruits of this expedition, in the promotion of which, there had been such an exalted display
of public spirit, both by the government and individuals."

Understandably, the British took a different view. Secretary of State
Lord Germain wrote, "The severe blow Sir George Collier has given to

Portrait of Jonathan Carnes, of Salem, circa 1785–1795. Carnes, first mate on the *Pickering* under Captain Jonathan Haraden, went on to captain other privateers and letters of marque. While he had a number of successful cruises, he also experienced some noted failures. He was captain of the privateer *Hector*, one of the vessels impressed into service by Massachusetts for the disastrous Penobscot Expedition. Later on in the war, as captain of the Salem privateer *Porus*, he led a group of six privateers in an ill-fated attempt to capture the British island of Tortola, now part of the British Virgin Islands. British naval ships, alerted to the presence of the Americans, ran them off.

the rebel force at Penobscot . . . must deprive the people of the New England provinces of their great resource for privateering, and prove a considerable security to the navigation of the King's faithful subjects." Captain Henry Mowat, who commanded the British sloop *Albany* under McClean, called "the attack on Penobscot . . . positively the severest blow received by the American naval force during the war." Indeed, many have labeled it the most devastating naval defeat the United States suffered up until the Japanese attack on Pearl Harbor on December 7, 1941.

The cost of the fiasco was nearly £1,750,000, and it fell most harshly on Massachusetts and the privateer owners. George Williams, part owner of the Salem privateer *Black Prince*, which was burned during the retreat, lamented, "We have lost our ships and improvement of them. If it rains porridge, we have no dishes to receive it." Fourteen years later, in 1793, both Massachusetts and the privateer owners finally received compensation when the United States Congress agreed to foot the bill for all the losses incurred during the catastrophic expedition.*

"SUCCEED OR DIE IN THE ATTEMPT"

Robert Wormsted's revolution started off with a bang and a near miss. As a member of an artillery unit from Marblehead, the twenty-year-old fought at the Battle of Bunker Hill and was wounded by a bursting shell. While he helped take other wounded men off the battlefield, a cannonball screamed by, striking the man standing next to him, removing his head entirely from his body.

After stints in the army and as a crewman in Washington's navy and on a privateer, Wormsted sailed in 1777 on a merchant schooner heading to Bilbao that was captured by a British privateer. Along with another man and a boy, he was kept on the schooner, as its new prize crew planned to take it to England. With the help of his fellow captives, Wormsted seized control of the vessel and sailed it to its original destination. Two years later, he found himself in a similar situation, and he hoped history would repeat itself.

In November 1779, Wormsted signed on as first mate to the Marblehead letter of marque *Freemason*, captain Benjamin Boden, bound for Martinique. It was not an imposing vessel, with only six cannons and fifteen men. Instead of finding a prize, the *Freemason* became one itself when a small, lightly crewed British privateer captured it off New York. Boden,

---

* In the late 1990s and early 2000s, archaeological studies in the Penobscot River conducted by federal and state agencies and the University of Maine found remains of some of the Penobscot fleet's vessels and arms.

the second mate, and a boy remained on board, but Wormsted and the rest of the crew were placed in handcuffs and thrown in the hold of the British privateer. A strong, lithe young man standing five feet eleven, Wormsted wriggled out of the restraints that night and helped set his fellows free. They all agreed to his proposal to rush the main deck the following morning when the hatch was opened. Wormsted told the others that they must "succeed or die in the attempt."

Succeed they did, and as soon as the captain and crew were subdued and locked in the main cabin under guard, Wormsted set off after the *Freemason*. Upon catching her, he ordered the prize crew to strike their colors, which they did with neither side firing a shot. Boden, overjoyed by this unexpected result, gladly took on the mantle of prize master of the British privateer. Sailing in tandem, the *Freemason* and its prize arrived in Guadeloupe a few weeks later, where the British crew were imprisoned and the privateer was sold.

Wormsted went on to captain a letter of marque and then a privateer, but in 1782, while first officer on yet another letter of marque, his luck turned. After its cargo was sold in Bilbao, the brig sailed for home. Off the Grand Banks, a violent gale sent the vessel to the bottom, and all hands, including Wormsted, were lost.

FRANKLIN'S PRIVATEERS

Luke Ryan, a pale, slight, twenty-nine-year-old Irishman, was in trouble. A successful smuggler of goods in the mid-1770s, operating between Dunkirk and his hometown, Rush, about fifteen miles north of Dublin, he had decided to change course and become a British privateersman, tasked with attacking American, French, and Spanish shipping. In late February 1779, Captain Ryan headed out on his first privateering cruise, on the cutter *Friendship*, with a crew of sixty and fourteen cannons. But he couldn't shake his old ways. He returned to Rush in April with no prize but plenty of contraband—French brandy and Dutch tea. Customs inspectors seized the *Friendship*, brought it to Dublin, and threw much of the crew into the Black Dog prison. Ryan was not among them—he had already gone ashore.

Ryan had no intention of giving himself up or letting his men face jus-

1. Captain Offin Boardman, by Christian Gullager, 1787. Board-man captained multiple privateers during the war and was twice captured and sent to Mill Prison in England, from which he escaped two times.

BRIG SUKEY, CAPTURED BY THE PRIVATEER WASHINGTON JAN? 15 1776, ENTERING NEWBURYPORT UNDER A PRIZE CREW.

2. A painting by an unknown artist, titled Brig "Sukey," captured by the privateer "Washington," Jan[uar]y 15, 1776, entering Newburyport under a prize crew. This painting is in the collection of President Franklin Delano Roosevelt, housed at the presidential library in Hyde Park, New York.

3. Painting, circa 1980s, by John Bentham-Dinsdale, titled *Action Between the American Brig Yankee Hero and the British Frigate Milford Off Cape Ann, 7th June 1776.*

4. Elias Hasket Derby, of Salem. One of the richest American merchants during the war, he later added to his wealth by becoming a major player in the burgeoning China trade.

5. Privateers preparing to board a prize, depicted in Frank Schoonover's painting *Man on the Bowsprit*, which graced the cover of the 1923 children's book *The Privateers of '76*, by Ralph D. Paine. Swashbuckling images like this no doubt contributed to the notion that privateers were pirates, although they were not. Privateer garb would not be so flamboyant (no bright sash or bandanna); it would instead be similar to that of other sailors of the day—simple trousers, a single- or double-breasted blue or brown jacket down to the waist or hips, and a knitted cap or a round-brimmed hat or tricorne made of felt or tarpaulin.

6. This painting has a fascinating history. Purchased for $1,300 in 1975 by Dr. Alexander McBurney, a Rhode Island urologist, it was thought at the time to be an image of a Black privateer during the American Revolution, which would make it the only such painting known to exist (paintings of white privateersmen are rare). Over the years, the painting appeared in a number of books and museum exhibitions, always identified as being an image of a Black privateer or mariner. In 2005, McBurney agreed to lend the painting to an exhibit to be held at the Fraunces Tavern Museum in New York City called *Fighting for Freedom: Black Patriots and Loyalists.* It was to be the signature painting of the exhibition. Before delivering it, McBurney

began to harbor some doubts about the painting's authenticity. He sent it out for a cleaning but also requested that the picture be examined closely. The art restorer began applying solvent to small areas of the face and hands and off came the black paint, revealing white skin beneath. The original had been painted over. The painting nevertheless likely hails from the Revolutionary War and, based on the ship in the lower left corner and the uniform, could originally have been a portrait of an American privateersman. The restorer surmised that the "cover-up work" must have been accomplished not long before McBurney bought the piece. The discovery knocked the painting out of the museum show and caused its value to remain around what McBurney had originally paid for it. Despite this dramatic fall, McBurney welcomed the painting back to his home. As he told a reporter for *The New Yorker*, "He's an old friend now. For more than thirty years, he's occupied a position of honor in the dining room, and he'll stay there" (Erik Baard, "A Painting's Secret," *The New Yorker*, May 7, 2006).

7. East India Company ship *Bridgewater* successfully beating off an attack by the American privateer *Hampden* on its way from St. Helena to England, March 8, 1779. Unsigned painting after Francis Holman.

8. *The Surrender of John Burgoyne at Saratoga*, by John Trumbull, circa 1826. The painting hangs in the U.S. Capitol Rotunda.

9. *Destruction of the American Fleet at Penobscot Bay, 14 August 1779*, painting by Dominic Serres the Elder, circa 1780s. The painting shows the bay viewed from the south. In the background at left is the *Raisonnable*, firing at the Massachusetts privateer brig *Hunter*. Fires from the British fortifications can be seen in the distance. To the right are the rest of the ships of the squadron chasing the enemy, many of whose vessels are already shown ablaze.

10. A view of His Majesty's brig *Observer* (left) engaging the privateer *Jack* on May 29, 1782, off Halifax Harbor. Aquatint by Robert Dodd, circa 1784.

11. Portrait of James Forten by an unidentified artist, circa 1818.

12. Colonel Benedict Arnold, by Thomas Hart, 1776.

13. View of Mill Prison by Henri Rodolphe de Gueydon, circa 1798.

14. Battle between Continental navy ship *Bonhomme Richard* and HMS *Serapis* on September 23, 1779. The painting depicts the *Bonhomme Richard* (*center, to the right of the moon*) closely engaged with the *Serapis*, commanded by Royal Navy captain Sir Richard Pearson, off Flamborough Head, England. Firing at right is the Continental frigate *Alliance*. Painted by Thomas Mitchell, 1780.

15. Elias Davis Sr., who was born in Gloucester and spent three months in the Continental army, captained three privateers, including Boston's *Tybalt*, which was commissioned in March 1783 and is thought to be the last privateer to receive a commission during the war. This portrait was made circa 1790.

Luke Ryan,
circa 1782.

tice. He concocted a plan and executed it in the early morning hours of
April 12. Assisted by armed men he had sent, his crew broke out of the Black
Dog. Commandeering a few boats, they rowed out to the *Friendship*, over-
powered the nine customs guards on board, cut the anchor cable, raised the
sails, and sailed out of the harbor. Farther up the coast, Ryan's men rowed
the guards ashore and gave them each a guinea to cover the cost of their
journey back to Dublin. The next stop was Rush, where Ryan was waiting.

Once aboard the *Friendship*, Ryan began implementing the second
phase of his plot. Smuggling was bad enough on its own, but now that his
men had escaped from prison, made off with the *Friendship*, and wounded
a few customs guards, there was no staying in Ireland. They were wanted
men, and if captured would certainly be tried for piracy and probably
hanged. The alternative Ryan had chosen, and which his men had agreed
to, was to sail to Dunkirk to become "American" privateersmen.

Ryan had many connections in Dunkirk, a famous smuggling depot.
Soon after arriving on the *Friendship*, now renamed the *Black Prince*, he
contacted Jean and Charles Torris, Flemish businessmen who had sup-

plied him with contraband in the past. Ryan proposed that the brothers purchase a 50 percent stake in the *Black Prince* and that they turn it into a privateer. A deal was struck. The Flemish brothers thought it would be easiest to secure a privateering commission from the French. Ryan demurred, fearing that if the *Black Prince* was stopped or captured, a crew comprised almost entirely of Irishmen could never pass for French. He had another idea. He had heard that Benjamin Franklin was interested in commissioning American privateers to sail from France—so why not ask him? Ryan and his men could certainly pretend to be American if they had to. The Torris brothers tapped connections who knew Franklin. They learned that the famous American was not allowed to grant privateering commissions to vessels captained by foreigners, much less Irish smugglers. The captain, at least, had to be American. Luckily for Ryan and his partners, Stephen Marchant, a Connecticut shipmaster, was in Dunkirk at that very moment and looking for a command.

A meeting was arranged, and Ryan concluded that Marchant was a weak-willed and easily manipulated man with an outsized ego whom they could use for their purposes. He would be presented to Franklin as captain, and another Connecticut man, Jonathan Arnold, would be offered as first mate, but in reality Ryan would be in charge. (Marchant and Arnold would not be privy to this fact.) Franklin met Marchant and granted the privateering commission—less because of his confidence in Marchant than because he wanted to help repatriate privateersmen and sailors from the Continental navy wasting away in British prisons.

Ever since arriving in France, Franklin had been disturbed by the idea of his countrymen languishing in British jails and had worked tirelessly to secure their release. His only real hope was to arrange for cartels, whereby British prisoners held in France were exchanged for Americans held in Britain. But there were two problems. First, British authorities were reluctant to release any prisoners, regardless of the circumstances. When Franklin had first approached Lord Stormont with the idea of conducting a prisoner swap, he had received a biting and dismissive reply from the British ambassador to France: "The King's ambassadors receive no applications from rebels, unless they come to implore his Majesty's mercy." Second, the number of American prisoners in Britain was far greater than the number of British ones in France.

Not long before Luke Ryan's arrival in Dunkirk, Franklin had finally convinced the British to agree to a cartel, and a single ship had delivered nearly one hundred Americans to freedom in France. Franklin expected there would be additional cartels, but for that to happen he would need more British prisoners to trade. This is where privateers entered his thinking. In granting commissions such as the one given to Marchant, he hoped that the privateers would come back not only with prizes but also loaded with prisoners he could use as bargaining chips.

ACROSS THE SPRING and summer of 1779, the *Black Prince* sailed on four cruises, capturing thirty-four prizes. The privateer also returned with more than fifty prisoners. Franklin had wanted more, but many potential prisoners had been allowed to depart with ransomed* prizes, because Ryan did not want to be bothered with manning the prize ships and sending them to Dunkirk.

Wherever the *Black Prince* struck along the coasts of England, Wales, Scotland, and Ireland, it left a terrorized local populace. A resident of Newquay, England, wrote to a friend after one of Ryan's raids on local shipping, during which thirteen vessels had been taken within sight of the town's harbor: "We are all in vast alarm here, for two nights the soldiers have been under arms." Local officials pleaded with the Admiralty to send ships to protect them, complaining that the coast was "totally defenseless, there not being one King's ship stationed between Bristol and Land's End."

During the first three cruises, it became clear to everyone, except, somewhat shockingly, Marchant, that Ryan was the true captain and the American a figurehead. Ryan gave orders that his Irish crew heeded, and more than a few paroled prisoners told authorities that they were certain Ryan, not Marchant, was actually in charge. By the fourth cruise, in September, Ryan could act no more. He despised the incompetent Marchant and told him the truth of his situation, that his position was a mirage. Marchant was despondent over the loss of the captaincy, but he stayed on

---

* Ransoming, in the privateering context, meant allowing a prize to depart after first obtaining a written promise from the captain of the vessel that the owner would pay a certain fee for the safe return of his vessel. In many instances the captain would be held captive to ensure that the ransom was paid. American privateers were not supposed to ransom prizes, per the privateering regulations they operated under, but they often did, which spared them the necessity of placing a prize crew on the vessel that would sail it into port.

board quietly sulking until the *Black Prince* returned to Dunkirk at the end of the month, after which he returned to America.

When Franklin was finally told about the trickery, and that all along the Irish smuggler Ryan had been the real captain, he was amused and accepting. He even congratulated Ryan and sent him a gift. In the letter accompanying the package, Franklin wrote, "Being much pleased with your activity and bravery, in distressing the enemy's trade, and beating their vessels of superior force by which you have done honor to the American flag, I beg you to accept my thankful acknowledgement together with the present of a night glass [binoculars] as a small mark of the esteem with which I have the honor to be, Sir, yours etc." At the same time, Franklin wrote to John Jay, the president of Congress, boasting about his star privateer's recent success. "We continue to insult the coasts of these *lords of the ocean* with our little cruisers. A small cutter, which was fitted out as a privateer at Dunkirk, called the *Black Prince*, has taken, ransomed, burnt, and destroyed above thirty sail of their vessels within these three months."

So happy was Franklin with the *Black Prince* that he commissioned a second privateer, the *Black Princess*, to be captained by Edward Macatter, Ryan's right-hand man and a fellow Irishman.* The two privateers went on a joint cruise from December 1779 to March 1780 without Ryan, who had taken ill and was replaced by his first lieutenant, Patrick Dowlin. It was another success. Twenty prizes were captured and sixty-eight prisoners brought in. According to a letter in the *London Courant*, "Complaints are very loud in the north part of this kingdom against the Admiralty" for not protecting the coast from the depredations of "the two American corsairs."

No sooner had the joint cruise ended than Franklin commissioned a third privateer, the *Fearnot*, commanded by Ryan, who had by then recuperated from his illness. The cutter had eighteen six-pounders, twenty swivel guns, and a crew of ninety-six. From March through the end of August, Franklin's "Irish" privateers conducted a total of six more cruises, capturing sixty prizes. Reflecting on the *Fearnot*'s actions off the coast of Inverness, Scotland, one local resident wrote to the *London Chronicle* that "on the west coast the *Fearnot* American privateer, Luke Ryan commander, reigns

---

* Franklin had, apparently, decided to disregard the stipulation that a privateer captain had to be American, and instead allowed Irishmen to fill that position.

uncontrolled." He had taken every ship belonging to the town of Stornway: "Scarce a day passes without his making a descent on some part of the coast."

The cruises were not a complete success, however. In April the *Black Prince* was chased by a frigate flying British colors. Thinking that the frigate might be French, Dowlin hoisted a French flag to signal that he was a friend, but still the frigate came on, forcing the *Black Prince* into very shallow water just a few hundred yards from land. Before the two vessels could engage, the *Black Prince* plowed into the rocks near Berck, France. All the men on the *Black Prince* made it to shore, but the cutter was a wreck. As for the frigate, moments after the crash, it sheared off, and its captain lowered the British flag and raised the fleur-de-lis, revealing its true identity: it was a French privateer, and its captain later claimed that he believed the *Black Prince* was a British ship that had raised the French flag as a ruse.

By September 1780, Franklin was done with privateering. French authorities had become annoyed with his cavalier manner in awarding commissions and adjudicating prizes; various controversies had arisen, among them a dispute over a neutral Dutch vessel improperly declared a prize. Furthermore, they were frustrated that so many Frenchmen had signed on to American privateers instead of serving in the French navy. Vergennes, the foreign minister, told Franklin that while he couldn't force him to recall the privateering commissions given to the *Black Princess* and the *Fearnot*, he recommended that he do so for the sake of Franco-American relations. Franklin, who had long wanted to devote more time to diplomacy, gladly complied.

There was yet another reason Franklin was eager to turn away from privateering. He had not been as successful as he had hoped in achieving his overriding goal of transforming captured British sailors into free Americans. While his three privateers had brought back 161 prisoners in total, that was a disappointingly low number, given how many prizes they had taken. Furthermore, a significant number of those prisoners had elected to sign on as crew members on one of the privateers. But even if the privateers had delivered more men, Franklin might not have been able to use them. The British continued to balk at cartels, and only two other small exchanges had taken place while Franklin's privateers were active.

Still, Franklin had cause to be proud of what the *Black Prince*, the *Black Princess*, and the *Fearnot* had accomplished. As historian William Bell

Clark concluded in his seminal book on Franklin's privateers, "Despite all Franklin's regrets, the accomplishments of his privateers he realized had been phenomenal." Combined, 114 "British vessels of all descriptions [had been] sent in, burned, scuttled, or ransomed. . . . Better than that, however, had been the consternation of British shipowners, the soaring of marine insurance rates, the havoc to the coastal trade in the English, Irish, and Scotch seas, and the discomfiture of the British admiralty."

With their American commissions clawed back, the owners of the *Black Princess* and the *Fearnot* obtained French privateering commissions and continued to send forth their vessels, under new names, to attack British shipping. Luke Ryan's luck ran out in April 1781, as captain of the French privateer *Calonne*. On the evening of the fourteenth, the *Calonne* captured the Scottish brig *Nancy*, just south of the Firth of Forth in Scotland. A few hours later, one of Ryan's men spotted the lights of two vessels in the distance. The captain of the *Nancy*, who was on board the *Calonne*, told Ryan that earlier that day he had seen two British whaleships heading north. Thinking that the two in the distance might be those vessels, Ryan set off after them.

As he got closer, he saw that the two ships were quite large and surmised that they were not whaleships but merchantmen loaded with valuable goods. His confidence that he could take them easily was understandable. The *Calonne* was a 400-ton frigate with 34 cannons and nearly 250 men. Ryan ordered a broadside and yelled across the water for the larger ship to surrender. So confident was he that his demand would be met that he had a boarding party crowd into one of the *Calonne*'s boats to prepare to claim the prize.

The "merchantman" suddenly sprang to life, as hundreds of marines were called to their battle stations. Ryan had chosen the wrong mark. This was no merchantman but rather the 74-gun third-rate ship of the line *Berwick*. Realizing the enormity of his mistake, Ryan fled so precipitously that he cut loose the boarding party, leaving them at the mercy of the British. Before the *Calonne* had gone too far, the *Berwick*'s escort, the thirty-six-gun *Belle Poule*, caught up, and for forty-five minutes the two ships traded cannon shots, giving the *Berwick* enough time to enter the fray and force Ryan to surrender.

According to the *Edinburgh Advertiser*, after being brought into Edinburgh, Ryan boasted that he would have beaten the *Belle Poule* had not the Berwick come to its aid. He added that he had not allowed his colors "to be struck till he was knocked down by one of his own men, and then he attempted to get hold of a match to blow up the powder-room and his ship."

Ryan was put on trial for piracy. He was found guilty and sentenced to death. But many notable figures, including representatives of the French government, pleaded with British officials on his behalf. In March 1783, with the final peace negotiations nearing, he was given a royal pardon as a gesture of goodwill toward the French and the Americans.

Ryan died in 1789 in debtors' prison. His obituary in London's *Gentlemen's Magazine* mentioned his poverty but also his string of successes as a privateersman, claiming that the *Black Prince* under his captaincy "captured more vessels belonging to Great Britain than any other single ship during the war," and that during his privateering career he "did more injury to the trade of these kingdoms than any other single commander ever did."

"BLOOD WAS SEEN TO RUN
OUT OF THE SCUPPERS"

John Adams, the country's most persistent and voluble promoter of privateering, was concerned that France was not paying enough attention to the exploits of America's privateers. So on May 3, 1780, he wrote a letter to Edmé Jacques Genet, head of the French Ministry of Foreign Affairs. Adams begged Genet to persuade French newspapers to print accounts of the "glorious combat and cruise" of Captain Daniel Waters and his privateer *Thorn*. Adams had picked a worthy subject.

In mid-afternoon on Christmas Day 1779, Waters attacked two New York privateers, the *Sir William Erskine* and the *Governor Tryon*, the latter one of the most successful and powerful British privateers launched by the city's loyalists. According to the *Thorn*'s first lieutenant, when the Americans came within hailing distance of the *Governor Tryon*, its captain, George Stebbins, asked Waters "what right he had to wear the thirteen stars in his pendant." Waters replied, "I'll let you know presently," and gave the British privateer a broadside that was quickly returned not only by the *Governor Tryon* but also by the *Sir William Erskine*, which was on the *Thorn*'s other side. For an hour the three vessels battled, repeatedly hammering each other with cannons and raking each other with musket fire. Waters was wounded in the knee about a half hour into the fight, which is when the men of the *Governor Tryon* attempted to board his ship. But they were "soon convinced of their error, receiving such a warm and well-directed fire from our marines." As Waters's first lieutenant described it, "seeing his men running about the deck with pikes in their backs instead of in their hands," Stebbins was "glad to get off again."

Although heavily damaged, the *Governor Tryon* renewed its attack, but after a few broadsides, it surrendered. "There must have been a great slaughter" on the New York privateer, "as the blood was seen to run out of the scuppers." Waters now set off after the *Sir William Erskine*, ordering the *Governor Tryon* to follow. After another battle, this one lasting two hours, the *Sir William Erskine* struck and Waters sent aboard a prize crew. In the meantime, however, the *Governor Tryon* began sailing away. The *Thorn* pursued but lost sight of the British privateer as the night closed in. The *Governor Tryon* ultimately made it to British-held Antigua, but it had paid a heavy toll, with twenty men killed and many more wounded. As for the *Thorn*, and its sole prize, the *Sir William Erskine*, they had, respectively, eighteen and twenty men killed or wounded.

"There has not been a more memorable action this war," Adams told Genet, "and the feats of our American frigates and privateers have not been sufficiently published in Europe. It would answer valuable purposes, both by encouraging their honest and brave hearts, and by exciting emula-

Painting by Irwin Bevan showing the American privateer *Thorn* capturing two British privateers, the *Governor Tryon* and the *Sir William Erskine*. The painting was done in the late 1800s or early 1900s.

tions elsewhere, to give them a little more than they have had, of the fame that they have deserved. Some of the most skillful, determined, persevering, and successful engagements that have ever happened upon the seas, have been performed by American privateers against the privateers from New York." Adams hoped that Genet could rectify the lack of coverage, at least in this case. Genet complied, and an account of the *Thorn*'s encounter with the *Governor Tryon* and the *Sir William Erskine* was published in the *Mercure de France*.

THE "MISCHIEVOUS *HOLKER*"

The Pennsylvania privateer brig *Holker* was cruising off the New Jersey coast late in the afternoon on July 6, 1780, when Captain Matthew Lawler recognized a ship in the distance. It was the former Pennsylvanian privateer sloop *Active*, which had been captured by the frigate HMS *Iris* just a few months earlier and was now the *Admiral Rodney*, a British privateer captained by Daniel Moore. The two privateers were almost evenly matched. The *Holker* had one hundred men, sixteen cannons, two cohorns, and a tier of swivels, while the *Admiral Rodney* had an equal number of cannons and eighty-three men. Both captains were up for a fight, and in short order "a very close and furious engagement" commenced.

Within twenty minutes, Moore had been struck in the head by swivel shot. Bleeding profusely, he continued to bark orders for a few minutes more before being relieved of his command and taken below. For another hour the two vessels pummeled each other at close range. How the battle ended depended on who was doing the telling. According to a British account in the *New-York Mercury*, the Americans fought bravely but turned tail first. "So much justice should be done the rebel crew as to say that, though in an infamous cause, they did not exhibit any symptoms of cowardice until half-past five o'clock; when, after receiving a well-directed broadside from the *Rodney*, they uttered a dreadful scream, made sail, and ran off." Lawler's account was much briefer, stating that "the enemy sheared off twice, at the same time an armed schooner coming down," at which point the *Holker* sailed away because it was in no shape to contend with two opponents.

Regardless of whose story is more accurate, the bloody result was the same. The *Holker* returned to Philadelphia with six dead and sixteen wounded, with Lawler among the latter. The *Admiral Rodney* returned to New York, carrying six dead crewmen and twenty wounded. As for Moore, he died of his injuries a few days after landing and was buried at Trinity Church after a well-attended funeral, featuring fine speeches about his courage and fidelity to Britain.

Such a disastrous encounter was the exception to the rule for the *Holker*, arguably the most successful privateer of the Revolution. Owned by Blair McClenachan, it brought in seventy-one prizes over four years, under four captains on eleven cruises, a few in the company of one or two other privateers. In one of its most triumphant cruises, it captured ten prizes, which realized nearly £2,000,000 at auction. One of the ships captured during this cruise had an enormous quantity of flour and beef on board, bound for the British army. Instead, the food was sold to the Continental army on good terms and delivered to Washington's troops.

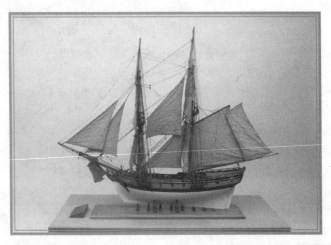

Model of the Philadelphia privateer *Fair American*. In addition to its highly successful joint cruise with the privateer *Holker*, the *Fair American* (sixteen guns), captained by Stephen Decatur, went on a cruise in 1780 that netted nine prizes. One of those prizes, the *Mercury*, had on board seven British officers' wives traveling to New York to join their husbands. When the prize was brought in to Philadelphia, the women were allowed by Congress to continue on to New York. According to one of the men on board the *Fair American*, as the Americans were attacking the *Mercury*, they "could hear the screeches of women." After surrendering, the captain of the *Mercury* said that he "would not have struck so soon if it had not been for the ladies being on board."

The only other vessel besides the *Admiral Rodney* that gave the *Holker* trouble was the *Richmond*, a Scottish privateer. Though relatively unimposing, with only ten cannons and thirty-four men, the *Richmond* put up a ferocious fight over two days just beyond the Charleston bar. The *Holker* and another American privateer, the *Fair American*, attacked first, at twilight on October 15, 1780, but they were beaten off. The next morning, the *Holker* and the *Fair American* attacked again, and after an hour and a half retreated to regroup, whereupon they renewed their attack, this time forcing the *Richmond* to strike its colors after another forty-five minutes of intermittent broadsides. Despite the intensity of the engagements, only one person on the *Richmond* died. Three were wounded. The *Holker* and the *Fair American* between them lost only one man and had one wounded.

The *Richmond* sailed for Philadelphia with a prize crew and eight prisoners on board. Though small in number, the prisoners were large in their resolve. They rose up and commandeered the arms locker, making themselves masters of the ship. A few of the Americans switched allegiance and joined the British, while the rest of the prize crew was loaded onto a jolly boat* with some food and set adrift. The *Richmond*'s new crew sailed to Charleston, their original destination, which was then occupied by the British. So relieved were the ship's owners that they gave each of the men who brought it in a reward of five guineas. No wonder the owners were delighted: the *Richmond*'s cargo, including silver bullion, two boxes of gold watches, and a great range of dry goods and wine, was worth about £175,000.

Two of the Americans in the prize crew who had joined the British proved to be rather foolhardy. A few months later, they returned to Philadelphia hoping to secure a cut of the prize money that the *Holker* and the *Fair American* had amassed in their recent cruise. The turncoats were seized by local authorities and tried for piracy. One was acquitted; the other, Thomas Wilkinson, found guilty "of joining with others of the crew in a revolt," was hanged.

LIKE MORE THAN a few other privateers, the *Holker* was willing to lend a hand to those in need. In August 1779, while cruising off the New Jersey

---

* A relatively small, clinker-built vessel—where the edges of the hull planks overlap each other—typically used to ferry personnel to and from the ship, or for other general-purpose work.

coast, Captain George Geddes saw a badly damaged ship riding low in the water and ordered his men to sail closer. It was a Boston brig captained by William Clark that had been en route to Port-au-Prince with a load of lumber. It had been nearly destroyed a few days earlier during a storm off North Carolina, with its mainmast and part of the upper hull ripped away. Clark's crew had tried to fill the breach by stuffing it with wooden shingles and oakum, but still the ocean kept rushing in, forcing them to pump continuously for forty hours while standing in water up to their necks until they "were faint and ready to expire."

A few men had been washed overboard, and one drowned, while many of those who remained were racked with dysentery. All of the brig's navigational equipment and maps had been lost, and the only sustenance left was a nearly empty barrel of salt pork, a few pieces of hardtack, and a limited supply of water—to lighten the brig, a number of hogsheads of water had been pitched over the side. Geddes gave Clark everything he asked for and helped repair some of the worst damage. He said that the brig could stay with the *Holker* until it returned to port, but Clark wanted to set off immediately. "He acknowledged with a grateful heart, the kindness he received from Captain Geddes, and took his leave." The brig arrived in Egg Harbor a few days later, having survived a squall.

About a week before this rescue at sea, the *Holker* captured the brig *Diana* off Sandy Hook, New Jersey. Its cargo included eighty cannons, ranging from two- to six-pounders, and more than 150 barrels of gunpowder and assorted goods from Europe and the Far East. Those munitions were a boon both to privateers and Continental forces, and in a gesture of respect, Geddes sent Washington a "pair of very elegant pistols" he had taken from the prize.

IN EARLY MAY 1781, McClenachan received distressing news. An article from *Rivington's New York Royal Gazette*, reprinted in the *Pennsylvania Gazette*, reported that the *Holker* had been captured by the HMS *Fox* and brought into the harbor at St. Lucia, putting an end to its days as a privateer. McClenachan grieved for the loss of his favorite and most profitable ship, but one month later, Captain Roger Keane sailed the *Holker* into Philadelphia, astonishing the city's residents and delighting McClenachan. In addition to bringing back a number of prizes, Keane told his boss that the British had taken to calling his vessel the "mischievous *Holker*." This surprising development led the *Pennsylvania Gazette*'s editor, John Dunlap, to do some crowing of his own; he wrote a piece to inform *Rivington's* of its egregiously mistaken notice of the *Holker*'s demise, noting that "after a successful cruise in the West-India seas (in which she was the terror of British commerce)," the *Holker* had "returned home in good condition to her native port."

The end finally came on March 2, 1783. The *Holker*'s fourth captain, John Quinlan, had just completed a productive six-week cruise in the Caribbean during which the privateer had captured sixteen prizes. He was heading back to Martinique when the HMS *Alcmene* gave chase through a storm. The *Holker* crowded on the sails, but the strain on the hull was too great, and some of its planking pulled apart, letting the water flood in, ultimately upsetting the privateer and pitching the crew into the ocean. The *Alcmene* launched its boats and managed to save fifty-one men, the remaining forty-three having gone down with their ship. The *Holker*'s spectacular run was over.

WHALEBOAT PRIVATEERSMEN AND OUTLAWS

During the Revolution, Connecticut governor Jonathan Trumbull Sr. issued more than a dozen privateering commissions to whaleboats, granting them permission to seize British shipping in Long Island Sound and adjacent waters and also to pillage those parts of Long Island under British control and take loyalist property on land. Many of the whaleboat privateers lived up to their commissions, restricting their attacks to British vessels and subjects. One of the most enterprising of these privateersmen was Ebenezer Jones, of Stamford.* His three whaleboats—the *Rattle-*

---

* A story about Jones, often repeated, says that he and his men rowed up to a British sloop of war with fifteen or twenty guns, the number varying depending on who is telling the tale. Jones went aboard, claiming that he was a British official, and upbraided the captain of the sloop for neglecting his watch, especially since there were so many rebel whaleboats about, looking to capture British ships that were not on guard. The flustered captain apologized profusely; all the while, Jones's armed men were climbing on board the sloop and taking up their positions. When enough of his men had boarded, Jones stamped his foot, and his men drew their weapons. The sloop was theirs. An exciting story, but there is no record that backs it up, and it almost certainly didn't happen.

Detail of a 1776 map by Thomas Jefferys showing Long Island Sound, where whaleboat privateers were particularly active. If you look closely, you will see that the sound was also called the Devil's Belt, a nod to the fast currents and shoals that mariners encountered there.

snake, the *Viper*, and the *Saratoga*—each crewed by ten heavily armed men, and boasting a single swivel gun, captured more than thirty vessels.

Not all whaleboat privateers, however, were so scrupulous about their targets. A few went beyond solely attacking loyalists and used their commissions as a license to raid fellow patriots on Long Island. In April 1781, New York's governor, George Clinton, wrote to Trumbull complaining that "it has been lately represented to me that several of the inhabitants of Suffolk County whose attachment to the cause of America is indisputable, have been divested of their property by parties acting under commission from your state." Clinton demanded that restitution be made, and that his fellow governor take action to prevent any more pillaging.

Reports of criminal acts were not news to Trumbull. In fact, a few months earlier he had revoked whaleboat privateering commissions due to the "many evils committed by the armed boats." But that action had not halted the attacks, and Trumbull had no interest in admitting to Clinton the scope of the problem. Instead, he deflected Clinton's claims, asserting that the whaleboat privateers had been issued clear instructions with their commissions, setting forth acceptable behavior, and that attacking fellow patriots was certainly not condoned. To guarantee adherence to those instructions, he added, the privateers had put up bonds of £2,000 each, which would be forfeited if they engaged in illicit activity. However, Trumbull did concede "that in some instances this good intention has by

Connecticut governor Jonathan Trumbull Sr., the only colonial governor to side with the colonists against Great Britain.

evil men been contravened," and that if any of Connecticut's whaleboat privateers had stepped over the line of legality, those harmed should support their grievances with proof so that "full justice may be obtained."

There it stood until August 1781, when Lieutenant Caleb Brewster, a member of the Culper Spy Ring, which gathered intelligence on British army operations in New York for General Washington, informed Clinton of a new round of "atrocities" committed by Connecticut's whaleboat privateersmen, who had been allowed by Trumbull to sally forth again with new commissions. Two whaleboats had landed at midnight on August 14 in Miller Place, on Long Island. The privateersmen marched to the houses of Captain Ebenezer Miller and his brother Andrew, both of whom had fought for the American cause. As they were confiscating Ebenezer's arms, his son William, hearing the commotion downstairs, raised the bedroom window to look outside. One of the whaleboatmen raised his gun and fired, killing the boy instantly. In the meantime, at Andrew's house the men didn't even ask him to turn over his weapons. Instead, as soon as he opened the door, "one of the party struck him with the breech of his gun, broke the bone over his eye, tore his eye all to pieces, broke his cheek bone and left him for dead." Both houses were then ransacked.

The same group of whaleboatmen, Brewster claimed, had crossed the sound multiple times on similar expeditions. In one instance they hung a patriot, army officer Richard Thorn, upside down to force him to divulge where he kept his money, until he passed out. They then cut him down, and when he revived slightly, one of the privateersmen slashed his neck. Next, the marauders attacked another patriot named Coulne in the same manner. "There's not a night but they are over," Brewster complained, and "if boats can cross, people can't ride the roads but what they are robbed."

Brewster's alarming report prompted Clinton to renew his remonstrations with Trumbull, urging him to revoke all whaleboat privateering commissions—or else, he warned, there would be an avalanche of lawsuits and a great rift between the two states. Trumbull revised the commissions to make it clear that privateers were prohibited from "landing or going on Long Island above high water mark." Nevertheless, the problems continued, and no doubt were exacerbated by raids conducted by noncommissioned or freelance whaleboat "privateers." Hoping to finally put an end to the raids, in November Trumbull voided all privateering commissions. According to historian Jackson Kuhl, "After this, complaints about the Connecticut boats vanish from the public records but raids . . . persisted into the following year, even if they became less frequent in the aftermath of Yorktown."

THE *CONGRESS* AND THE *SAVAGE*

Captain Thomas Graves,* of the British sloop of war *HMS Savage*, sixteen six-pounders, had done an excellent job terrorizing Americans and destroying their property. In the company of two other British naval ships, he sailed up and down the Potomac River for five weeks in the spring of 1781, burning plantations, houses, warehouses, and any other rebel property within a short distance from the riverbank. Graves also welcomed any Black enslaved persons seeking to take advantage of the offer of protection and freedom if they came over to the British side. One of the only planta-

---

* His uncle was Admiral Samuel Graves, who had commanded the Royal Navy's North American Station in Boston from 1774 to 1776, and his first cousin once removed was Lord Thomas Graves, who commanded British naval forces in North America during their decisive loss at the Battle of the Chesapeake.

A View of Mount Vernon with the Washington Family, by Benjamin Latrobe, 1796.

tions that Graves didn't burn was George Washington's home, Mount Vernon. And that made Washington furious.

While he was off fighting, Washington had left his home and plantation in the care of his cousin Lund Washington. On April 14, Lund watched as Graves's men landed across the river on the Maryland shore and torched a number of houses. Graves, who knew full well who owned Mount Vernon, sent marines ashore on the Virginia side. The men demanded that Lund provide them with food, and threatened to burn the plantation to the ground if the demand was not met. Lund replied "that when the General engaged in the contest, he had put all to stake, and was well aware of the exposed situation of his house and property, in consequence of which he had given him orders by no means to comply with any such demands, for that he would make no unworthy compromise with the enemy, and was ready to meet the fate of his neighbors."

When the marines returned and told Graves what had transpired, he ordered the *Savage* to sail across the Potomac and moor directly in front of Mount Vernon, whereupon he invited Lund on board. Hoping to calm tempers, Lund brought with him a live chicken as a present for the captain. Lund repeated the bold words he had offered to the marines, and

Graves treated him with great kindness and deference, stating that he had the utmost respect for General Washington and would never entertain the idea of burning his plantation. Graves's warm treatment had a transformative effect on Lund, who, after returning to shore, immediately sent a boat to the *Savage* filled with sheep, hogs, and other provisions. Seventeen of Washington's enslaved people also escaped, throwing in their lot with the British. With that, Graves's mini-armada departed downriver, continuing to light up the countryside.

If Lund thought he would be thanked for having saved Mount Vernon from being torched, he was badly mistaken. When Washington heard of these events, he dashed off an angry letter to his cousin. "It would have been a less painful circumstance to me, to have heard, that, in consequence of your noncompliance with their request, they had burnt my house, and laid the plantation in ruins. You ought to have considered yourself as my representative, and should have reflected on the bad example of communicating with the enemy, and making a voluntary offer of refreshments to them, with a view to prevent a conflagration." He continued: "But to go on board their vessels, carry them refreshments, commune with a parcel of plundering scoundrels, and request a favor, by asking a surrender of my negroes, was exceedingly ill judged, and, it is to be feared, will be unhappy in its consequence, as it will be a precedent for others, and, may be, become a subject of animadversion [criticism or censure]."

Washington had reason to be concerned about his reputation. One of his closest confidants, the Marquis de Lafayette, wrote to him about the affair: "You cannot conceive how unhappy I have been, to hear that Mr. Lund Washington went on board the enemy's vessels, and consented to give them provisions. This being done by the gentleman, who, in some measure, represents you at your house, will certainly have a bad effect, and contrasts with spirited answers from some neighbors, that have had their houses burnt, accordingly." Washington's reputation, of course, remained intact, and he must have experienced some measure of satisfaction when he heard what happened to the *Savage* a few months later.

AFTER LEAVING THE POTOMAC, the *Savage* sailed south. Graves was transferred to another ship and replaced by Charles Stirling, who now had command of the *Savage*'s 125 men. On September 6, about thirty-five miles east of Charleston, Stirling saw the Pennsylvania privateer *Congress* bearing down in full sail. It was a menacing sight. The *Congress* was one of the most powerful privateers in service during the Revolution. Ninety-two feet at the keel, and with a beam of thirty-one feet, it bristled with twenty twelve-pounders on the main deck and four five-pounders on the quarter-deck. With a crew of two hundred and an experienced captain—George Geddes of *Holker* fame—the *Congress* had cost upward of £20,000 to fit out. Its primary owner was Blair McClenachan, though General Nathanael Greene, along with two other army officers, owned one-sixteenth of this particular cruise.

Stirling could see that *Congress* was a formidable vessel, and though he originally thought he could take her, his confidence waned as the *Congress* approached. By the time he realized the privateer "was far superior to what we imagined," it was too late to flee. The *Congress* was a much swifter vessel, and soon the *Savage* was being raked with muskets and bow chasers and pounded by heavy cannonades. Within an hour, Stirling later recalled, "I had the mortification to see our braces and bow lines shot away, and not a rope left to trim the sail with." Yet the *Savage* kept up a steady barrage of fire of its own, which was returned by the *Congress*. The two vessels came so close to each other that "the fire from each ship's guns [was] scorching the men who opposed them." Multiple cannons on both sides were "rendered useless," and amid the smoke and the deafening roar of the cannons, men resorted to throwing anything they could grab at their foes, hoping to land an injurious blow. With only forty men still fit for duty, the *Savage*'s mainmast tottering, its mizzenmast shot away, a fire raging, and the Americans attempting to board at multiple points, Stirling surrendered four hours after the battle had begun.

The carnage was incredible. On the *Savage*, eight men were dead and thirty-four wounded, including Stirling. As for the *Congress*, eleven men were killed and thirty wounded. The *Congress*'s rigging and masts were almost in as bad shape as the *Savage*'s. It took three days of repair work merely to allow the *Congress* to limp back to port. The *Savage* required five days of mending before the prize crew could begin to bring it in. But a prize it wouldn't be. As the Americans were sailing the *Savage* back to Philadelphia, it was recaptured by the HMS *Solebay*. Nevertheless, the battle of the *Congress* and the *Savage* would rank as one of the fiercest maritime contests of the war.

BLACK PATRIOT

He heard the commotion coming from the square outside the Philadelphia statehouse and went to investigate. It was July 8, 1776, and James Forten was nearly ten years old. As he listened to the man speak to the large crowd, he was transfixed. "All men are created equal, that they are endowed by their creator with certain unalienable rights, that among these are life, liberty and the pursuit of happiness." The entire Declaration of Independence was momentous, but those words must have rung in young Forten's ears. Could they apply to him, a Black boy in colonial America?

Forten was a most unusual child in a most unusual family. As he proudly recalled late in life, "My great-grandfather was brought to this county as a slave from Africa. My grandfather obtained his own freedom. My father never wore the yoke." His mother was free, too, at least by the time he was born, making Forten's family one of the few free Black families in Philadelphia at the beginning of the Revolution. However, even though they were free, they were not equal in the eyes of the vast majority of white colonists or in how they were treated by the law. The Fortens were certainly far better off than most of their Black contemporaries, but they were still second-class members of society.

From an early age, according to his son-in-law Robert Purvis, Forten "was marked for great sprightliness and energy of character, a generous disposition, and indomitable courage"; he was "always frank, kind, courteous, and disinterested."* He left school in 1775 when his mother could no longer afford the fees and worked for the next few years in a grocery store and doing menial jobs, even though he could read and write.

In 1780, Forten's small world shifted slightly when the Pennsylvania Assembly passed An Act for the Gradual Abolition of Slavery, the first abolition law in America. "Gradual" was the key word. The act did not free the currently enslaved but did emancipate their children when they

---

* In the late 1700s, "disinterested" most often meant virtuous or self-sacrificing, and out for the public good, not profit.

reached the age of twenty-eight. Although it didn't confer any new rights of citizenship upon free Black people like Forten, it did hold out the promise of better times ahead. According to historian Julie Winch, "What the quality of citizenship might be for a black Patriot he [Forten] would have to wait and see, but the abolition law, with its statements about justice and an end to prejudice, evidently convinced him that society was being reordered, and that merit, rather than complexion and condition, would be rewarded in the new republic. He had made his choice of loyalties."

That choice led him in July 1781 to sign on to the 450-ton Pennsylvania privateer *Royal Louis*, sporting 22 cannons and with a crew of 200. Its captain was Stephen Decatur Sr., the father of Stephen Decatur Jr., who would win fame as a naval commander during the first Barbary War (1801–1805) and the War of 1812. As Purvis put it, in taking this step, fourteen-year-old Forten was "fired with the enthusiasm and feeling of the patriots and revolutionists of the day." As a "powder boy," his job was to bring gunpowder from the ship's magazine to the cannons.

The cruise was a triumph. In company with one or two other privateers at a time and on its own, the *Royal Louis* captured seven vessels. Most gave up without much of a fight, though not the British sloop of war *Active*, which engaged the *Royal Louis* in a nasty battle, during which, according to Forten's recollection, everyone at his gun station except he himself was killed, and many others on board were wounded.

Upon returning to Philadelphia, the *Royal Louis* was greeted with "loud huzzas and acclamations of the crowds that had assembled upon the occasion." Confident in Decatur, and with "an unquenchable devotedness to the interests of his native land" and a desire to earn more prize money, Forten embarked on another cruise.

Barely a day out from Delaware Bay, the HMS *Amphion*, with thirty-two cannons, spotted the *Royal Louis* and started its pursuit. Five and a half hours later, the *Amphion* had closed in, and its captain, John Bazely, fired a chase gun to force the issue, raising the French colors in an attempt to appear as friend, not foe. But Decatur had no doubt he was facing a British warship. He hoisted the American colors and fired his stern chaser in a futile gesture. Decatur knew that the *Royal Louis* was no match for the much larger ship, and when the *Amphion* raised the Union Jack and fired a few more rounds, he surrendered.

Forten soon found himself a prisoner on the *Amphion*. "His mind was harassed with the most painful forebodings," Purvis later wrote, "from a knowledge of the fact that rarely, if ever, were prisoners of his complexion exchanged; they were sent to the West Indies, and there doomed to a life of slavery." Yet Forten's situation soon brightened.

Bazely was accompanied by his two sons. The older boy, John Jr., was fourteen and had been on a number of cruises already, rising to the rank of midshipman. The younger, Henry, was twelve, and this was his first time on a ship. His official job was to be his father's servant, but that didn't come with many responsibilities, so he had considerable free time. To keep him out of mischief, Captain Bazely tapped Forten to be Henry's companion.

While the *Amphion* took more prizes and more prisoners, Henry and Forten spent a great deal of time together, getting along well. So impressed was Henry with Forten's skill at marbles that he called his father to come see. Captain Bazely was equally impressed, not only by Forten's marble-shooting ability but also by his mature demeanor and the deference he had shown his son. When the *Amphion* sailed into New York Harbor on October 21 to join up with Admiral Graves's fleet, Bazely offered Forten a choice. He could join the other prisoners and be transferred to the *Jersey* prison ship, or he could be sent off with Henry back to England, where he would be under Henry's "patronage" and have the "advantages of a good education, and freedom, equality, and happiness forever."

Forten didn't take long in answering. "I am here a prisoner for the liberties of my country. I never, never shall prove a traitor to her interests." With that, he was taken to the *Jersey* with the others. But Bazely did not forget the companionship and kindness Forten had shown his son, and he sent a note to the commander of the *Jersey* that was highly complimentary of Forten, and that urged the commander to remember him if there were any prisoner exchanges.

Forten spent nearly eight months on the *Jersey*, enduring horrific conditions. Amid his suffering, he performed a noble act. An American officer was selected for exchange with a British prisoner of equal rank. Forten approached the officer and asked if he could hide in his sea chest, which would accompany its owner off the ship. The officer consented, but Forten changed his mind. He had become friendly with another prisoner a few years his junior named Daniel Brewton. Forten offered his spot in the chest to Brewton, who accepted. Forten had the satisfaction of helping carry the chest to the longboat waiting to facilitate the exchange.

Forten was finally released in the spring of 1782, and after weeks of traveling on foot he arrived back in Philadelphia, much to the relief of his mother, who had heard that her son had been shot and killed during the capture of the *Royal Louis*. Forten lived till 1842, and while the country that he fought for did not live up to the soaring rhetoric of the Declaration of Independence during his lifetime, he remained a loyal and proud American. And a very successful one, too: he became Philadelphia's leading sailmaker, leaving behind an estate that by one estimate was worth nearly $70,000. But his legacy was much broader than that. He was a leader in the city's Black community and was active in the abolitionist movement, even giving his friend William Lloyd Garrison money to help him launch *The Liberator*, which would become one of the loudest voices in the fight to end slavery.

NO GOOD DEED . . .

The Salem privateer *Jack*, with fourteen cannons and a crew of sixty, was cruising off Halifax in the early evening on May 29, 1782, when its captain, David Ropes, spied the British sloop of war *Observer* in the distance. He noticed that the *Observer* was copper-bottomed, a relatively new technology that eliminated fouling by marine organisms, thereby protecting the wooden hulls from deterioration and making vessels faster. The sloop also had sixteen cannons, but what really caught Ropes's attention was the size of the crew. Men were swarming the main deck, and although he didn't know the exact number at the time, there were 175 marines on board.

The *Observer* chased the *Jack* for nearly two hours before coming up alongside and unleashing a broadside, which mortally wounded Ropes and injured many others, including Lieutenant William Gray, who assumed command. The fight continued for two hours. The British attempted to board but—amazingly, given the difference in manpower—they were repulsed. While fighting at the rails, Gray later recalled that he "received a wound by a bayonet fixed on a musket which was hove with such force, as entering my thigh close to the bone, entered the carriage of a bow gun where I was fastened, and it was out of my power to get clear until assisted by one of the prize masters."

Despite his grievous wound, Gray continued to rally his men, who maneuvered the *Jack* into position for another broadside. But after getting off a few well-aimed shots, the *Jack*'s crew ran out of match rope, the slow-burning cord used to ignite the gunpowder in the touchholes of the cannons. Its fighting capability crippled, the *Jack* bore away, trying to escape its antagonist. The *Observer* pursued and again overtook the privateer, the British readying themselves for another boarding attempt.

Gray called his men together, urging them to fight on and raising, as motivation, the specter of being sent to a prison ship. That fear was not enough for many of the foreigners on board, likely French and Spanish recruits, who promptly deserted their quarters. With no other choice available to him, Gray "had the inexpressible mortification to deliver up the vessel." The final death toll was seven on the *Jack* and fourteen on the *Observer*. There were many injured on both sides.

American compassion, oddly enough, contributed to the *Jack*'s defeat. A few weeks earlier, two other American privateers—the *Lively*, from Salem, captained by Daniel Adams, and the *Scammel*, from Boston, captained by Noah Stoddart—had rescued the crew of the British naval frigate *Blonde* and all sixty-four American privateersmen held prisoner on it. The frigate had wrecked on Seal Island, off the southern tip of Nova Scotia. The *Blonde*'s commander, Edward Thornbrough, unreservedly praised the Americans who had saved his crew. In a letter later published in the *Nova Scotia Gazette*, he thanked Captains Adams and Stoddart for "the relief and comfort they so kindly afforded us in our accumulated sufferings and distress." They had fed the *Blonde*'s crew with provisions until they landed at Yarmouth, and they had given Thornbrough a passport to use when he and his men sailed to Halifax; the passport would keep them from being plundered or taken prisoner by American privateers that might cross their path.

Thornbrough also thanked his American prisoners. They had been taken from the prize ship *Lyon*, of Beverly, Massachusetts. When the *Blonde* ran aground on Seal Island, the prisoners had helped their captors man the pumps day and night to keep the ship from sinking "till all but one got out of her, and by the blessing of God saved our lives." As a gesture of appreciation, Thornbrough had provided the *Lively* and the *Scammel* with passports intended to protect them and the sixty-four repatriated Americans from British cruisers in Massachusetts Bay.

When the bulk of the *Blonde*'s crew finally got to Halifax, Lieutenant

Governor Sir Andrew Snape Hamond ordered them onto the *Observer* and sent them out to escort Thornbrough and the rest of the crew into port; they had left Yarmouth on another ship. The *Observer* soon found the ship and took aboard Thornbrough and some of his men, greatly increasing the number on the *Observer*. Thus when the *Observer* battled the *Jack* just a few hours later, its strength was enhanced by the addition of the men who had earlier been saved by the American privateers.

The Lion Roars

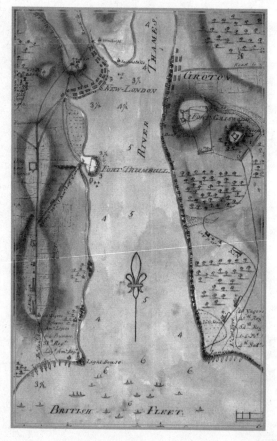

Detail of *A sketch of New London & Groton with the attacks made on Forts Trumbull & Griswold by the British troops under the command of Brigadier General Benedict Arnold, September 6, 1781,* by Daniel Lyman, circa 1781.

OLIVER WOLCOTT WAS A MEMBER OF THE CONTINENTAL CON-
gress, a signer of the Declaration of Independence, and a brigadier general
in the Connecticut militia. In April 1777, he wrote that "nothing had given
such surprise through Europe as the success of our privateering business."
Nobody was more surprised than the British. As David Ramsay, a South
Carolina delegate to the Continental Congress and one of the first historians of the Revolution, observed, "Naval captures, being unexpected, were
[a] matter of triumph to the Americans." The British "scarcely believed
that the former would oppose them by land with a regular army, but never
suspected that a people so unfurnished as they were with many things necessary for arming vessels, would presume to attempt anything on water."

The success of American privateers was reflected in the large number
of British prizes they captured. Determining the exact figure, however,
is a tricky proposition. Information about prizes, to the extent that it is
still available, is spread across thousands of eighteenth-century newspaper accounts, admiralty court records, and other sources, many of which
are in a sorry state. Even if it were possible to easily collect all this material, it would necessarily be incomplete because of poor record-keeping,
duplicative listings, and the fact that some number of prizes were not taken
into colonial ports to be adjudicated but rather were sold secretly or with
scant paper trails in the West Indies and France. Still, we can arrive at a
rough notion of how many British prizes the Americans took during the
Revolution.

One of the most oft-mentioned numbers is six hundred. The figure
comes from Edgar Stanton Maclay's widely quoted *A History of American
Privateers.* Maclay offers no source; and, given that he claims that there
were only 792 American privateers during the Revolution, an estimate that
is far too low, we can safely assume that his number of captures is low as
well.

Arguably the single best source regarding captures comes from a tabu-
lation in the early 1800s by John Bennett Jr., the first secretary of Lloyd's
of London, the world's largest insurance marketplace. Bennett concluded
that 3,386 British vessels were captured during the Revolution, 1,002 of
which were either recaptured or ransomed. That leaves a total of 2,384

British prizes remaining in enemy hands. Yet that number includes captures not only by American privateers but also by Continental and state navy vessels, Washington's navy, and French and Spanish vessels, which preyed on British shipping after France and Spain allied with the Americans. However, because American privateers accounted for the vast majority of the captures, it is reasonable to estimate that they brought in somewhere in the neighborhood of 1,600 to 1,800 prizes, if not more.

The financial damage caused by American privateering is likewise difficult to calculate. At the end of the war, British sources did not tally the overall cost of all the ships captured by the Americans. Still, there is an important clue. In February 1778, during a heated debate on the floor of Parliament, statistics were presented showing that the 559 vessels captured by American privateers and Continental navy ships resulted in a loss of at least £2.6 million. This suggests that the average value of each vessel was £4,651; and if Americans brought in roughly 1,600 to 1,800 prizes, then the overall value of prizes would be between £7.4 and £8.4 million (between $1.4 and $1.6 billion today). A considerable amount of money, yet there is good reason to believe that these numbers are too low. There are many records of American prizes earning their owners and crews much more than £4,651, including the value of the cargo *and* the vessel. Take, for example, the British merchantman *Hannah*, brought into New London, whose cargo alone was worth £80,000, and the haul of the *Holker*, which, as we have seen, captured ten prizes in a single cruise that sold for nearly £2,000,000 in total.

At that same parliamentary debate in 1778, the Earl of Sandwich argued that, since British losses to privateers were nearly equal to the number of American vessels captured by the British, the impact of American privateers was minimal. Captures on both sides essentially canceled each other out, and there was no loss to Britain as a whole. The Duke of Richmond pointed out the nonsensical nature of that argument when he rose to respond. "When the merchants of this country have lost . . . ships, valued at above two millions of money; to say that the commerce of this country is not affected by such a loss, because an equal number of ships have been taken from the enemy, and the prizes distributed to British seamen!* This

---

* British privateers and British naval ships were awarded 100 percent of the proceeds of all prizes taken.

is so far from being a balance in our favor, it adds to our loss, for if we were not at war with America, the value of all these cargoes in the circuitous course of trade must center with Great Britain."

But the earl's argument was even weaker than that. He was wrong about the supposed parity in captures between America and Britain. By 1778, the Americans had brought in far more British prizes than the British had brought in American. And that imbalance persisted in subsequent years. At war's end, the tally for American prizes condemned at the prize court in London stood at 376. If we add to that the prizes condemned at the two other most active British prize courts, in New York and Nova Scotia, the number increases to around 600 to 700—still far less than the roughly 1,600 to 1,800 British prizes taken by the Americans.

One other consideration is the nature of the prizes taken by each side. Here, too, there was an imbalance that favored the Americans. Most of the prizes seized by American privateers were merchantmen full of goods that were both inherently valuable and much in demand in the states. In contrast, many of prizes captured by the British were American privateers, as opposed to letters of marque, which had nothing that was of value to the British beyond the vessels themselves and perhaps their armaments. Even American letters of marque, which did have goods on board, were rarely as rich a prize as the British merchantmen taken by American privateers. According to the *London Advertiser*, in July 1776 "the value of the [American] vessels, and the cargoes taken from them is trifling, whereas those they take are worth more in proportion than ten to one." This difference created an unusual situation. As James Fenimore Cooper observed, "it is a proof of the efficiency of [American privateers] . . . that small [British] privateers constantly sailed out of the English ports, with a view to make money by recapturing their own vessels; the trade of America, at this time, offering but few inducements to such undertakings."

American privateers inflicted economic pain on numerous British merchants, even though many were compensated partially or in whole by insurance claims. According to Lloyd's, between 1779 and 1782, the years in which losses to American privateers were greatest, the number of British vessels captured annually was equal to roughly 8 percent of the British merchant fleet. Such losses were certainly significant, because they were concentrated in the extremely valuable Caribbean trade. As a Briton in Grenada noted in 1778, "From London, we hear of nothing but stoppages, bankruptcies, want of money, universal diffidence in the commercial world, West India produce daily failing, and in a word, a picture of horror for all of us who are interested in these islands."

Aggrieved merchants pressured politicians to do something, contributing to an overall war-weariness in Britain. The desire to return to the days when trade with America was one of the mainstays of the British economy only increased. Of course, it was preferrable to trade with British colonies rather than with an independent country, but above all else, the merchant class wanted safe trade to resume. This was one of the key factors that created an atmosphere conducive to finalizing the peace. As an early twentieth-century military historian observed: "The widespread losses inflicted upon British commerce provided the argument for setting free an obstinate people, who not only had shown they refused to submit on the land, but also continued to destroy shipping in increasing totals on the sea."

DESPAIR WAS NOT the only, or even the primary, British response, however. Initially shocked by the courageousness, resolve, and success of America's privateers, Britain soon began fighting back, using its navy, army, and privateers to retaliate.

While the Royal Navy was the world's largest naval force at the outset of the Revolution, it was in poor shape, with fewer than 100 of its 270 ships ready for immediate service. By war's end, it had been revitalized and greatly expanded, ballooning to 468 vessels, including 174 ships of the line and 110,000 men. Of those vessels, more than 300 were in fighting form. Of course, all of that firepower was not trained on American privateers. The Royal Navy's primary tasks included supporting land forces in America, battling France and Spain in a world war that stretched from the Atlantic to the Indian Ocean, and attacking Continental navy ships. Privateers, however, were a serious concern, and the Royal Navy confronted the threat in three ways. First, reacting to the angry chorus of merchants demanding protection, it diverted a considerable number of ships to convoy duty. The presence of one or more naval ships was usually enough to scare off any privateer, but convoys were not always effective. Privateers sometimes picked off laggards that had drifted too far away from their protectors.

HMS *Brune* (*left*) capturing French ship *L'oiseau* in 1762, during the Seven Years' War. Painting by John Cleveley the Elder (circa 1712–1777).

The second way the Royal Navy dealt with American privateers was by attacking them. The admiralty instructed their captains to "use your best endeavors to take or destroy any ships or vessels belonging to the rebellious colonies of North America." One captain who took those instructions to heart was James Ferguson, of the 32-gun HMS *Brune*.

In September 1777 the *Brune* caught up with the *Volunteer*, a privateer schooner from Charleston with twelve four-pounders, sixteen swivels, ten cohorns, and sixty-one men. Ferguson hailed the *Volunteer*, demanding to know its identity, whereupon Captain Eliphalet Smith replied, "The *Lord Howe* from St. Augustine, bound for New-York." Ferguson wasn't convinced. He ordered Smith to lower his sails and come aboard the *Brune* for questioning. Far from complying, Smith's men raised more sails, and in reply, the *Brune* fired a single six-pounder at the privateer. When that didn't have the desired effect, and with the *Volunteer* "dropping fast astern," Ferguson ordered a tremendous broadside—seventeen shots from twelve-pounders, sixteen from six-pounders, and, to top it off, several volleys of small arms fire. Amazingly, this torrential fusillade of iron and lead killed only one person, Smith, and wounded another. The schooner was another story. Its hull was punctured with so many holes that it began to sink. The officer who replaced Smith called for quarter, and Ferguson sent over boats to gather the prisoners. No sooner had all the Americans climbed aboard the *Brune* than the *Volunteer* "went to the bottom." When the people of Charleston learned from a New York paper of the destruction of the *Volunteer*, they lamented the brutality of the British. The editors of the *Gazette of the State of South-Carolina* observed that "there does not appear much humanity in firing a whole broadside of a frigate's cannon upon a small schooner that appears to have been within musket shot."

An even greater imbalance of power was on display in April 1777, when the 74-gun HMS *Terrible* captured the privateer brigantine *Rising States* in the Bay of Biscay. In the weeks leading up to the capture, the privateer, armed with eighteen six-pounders, seized three prizes. Manning those prizes reduced the *Rising States* crew from sixty-one to fewer than forty, which was its complement when the *Terrible* appeared ominously on the horizon on April 15. Captain James Thompson, realizing that escape was his only option, called all hands on deck to put the vessel under full sail. Still the *Terrible* gained. To lighten the vessel, the crew threw eight of their cannons and much of their supplies overboard, but to no avail. When the *Terrible* was within range it fired a couple of times, intentionally missing the *Rising States*, to encourage it to strike its colors. Foolishly, even though he knew he was caught and greatly overmatched, Thompson ordered his men to return fire with the privateer's two stern chasers. This defiant behavior from such a small vessel enraged the *Terrible*'s captain, Sir Richard Bickerton, who ordered his gunners to haul out three eighteen-pounders and sink the privateer. But the order was rescinded when Thompson told Bickerton that there were nineteen English prisoners on board. The *Rising States* struck, and its English prisoners were transferred to the *Terrible*. A prize crew sailed the *Rising States* to Spithead, England, where it was sold by a court of admiralty and put into service as a British letter of marque.

Finally, the Royal Navy and the British army set out to destroy American privateers by targeting their bases. This tactic was not immediately embraced by the navy; it would have much preferred a major engagement at sea. In the summer of 1778, Rear Admiral James Gambier, stationed in New York City, complained about the numerous privateers "vegetating in every harbor and creek"—he wished they would come out as a single force and fight. He claimed that the "rebels could muster threescore sail from their different ports [with] from" eighteen to thirty-six cannons each, "and

The 32-gun frigate HMS *Pearl* (*left*) captures the 26-gun
American privateer *Industry* off Sandy Hook on July 25, 1778.

yet I will venture to affirm that a third of that number of our frigates would
take them all, would each party agree to meet." But American privateersmen were too smart to pursue such a rash course, which is why the British
navy and the army decided to go to their sources.

In early September 1778, Gambier dispatched a large fleet of ships east-
ward from New York, destination Bedford (present-day New Bedford),
Massachusetts. On board were four thousand army troops, led by Major
General Charles Grey, whose main goal was to "to exterminate the nests of
some rebel privateers, which abounded in the harbors, rivers, and creeks
about Buzzard's Bay, in the old colony of Plymouth." At about six in the
evening on September 5, a portion of the fleet anchored in Clark's Cove,
on the outskirts of Bedford. Facing virtually no resistance, Grey and his
men disembarked in boats and over the next eighteen hours ranged up
and down the Acushnet River, burning buildings and vessels and looting
warehouses in Bedford and Fairhaven. The fires were so massive, their
flames licking the sky, that the glow could be seen twenty miles away in
Newport. In his report to Sir Henry Clinton, commander in chief of British troops in America, Grey stated that "the stores destroyed were valuable, and the number of ships burnt about seventy, privateers and other
ships, ready with their cargoes in for sailing." Having ravaged Bedford,

Major General
Charles Grey.

the British sailed to Falmouth, taking three vessels and burning one. Then it was on to Martha's Vineyard, where they destroyed six ships, a salt-works, and twenty-eight whaleboats. They also seized 10,574 sheep, 315 cattle, 52 tons of hay, and a variety of arms and munitions.

Germain was thrilled with Grey's marauding. "The keeping the coasts of the enemy constantly alarmed, the destroying of their ships and magazines, and by that means preventing the rebels becoming a formidable maritime power and obstructing commerce of his majesty's subjects," were accomplishments of great importance. Even if such actions didn't cause the Americans to give up their fight, Germain thought British activity would at least "prevent their sending out that swarm of privateers, the success of which has enabled and encouraged the rebels to persevere in their revolt."

The British were not done yet. Soon after the fleet returned from its New England foray, another nine naval vessels were sent south from New York to attack the privateers that had long been operating out of Little Egg Harbor, New Jersey. Just a few months earlier, privateers from the harbor had captured two very valuable British merchantmen, finally convincing Clinton and Gambier that the time had come for direct retaliation. Led by Captain Patrick Ferguson, reputed to be the best marksman in the British army, four hundred soldiers were brought by ship into Little Egg Harbor on October 6. Transferring to smaller boats, they ascended the Mullica River to Chestnut Neck (near present-day Port Republic), a small community that was a key launching point for privateering raids. Bad weather delayed the British force's arrival, giving American spies enough time to tip off residents of Chestnut Neck about the impending attack. Three privateers had already headed out to sea, a few moved upriver, and those that remained had been stripped of their weapons and cargoes, dismasted, and scuttled to keep the British from taking them.

The soldiers quickly overwhelmed the few Americans defending the town, and the "skulking banditti," as Ferguson called them, fled into the woods. Frustrated in their attempt to recover the two merchantmen, the soldiers burned eight privateers and two prize ships, or at least those parts of the vessels still peeking above the waterline. They also torched the little village, leaving a lone house standing.

Ferguson had originally planned to destroy other privateer bases farther up the Mullica, but because he had lost the element of surprise and military detachments from nearby Philadelphia were coming to reinforce the local militia, he decided to retreat—but not before a quick sally into the

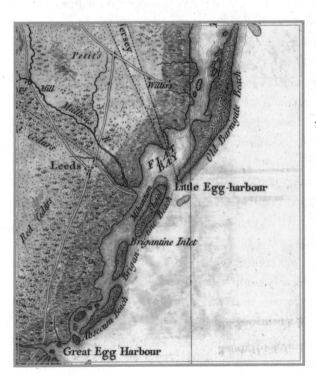

Detail of 1777 map *The Province of New Jersey, Divided into East and West, Commonly Called the Jerseys,* showing Little Egg Harbor and the Mullica River (here labeled Mullicus).

countryside to damage three saltworks and burn the homes of rebel leaders who had invested heavily in privateering activities.

In subsequent years, the British launched additional attacks on American-held coastal ports, designed in part to root out privateers. These included General William Tryon's raids on New Haven, Fairfield, and Norwalk in the summer of 1779. But the deadliest raid of all was the one spearheaded by the traitor Benedict Arnold in early September 1781, which targeted New London.

THE ASSAULT ON New London was intended to achieve two goals. Clinton had been worried that Washington planned to attack New York City, and he hoped that Arnold's raid would draw American forces away from the city. The second goal was more punitive. Almost from the start of the Revolution, New London had been a major center for privateering. Most recently, in July 1781, the New London privateer brigantine *Minerva*, captained by Dudley Saltonstall, of Penobscot Expedition infamy, captured the British merchantman *Hannah* while it was heading to New York from London. The *Hannah*'s £80,000 cargo made it the richest prize brought in to New London during the war. By attacking New London, Britain also hoped to land a significant blow in its continuing fight against American privateers.

By the time Arnold was ready to depart on his mission, however, the potential value of the raid as a diversionary tactic was considerably diminished. Clinton had learned that Washington wasn't going to attack New York but rather was already heading to Virginia to confront Cornwallis at Yorktown. Nevertheless, Clinton still wanted, in his own words, to "annoy the enemy's coasts and endeavor to cause a diversion somewhere," so he sent Arnold, along with about 1,850 men under his command, to New London "with directions to . . . bring off or destroy the prize vessels, traders, or privateers." Arnold's forces, on board two dozen vessels, sailed from New York on September 4.

Arnold, in a sense, was coming home. He was born twelve miles up the Thames River from New London in the town of Norwich, Connecticut, on January 14, 1741. Nowhere in America had news of his treason caused more pain than in his hometown. When the people of Norwich heard that Arnold had left his post as commander of West Point in late September 1780 and had defected to the British, they were apoplectic. Making their anger and disgust clear, they marched to the graveyard where his father and brother were buried and desecrated their graves.

The British fleet arrived off New London at about 1:00 a.m. on September 6, but contrary winds kept them from entering the harbor until 9:00 a.m. It was a costly delay. At Fort Griswold, located across the Thames from New London in Groton, Sergeant Rufus Avery had seen the British ships at 3:00 a.m. and had immediately dispatched a rider to the nearby home of Captain William Latham, the fort's commander, with the news. Latham soon arrived and sent a message to William Ledyard, lieutenant colonel in the Connecticut militia, who was staying in New London. When Ledyard reached the fort, he dispatched express riders to alert militias in neighboring towns to come to his aid. He also ordered that two cannons be fired in quick succession, the signal for a general alarm. But Arnold knew what that signal meant and ordered that one of his own cannons be fired, since three blasts meant that a prize ship was sailing into the harbor, a common occurrence. The decoy seemed to work, and many people in New London, Groton, and nearby towns remained in bed. But others were not fooled, and they began preparing for the battle to come. More than a few privateer owners hastily sailed their vessels upriver to avoid the British.

Arnold split his forces in two, landing them on both sides of the river at 10:00 a.m. Leading his men on the New London side, he quickly over-

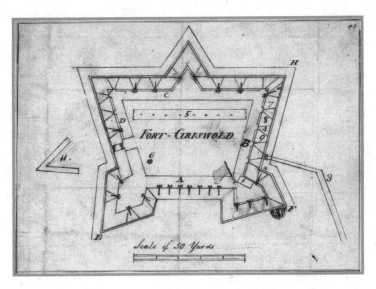

Plan of Fort Griswold, Connecticut, circa 1781.

whelmed the scattered and disorganized resistance along the city's roads and at its two small forts. Most of the residents fled, some of them taking advantage of the confusion by plundering warehouses and the homes of fellow citizens. Arnold forbade his men from taking private property, and for the most part they complied.

With the city subdued, Arnold sent out parties to selectively torch structures of military or economic importance, including the homes of militia leaders and privateer owners, warehouses, the town mill, and the printing office, as well as vessels tied up at the wharves. A massive conflagration ensued, and Arnold, defending his actions, later claimed that things got out of hand when a hidden store of gunpowder ignited and a shift in the wind caused the flames to reach parts of city he had not meant to burn. The residents, whose property was destroyed, thought that Arnold's post hoc explanation was a sham, and that he and his men had deliberately tried to incinerate the entire city. Ever since, historians have argued over Arnold's intentions.

The attack left New London in ruins. Arnold's men had burned twelve vessels, mostly privateers, including the *Hannah*. A total of 143 buildings were destroyed and nearly one hundred families left homeless. Fourteen British soldiers were killed or wounded and eight taken prisoner. On the American side, four were killed and twelve wounded.

In the meantime, Arnold's forces in Groton, led by Lieutenant Colonel Edmund Eyre, marched on Fort Griswold. Unfortunately for the Americans, Ledyard's call for reinforcements yielded a weak response. He had only about 170 men to defend the fort, most of whom had little or no combat experience. Making matters worse, the fort was low on ammunition and powder.

Once his eight hundred men were in position down the slope from the fort, Eyre demanded that the Americans surrender. The call was refused. Eyre then informed Ledyard that if the fight commenced, no quarter would be given, to which Ledyard responded, "We will not give up the fort, let the consequences be what they may." Ledyard's seemingly foolhardy stance, given the overwhelming force arrayed against him, was based in part on his mistaken belief that the much hoped-for reinforcements would soon—finally—arrive.

While this exchange was taking place, Arnold was watching from across the river. He didn't like what he saw. Based on advance intelligence, he assumed that the fort was rather insubstantial and could easily be taken. But now he realized that it was "more formidable" than he had expected. He immediately dispatched one of his officers on a boat to reach Eyre and instruct him to call off the attack. The message arrived too late; the battle had already begun.

The British attacked the fort from three sides, repeatedly charging and trying to climb over the ramparts. The Americans used their light arms and cannons to good effect and also employed sharp pikes to beat back the British. At one point, a stray bullet cut the halyard holding up the American colors, which fluttered to the ground. Even though the flag was quickly remounted on a pole, the British assumed that its initial fall meant that the fort had surrendered. They rushed forward in jubilation, only to be cut down by the Americans. The apparent duplicity enraged the British soldiers, who redoubled their assault, finally broke open the fort's main gate, and started streaming in. Ledyard realized that there was no use fighting anymore and called for his men to surrender. Amid the chaos, not all of them heard the command, and the battle continued.

The most controversial moment of the battle soon arrived. According to an account by an eyewitness, published well after the war when the man was quite old, British major Stephen Bromfield, who had taken command after Eyre was wounded, entered the fort and asked, "Who commands this fort?" Ledyard stepped forward and said, "I did, but *you* do now." At the same time, Ledyard presented his sword, hilt first, to Bromfield, and as the story goes, the major grabbed the sword and thrust it clear through Ledyard's body, murdering him. However, Walter L. Powell, in his authoritative review of the event, notes that contemporary accounts don't mention this conversation, or Ledyard being run through with his own sword by Bromfield. Instead, what probably happened was that Ledyard "was bayoneted, with several other men, while begging for quarter."* Still, it was a terrible end.

---

* William Pynchon, in his diary entry for September 13, 1781, does say that "the commander of the fort was stabbed upon resigning his sword," but it is not clear whether this means he was stabbed with his own sword or by a bayonet. The exact cause of death is less important than the fact that he was killed in a dishonorable manner. See William Pynchon, *The Diary of William Pynchon of Salem*, ed. Fitch Edward Oliver (Boston: Houghton, Mifflin and Company, 1890), 105.

It was after Ledyard was killed and the Americans had laid down their arms that the worst atrocities began. According to Stephen Hempstead, one of the American survivors, the British "wantonly went to shooting and bayonetting us though quarters was continuously cried for from everyone but to no purpose." Arnold viewed the battle in a completely different light, later claiming that "the attack was judicious and spirited, and reflects the highest honor on the officers of the troops engaged."

The slaughter finally ended at about 2:00 p.m. Eighty-three Americans were dead and thirty-six wounded; a few would later succumb to their injuries. British losses were comparable, with 48 killed and 145 wounded, three of whom later died. Arnold's two forces reconnected later that day and sailed back to New York the following morning, leaving behind a gruesome scene. According to historian Eric D. Lehman, "The Battle of Groton Heights was the bloodiest battle of the entire war, with the highest percentage of soldiers participating killed. . . . New London suffered the highest percentage of destruction of any American city."

British attacks on the "nests" of rebel privateers had little impact on the war because they barely put a dent in American privateering. The sites raided, including devastated New London, continued to send out privateers, and there were plenty of other active privateering ports that were spared. What the raids did do, however, was further inflame the patriotic passion of many Americans.

THOUGH IT WAS the birthplace of privateering, Britain was slow to send out its own privateers against its former colonial subjects. Finally, on March 11, 1777, Parliament passed a law authorizing the Lords of the Admiralty to issue letters of marque to vessels sailing from England, Wales, and Scotland giving the bearers permission to attack any shipping belonging to "the rebellious colonies." Adding privateers into the mix made good sense militarily. As the conflict wore on, the Royal Navy found itself transporting and supplying armed forces in America, convoying merchant vessels, and defending its far-flung colonies around the world. Even as the navy expanded, it needed help in prosecuting the war, and privateering was a well-worn British tradition.

British shipowners and sailors eagerly responded to the opportunity, sending forth numerous vessels to do battle with the Americans. When

France, Spain, and the Dutch Republic* allied with the Americans, it gave a significant boost to British privateers, who now had three more targets of opportunity. Between 1777 and 1783, Britain issued a staggering 7,352 privateering commissions. Each specificized a particular enemy nation to target: 2,285 commissions were granted to privateers to prey on American shipping, while the numbers for France, Spain, and the Dutch Republic were 2,328, 1506, and 1,233, respectively. But these figures overstate the true size of Britain's privateering force, because roughly two-thirds of the commissions were duplicates or recommissions. Still, there were 2,676 unique British privateering vessels during the war, an impressive total.

Nowhere in Britain was the privateering spirit stronger than in Liverpool. A bustling shipping port before the war, the onset of hostilities brought much of the city's maritime commerce and slave trading to a halt. Liverpudlians, many of whom were opposed to the war with America because it would cripple business, now had no alternative and channeled their anger and frustration into privateering, and in time, valuable prizes helped to buoy the local economy. Between August 1778 and April 1779 alone, the city sent out at least 120 privateers, carrying nearly 2,000 cannons and 9,000 men. One Liverpudlian wrote in late 1778 that "the privateering trade is the best trade going on at this time, for we have but little other. Half the people must have been bankrupt, had it not been for the great success our armed ships have met with." The most spectacular battle involved the privateer *Watt* and the Continental navy frigate *Trumbull*.

In early June 1780, the *Watt*, an imposing privateer with 32 cannons and 164 men, was north of Bermuda sailing for New York when Captain John Coulthard spotted a large vessel heading in his direction with no colors flying. Unsure of the other ship's intentions, Coulthard raised the British flag and fired one of his cannons as a warning. The mystery vessel quickly ran up British colors as well, but Coulthard was still suspicious, as well he should have been.

Captain James Nicholson of the *Trumbull* was playing for time so he could maneuver into a better position. One of the original thirteen frigates built by Congress, the *Trumbull* had 30 cannons and a complement of 199 men. Nicholson could tell that the *Watt* was a formidable foe, but

---

* Britain declared war on the Dutch Republic in 1780 in response to the Dutch providing the Americans with arms and supplies.

he judged the *Trumbull* a better sailer, and when he exhorted his men to fight, they heartily agreed. Nicholson edged the *Trumbull* to within firing range.

To either confirm his suspicions or put them to rest, Coulthard signaled the *Trumbull* in a manner that only another British ship, familiar with British signs, would understand. When the *Trumbull* failed to respond, Coulthard and his men "instantly gave her three cheers and a broadside." Nicholson raised the American colors and promptly fired back. For two and a half hours, within one hundred yards of one another and at times "yardarm to yardarm," the two vessels fought. According to Gilbert Saltonstall, captain of marines on the *Trumbull*, "It is beyond my power to give an adequate idea of the carnage, slaughter, havoc, and destruction that ensued. Let your imagination do its best, it will fall short. We were literally cut all to pieces; not a shroud, stay, brace, bowling, or any of our other rigging standing; our maintop mast shot away; our fore, main, mizzen, and jigger masts going by the board; some of our quarter-deck guns disabled." Saltonstall later examined the frigate's flag and just three of its sails and counted 959 holes. Ten cannonballs had penetrated the hull, all above the waterline.

The *Watt* didn't fare any better. Its rigging and sails were shot to pieces, and it had multiple holes in the hull, including a few below the waterline. Four cannonballs had entered the ship's powder magazine, but incredibly it did not explode. With water flooding in, the *Watt* was in danger of sinking, a situation made worse because the *Trumbull*'s cannons had disabled all of the privateer's pumps save one.

Nicholson had had enough. The *Trumbull* put before the wind and sailed off. But Coulthard was not ready to give up, and for eight hours the *Watt* chased the *Trumbull* until it disappeared over the horizon. Now both vessels focused on their most immediate goal: staying afloat and avoiding capture until they could get to a friendly port. The *Watt* finally limped into New York on June 11 and received a warm welcome from a crowd that delighted in hearing of the great damage it had inflicted on the rebel frigate. New Yorkers crowned Coulthard and his crew as heroes. Three days later, after weathering a gale, the *Trumbull* arrived in Boston. When interviewed later on, Nicholson said, "I give you my honor, that was I to have my choice tomorrow, I would sooner fight any two-and-thirty-gun frigate that they have on the coast of America, than to fight that ship over again."

The final toll on the *Trumbull* was eight killed and thirty-one wounded. For the *Watt*, the numbers were thirteen and seventy-nine.*

WHILE MOST BRITISH PRIVATEERS sailed from ports in England, Wales, and Scotland, others set off from the North American colonies Britain still controlled, whether completely or partially, including Nova Scotia, New York, the Bahamas, Florida, and Jamaica. On August 5, 1778, Lord Germain sent a confidential circular to the British governors of these colonies, giving them permission to authorize privateers. Of all the loyal colonies that sent forth privateers, Nova Scotia and New York pursued this form of warfare with the most zeal.

For a brief moment at the outset of the Revolution there had been a slight possibility that Nova Scotia might become America's fourteenth colony, joining the battle against Britain. Roughly three-quarters of Nova Scotia's 20,000 citizens had migrated from New England in the aftermath of the Seven Years' War, and in the years leading up to the Revolution the personal and trading ties between Nova Scotia and New England grew stronger. Many Nova Scotians also had their own complaints about British rule and were quite sympathetic to the American cause. Delegates from Nova Scotia even sent out feelers to determine if such a union was possible, as did the Americans.

Discussions never got very far for a number of reasons, one of the most compelling being the actions of American privateers. As early as 1775, they began attacking Nova Scotian ships, taking them as prizes and greatly damaging Nova Scotia's economy in the process. Worse still were the renegade actions of more than a few privateers that went well beyond the terms of their commissions. The captains of these ships landed in Nova Scotian towns for the sole purpose of terrorizing and pillaging the locals, behavior that virtually extinguished any thoughts Nova Scotians had of aligning with the Americans. As a Nova Scotian commented at the time, "robbing poor innocent ones has been a great means to cool the affection of many well-wishers to the just proceedings of America." Instead of joining the

---

* On September 20, 1780, the *Watt* sank when it struck a shoal off Montauk Point, Long Island. Captain Coulthard and twenty of his men drowned. See "The Story of the Vessels Built in Connecticut for the Continental Navy, the *Trumbull*," *Records and Papers of the New London County Historical Society*, part 1, vol. 1 (New London, CT: Published by the Society, 1890), 60.

Americans, the Nova Scotians decided to launch their own privateers and attack them.

They had considerable success. Between 1779 and 1781, they brought in forty-two prizes, the majority of which were American privateers. Some Nova Scotian privateers were captured as well, often after bloody battles. Of the latter, the most notable was the fight between the Nova Scotian privateer *Resolution* and the Boston privateer *Viper*, both mounting sixteen cannons. On July 10, 1780, the two vessels met in a "hot engagement" within sight of Sambro Island Lighthouse, near Halifax, with the

Early twentieth-century painting of the Raid on Lunenburg (also called the Sack of Lunenburg) by American privateers on July 1, 1782—one of the worst privateer attacks on Nova Scotia during the war. Early that morning, five American privateers—the *Hope, Hero, Scammel, Dolphin,* and *Swallow*—landed nearly a hundred men who laid siege to the town, located about fifty miles southwest of Halifax. Resistance by the locals was cut short when the privateers overwhelmed the handful of defenders, burned the blockhouse, and threatened to burn the rest of the town if the Nova Scotians didn't give up. The privateers then landed two cannons and trained them on the town while the they ransacked houses, stole valuables, furniture, clothes, liquor, and food, destroyed weapons, took a couple of hostages, and forced the locals to pay a ransom of £1,000 before they would leave.

Viper emerging victorious. The American privateer had one dead and two injured, while on the *Resolution*, eight were killed and ten wounded.

But it was British-held New York City that took up the privateering banner with the most fervor and success. From the moment they learned that Parliament had authorized privateers to sail from ports in England, Wales, and Scotland, prominent loyalist New Yorkers had been lobbying London to allow them to send out privateers, too. Their motivations were clear. With the merchant class hemorrhaging money, privateering offered a means of recouping some of their losses and maintaining their business. At the same time, they could contribute to the defense of their country while inflicting pain on the much-despised rebels and other enemies of the Crown.

Nobody pushed for privateering more ardently than William Tryon, the loyalist governor of New York. In the summer of 1778, when Parliament finally assented, Tryon wasted no time. He went on to authorize at least 185 privateers that carried a total of six thousand men. They assembled an enviable record. Between September 1778 and March 1779, they captured 165 prizes valued at £600,000, and many of the captured ships were American privateers. At one point, in a rousing proclamation, Tryon encouraged his fellow New York city residents to become privateersmen, inviting "all those who are inclined to escape from the barbarous domination of the usurpers, and are desirous to contribute their aid to its speedy subversion, and the reestablishment of the harmony, tranquility, and prosperity of the empire," to join one of the many ships fitting out to fight Britain's foes. A recruiting advertisement for privateers emphasized the immense rewards that awaited those who signed on, claiming that the "never exhausted floating wealth of the Spaniard, the Frenchman, and the remnant of the Rebel, points out an ample field upon which the seaman may reap a golden harvest."

The success of New York privateers came at a cost: the lure of privateering caused many Royal Navy crewmen to desert their posts. In late 1778, the navy got so angry over the defections that it offered a reward of twenty guineas "to any person who will give information against any owner or master of a privateer . . . concerned in such daring and villainous proceedings, so that they may be convicted and brought to justice." This didn't solve the problem, and five months later Sir George Collier, who was stationed in New York, took a different tack. Because some deserters wanted to return to naval service, but hesitated because the penalty for desertion was "death by the sentence of a court martial," Collier offered a deal. If the deserters came back and acknowledged their crime, then they would be pardoned. Whether such clemency was effective, it still didn't eliminate the problem. Loyalist privateering out of New York continued, and navy men still found their way onto cruises.

The most remarkable New York privateer was the schooner *Royal Charlotte*, mounting eighteen cannons and two swivel guns. It was launched in 1779 by three "loyal ladies residing" in New York City who paid for the venture with their own money.* In so doing, they were following the example of King George III's wife, Queen Charlotte, as well as six "respectable ladies of Westminster," who had equipped privateers at their own expense "to assist in humbling the pride and perfidy of France, and in chastising the rebels of America." In announcing the commissioning of the *Royal Charlotte*, the editors of New York's *Royal Gazette* opined, "This instance, while it reflects great credit on the patriotism of the ladies, ought to be considered by the rebels as a proof of the flagrancy of their own insolence and obstinacy, in rejecting such generous offers of reconciliation, as to excite the indignation of the FAIR SEX; whose natural characteristics are gentleness and benevolence." A Long Island bard even penned a poem in honor of the women and offered it to them "as a New-Year's gift." It read, in part:

> *Brave loyal tars, and hearts of oak, will vie*
> *For you to fight or conquer, live or die;*
> *By you inspir'd, they'll plead our common cause,*
> *With vengeful thunder, 'gainst the Congress' laws.*

The *Royal Charlotte* had a couple of successful cruises, capturing a Spanish and an American privateer, both of which were brought into New York City and auctioned. Among the items listed at the sale of the Spanish ship was "choice Tenerife Wine." Come November 1779, the *Royal Charlotte* itself was placed on the auction block at the city's Merchants' Cof-

---

* A few newspaper articles announcing this privateer called it the *Fair American*, but later government documents and newspaper articles refer to it as the *Royal Charlotte*, meaning that the name must have been changed.

fee House. The advertisement announcing the event noted that "she is a fast-sailing vessel and well calculated for a privateer." Whether the *Royal Charlotte* sold and was sent out again as a privateer under a different name is not known.

THE SKILLFUL ACTIONS OF British privateers and the Royal Navy resulted in the capture of many American mariners during the war, which raised a critical question: What should be done with rebel prisoners? The British government's answer was to send them to land-based prisons in England and prison ships in North America. With the latter, in particular, Britain authored one of the most horrific and shameful chapters in the history of the Revolution.

CHAPTER
8

"Hell Afloat"

Early twentieth-century engraving
of the prison ship *Jersey*.

BRITAIN HAD A PROBLEM. IF CAPTURED AMERICAN SOLDIERS AND mariners—navy men and privateersmen—were treated as prisoners of war under international law, it would mean that Britain regarded the colonies as a foreign sovereign power; and of course neither the Crown nor Parliament was willing to recognize American independence. Other difficulties arose if the American prisoners were viewed as regular British citizens. In that case, they would have a constitutional right to habeas corpus: they couldn't be held indefinitely and could instead petition to be brought before a judge to determine if there were lawful grounds for their imprisonment. If there weren't, they would be set free. Were such a right to be made available to the crush of American prisoners, the courts would soon be overwhelmed with cases, and either many prisoners would go free or Britain might find itself violating its own constitution.

Because neither option for the treatment of American prisoners was practical or appealing, Lord North's administration passed a law early in 1777 that empowered the king to "secure and detain persons charged with, or suspected of, the crime of high treason committed in North America, or on the high seas, or the crime of piracy." In effect, the law allowed the British to hold American prisoners as long as they wanted to without access to the courts. This had the added benefit, from the British perspective, of avoiding the troubling prospect of trying Americans, finding them guilty, and hanging them—which would not only cause an uproar among the significant portion of the British public still sympathetic to their American brethren but also dim the chances for reconciliation. Furthermore, if the British started hanging American prisoners, it would raise the alarming specter of Americans retaliating in kind.

There was spirited opposition to the law, mainly focused on its suspension of habeas corpus, that "great bulwark of English liberty." Nevertheless, the bill passed with a large majority. In fighting for its adoption, Lord North argued that the law was a temporary expedient to deal with the flood of prisoners, and that it would only be in effect for a short time, as he believed that the American rebels would soon be subdued and the empire reunited. At that point, the prisoners could be dealt with appropriately, perhaps even summarily released. But North's optimism proved unwarranted. North's Act, as it was known, remained in force for nearly five years. During that period and even beyond, American prisoners in England were often treated poorly, but not horrifically so. The conditions on British prison ships in America, however, could only be described as abominable. American soldiers, navy men, and privateersmen alike suffered in the prisons and on the prison ships, but pri-

vateersmen made up the majority of the inmates, and they are the ones
who concern us here.

THE TWO MAIN PRISONS in Britain where privateersmen were sent
were called Mill* and Forton, and together they held 2,500 to 3,000 men
in total over the course of the war. Even before arriving at either prison,
privateersmen were already in miserable shape, after their experiences
on board the ships that captured them and transported them to shore.
Typically men were stripped of all belongings except the clothes on their
backs, though sometimes they were not even afforded that luxury. Then
they were thrown into the ship's hold, where they were crowded together
and chained, which was singularly unbearable in the sweltering summer
months. Rations were uniformly poor to execrable, usually just enough to
keep the men alive until reaching port.

Upon reaching their destination, privateersmen were customar-
ily detained on the ships they came in on while awaiting processing by
local authorities, which was a fairly routine business. The privateers were
brought before a judge or justice of the peace and asked a number of questions, including where they were born, whether they had a privateering
commission from Congress, and how they had been captured. If the men
had been born in England, as opposed to the North American colonies,
they were often impressed directly into the Royal Navy. Although Americans were urged to enlist, they rarely did. After the privateers' answers
were read back to them, the judge declared their fate. Charles Herbert, a
crewman on the Newburyport privateer *Dalton*, was told by a judge that
"you are supposed to be guilty of the crime of high treason, and committed to prison for the same until the time of trial" (a trial, of course, that
would never come). The men would then be marched under armed guard
to their assigned prison.

Wives of the British officers and crew visited their husbands on board
the ship where Herbert and his fellows were being kept. When the women
heard that there were American prisoners, their curiosity was piqued.
"What sort of people are they?" asked one, while another inquired, "Are
they white?" and "Can they talk?" A navy man pointed to a few Ameri-

---

* Also sometimes referred to as Old Mill or Millbay Prison.

cans who were on the deck. " 'Why!' " exclaimed [the women], " 'they look like our people, and they talk English.' " This was not a unique reaction. Amazingly, there are other instances of Britons expressing shock upon seeing privateersmen.

Herbert was sent to Mill Prison. It had four main buildings, housing the prison itself, the hospital, the commissary, and administrative offices. These surrounded a sizable courtyard, roughly 250 feet by 150 feet. Inner and outer stone walls were ten to fourteen feet high, their tops encrusted with broken shards of glass to discourage escapes. Guards patrolled the grounds. Mill could hold up to 800 prisoners, but the number never rose higher than 625. In addition to the American privateers and naval personnel, it held French, Spanish, and Dutch inmates. Privateersmen were considered lower-class prisoners and slept on hammocks or straw beds, typically without covers, while naval officers were afforded pillows and blankets. In addition to the clothes they walked in with, prisoners were given shirts, jackets, caps, socks, and, beginning in 1781, shoes.

Forton Prison was in Gosport, on the other side of Portsmouth Harbor from Portsmouth. Formerly a hospital for sick and wounded men from the Royal Navy, it was similar to Mill in size and layout, but instead of stone walls, the prison was surrounded by eight-foot-high iron pickets driven into the ground with two-inch gaps between them. The population of American prisoners rarely exceed four hundred and was usually closer to two hundred. As at Mill, the Americans were thrown in with inmates of other nationalities, there were plenty of guards, and the accommodations and clothing were basic, while always slightly better for officers.

Upon entering either prison, the privateers were read the regulations. They were expected to obey the keeper (warden) and guards without complaining, muster when called, refrain from fighting with one another, and clean up their quarters. They were also told that nobody had the right to "beat or in any manner ill-treat them." The prisoners could choose two from among themselves to watch their food being prepared to make sure that it was in the proper amount, as per regulations, and of good quality. If there was a problem, they could lodge a complaint with the keeper. The rations were as follows: each day from Sunday through Friday the men were to get one quart of beer, one pound of bread, three-quarters of a pound of beef (boiled and served with the broth), and half a pint of peas.

On Saturday the fare was the same, minus the beef, which was replaced with four ounces of butter or six ounces of cheese.

The amount of food actually provided was typically a fraction of the stated rations, and of wretched quality. Moldy bread, diluted beer, inedible cheese, putrid water "thick with animalcules," and "stinking beef" were routine. To supplement their meager fare, the men were sometimes driven to eat grass and snails found in the courtyards, and to gnaw at old bones. Captured rats, stewed, added to the menu, and on one occasion, the men at Mill grabbed one of the guard's dogs and cooked it. There was, however, one additional source of food. Every day from nine to two in the afternoon the prisoners were allowed to attend an open market held at the front gate of the prison, where they could buy fruit, beverages, and other refreshments, as well as clothes, using their own money.

That money came from three sources. A few prisoners who were not fully divested of their belongings prior to entering the prison brought the money in with them. Men were allowed to use their ample free time making things, such as boxes or model ships, which they could sell to visitors. Finally, and most importantly, outside groups, including church groups, friends, escaped prisoners, and sympathetic Englishmen, provided money for prisoner support. Special subscriptions taken up in the areas surrounding the prisons often raised a considerable amount. Benjamin Franklin, whose concern for the plight of American prisoners ran deep, worked through his friend David Hartley, a member of Parliament and fierce critic of the war, to funnel money, tobacco, and coats, among other items, to his countrymen.

The regulation requiring that the prisoners be treated well was not always observed. Guards would occasionally beat or insult their charges. The worst example occurred in Forton, where one particularly notorious and vile captain of the guards, who had expressed his desire to kill some of the prisoners, decided to provoke them into conflict. He used a red-hot poker to burn holes in the Americans' shirts, which were hanging on the pickets to dry. The men pleaded with the guard to stop but he ignored their cries. Trying to salvage their shirts before they were unwearable, the men rushed forward and grabbed them, careful not to incite the captain further. But he ordered a sentinel to fire; one prisoner was killed and another wounded. To stop the "uprising" from going any further, the guards rushed the Americans, bayonets first, forcing them back into their quarters. The next day a trial by jury was convened, overseen by the warden. Despite the fact that numerous eyewitnesses from the town testified that they saw the sentinel fire his weapon, reload, and threaten the Americans that he would fire again if they did not end their protest, the verdict was manslaughter instead of murder.

That guards would act cruelly was not a surprise, given the personalities of their bosses. John Newsham and William Cowdry, the keepers at Forton and Mill, respectively, were roundly reviled by the prisoners, with Cowdry viewed as the worse of the two. Newsham earned the nickname "the old crab" because he was, according to one of the prisoners, "very old and ugly, and used to creep over the ground not unlike a large crab. He was also very boisterous and ill-natured towards all of us." As for Cowdry, an American privateersman called him "as great a tyrant as any in England," someone who "uses us with the greatest severity." According to a number of accounts, Cowdry also stole items from the inmates, including money, which led to accusations of corruption.

Even with the often-dreadful food and at times ill-treatment, the prisoners were fairly healthy. In Forton, for example, the death rate for Americans was just under 6 percent, and at Mill it was 3.5 percent, relatively low numbers compared with most prisoner-of-war settings of the era. Medical treatment, of course, was not cutting-edge. One American privateersman at Mill complained that whatever one's ailment, the doctor's prescription was the same.

One of our men said to the Doctor,
"Doctor, I've a violent pain in my Head."
Reply: "Take some Mixture."
"Doctor, I've a sour Stomach."
Reply: "Take some Mixture."
Doctor, "I've a violent Fever on me every Night."
Reply: "Take some Mixture."

In short let the disease be what it will, you must take his Mixture.

That all-powerful "mixture" was a combination of salts, balsam, crushed roses mixed with sugar (marinated for three months), and Jalap, a laxative made from the dried roots of a Mexican plant in the morning glory family.

In addition to eating, building things for sale, and visiting the market, prisoners filled their days by writing letters, reading local newspapers or books, wrestling, gambling, cleaning their barracks, talking among themselves, or just doing nothing. Some prisoners even ran makeshift schools, teaching their illiterate peers how to read and write. Visitors also provided a pleasant diversion. Perhaps the most enthusiastic visitor of the war was Thomas Wren, a Presbyterian minister in Portsmouth. He began appearing at Forton early on, giving the Americans money, clothes, and medicine collected from the locals. He also offered the prisoners spiritual counsel and shared news of the war or from their friends back home.*

There was one other activity that took up a great deal of the typical prisoner's day: dreaming of freedom. The easiest method to escape the confined life of a prisoner was to sign on to a British naval ship. American prisoners were often urged to do so by visiting British naval officers, but not many took the opportunity. Various analyses estimate that the defection rate of Americans at the two prisons in Britain ranged from 5 to 8 percent, while one study claims that the figure for Mill Prison was around 12 percent. Such relatively low numbers are hardly surprising. Many American prisoners were fiercely loyal to their new country and the cause of independence, and they looked down on fellow countrymen who switched sides. Caleb Foot, who was captured on the Salem privateer sloop *Gates* and sent to Forton, noted that some of his fellow crewmen had "entered on board of his majesty's ships . . . which is to the shame of America."

In late December 1778, a group of Americans at Mill Prison drew up a statement that decried defections and proclaimed their collective resolve to not be seduced into British service. "We, whose names are hereunto subscribed, do, of our own free and voluntary consent, agree firmly with each other, and hereby solemnly swear, that we are fully determined to stand, and so remain as long as we live, true and loyal to our Congress, our country, our wives, children and friends, and never to petition to enter on board any of His Britannic Majesty's ships or vessels." More than one

---

* So thankful was Benjamin Franklin for the solace and support freely offered by Wren that at the end of the war he urged Congress to recognize his service. Franklin also felt that an American university should give Wren an honorary doctorate. Congress produced a letter of thanks from the body's president, and the College of New Jersey (today Princeton University) awarded Wren an honorary Doctor of Divinity degree, the first doctorate awarded to an Englishman by an American college or university after the Revolution.

hundred men signed the document. Forton's American inmates signed a more threatening document in which they promised to give any turncoat thirty-nine lashes and lop off one of his ears. Years after the war's end, Franklin praised American prisoners in England who "refused all the allurements that were made use of, to draw them from their allegiance to their country—threatened with ignominious halters, they still refused."

The patriotism of American prisoners was most apparent on their nation's birthday. William Russell, captured on the privateer *Jason* and sent to Mill Prison, wrote in his journal on July 4, 1780, "To-day being the anniversary of American independence, the American prisoners wore the thirteen stars and stripes drawn on pieces of paper on their hats with the motto, Independence, Liberty or Death. Just before one o'clock we drew up in line in the yard and gave thirteen cheers for the thirteen United States of America and were answered by the French prisoners. The whole was conducted in a decent manner and the day spent in mirth."

Another path out of prison was to be traded for British prisoners being held in France. Franklin worked tirelessly to affect such trades, but these cartels were rare occurrences nonetheless, and barely lessened prison populations. The last option for getting out of jail was to escape, which a surprising number of Americans were able to do.

Although solid figures are hard to come by, British records for Forton claim that 536 prisoners escaped between June 1777 and April 1782. But this number cannot be treated as accurate. It counts multiple attempts by the same individuals, and there is no information on how many were recaptured—and many certainly were, given the number of entries in prisoner diaries mentioning escapees being brought back and punished. Another source estimates that as many as eight hundred men escaped from Mill and Forton during the war, and that escape rates were on the order of 18 and 30 percent, respectively. But these numbers are unreliable, too, for the same reasons. Despite the lack of firm statistics, it is clear that escape attempts were numerous, and that many were successful.

Prisoners jumped the wall, dug tunnels, slipped out of the hospitals where security was lax, and broke into underground sewer pipes, wading through offal until reaching the nearby bodies of water and swimming to freedom. They also employed what was referred to as a "gold key," bribing guards to look the other way while they walked out through the main gate.

Once outside the prison walls, the escapees needed help. This often came in the form of sympathetic Englishmen, including Wren and other ministers, who would shelter them and provide food, money, and connections that enabled them to make it onto a boat and out of Britain.

Many escapees were captured not far from the prison by so-called five pounders, area residents who would turn them in for the £5 reward given by the Admiralty. Capturing prison escapees became a lucrative pastime for anti-American locals, and sometimes they got help from the prisoners themselves, who would connive with their captors and split the money. In the bargain, the prisoner got a little time outside the prison walls and a night of carousing before returning to prison a bit richer than before. Many of these entrepreneurial partiers were repeat offenders, with some performing the charade fifteen times.

But such actions had a cost. Escapees who were caught were cut to half rations and thrown into "stricter confinement" for as long as forty days, though usually far less time. Such confinement meant being put in the "black hole," a pit that often had standing water within. Once there, a prisoner was allowed to climb out for only an hour a day to stretch his legs and get some fresh air.

One lucky prisoner who escaped from Mill was Samuel Cutler, a crewman on the *Dalton*. After spending months thinking about escaping and watching many of his fellow prisoners try—most were recaptured—Cutler's turn came on the evening of October 26, 1777. With a steady rain and dark skies offering cover, he and fellow inmate William Morris bolted from the hospital. This was no spur-of-the-moment breakout but a long-planned attempt. Morris's uncle was the famed American artist Benjamin West, who lived in London, and it was with the help of Morris's connections that he and Cutler were able to pull off their daring escape. Friends on the outside, including West, collected £77 to finance the venture. Some of the money funded a well-placed bribe for a guard, which gave the Americans the opportunity they needed to squeeze through the (ineffective) prison bars on the window of their hospital room. The rest of the money paid for a new set of clothes—Cutler and Morris passed themselves off as Quakers—and the costs associated with their journey to freedom. It wasn't only money that was critical but also the sympathizers offering shelter to the escapees.

At one point, Cutler and Morris nearly blew their cover. Traveling through Exeter, they took a room at an inn and asked the landlord, "What is the news?" The landlord gave them a searching look and replied, "The news is that two Americans have escaped from Mill Prison." Fortunately for them, this gentleman was a friend to the American cause and didn't expose them but rather urged them to be more careful in the future.

It took them nearly fourteen days to make it to London. They stayed with friends in the city for a little more than a week and even were bold enough to dine out, visit Lloyd's Coffee House, and take in a play. Finally, on November 14, Cutler and Morris boarded a ship to Rotterdam, where more friends added to their funds and sent them off via coach to Paris. Both ultimately returned to America.

One of the largest escapes occurred at Forton not long after fifty-eight men from the North Carolina privateer *Fair American* entered the prison in November 1780. There were British locals living just fifty feet from the prison's outer fence, and the men of the *Fair American* decided to make their escape by tunneling to one of those homes. The main problem was where to put all the soil. They solved it in a clever manner. The ceilings in the prisoner's quarters contained multiple eighteen-inch-square openings for ventilators that extended to the roof and exhausted foul air from the prison. By removing the ventilator grates, the prisoners could get access to the attic. Digging as quietly as possible in the early morning hours, the men placed the extracted soil in bags, which were passed up into the attic, where the dirt was dumped. It was an impressive operation. A typical night's haul was one hundred bags. They had tunneled forty feet when disaster struck. A roof tile that was dislodged when they replaced one of the grates fell onto the head of a guard who was standing watch outside. He rushed into the building so quickly that the men didn't have time to cover their hole, and their plot was discovered. Later, when a contingent of guards asked the men where they had put all the dirt, they said that they had eaten it. Failing to discover the soil-filled attic, the guards apparently took the men at their word and forced the them to fill the tunnel with new dirt brought from outside.

The *Fair American* prisoners laid low for a while but then began digging another tunnel, this one a success. They broke through to the cellar kitchen of a nearby house and surprised an old woman, who started screaming for the prison guards. The prisoners quickly gagged her. Almost the entire crew of the *Fair American* emerged out of the hole, along with a few other privateersmen. All but two of them were soon recaptured, and many of them gave up voluntarily to share in the £5 reward.* One of the men who escaped, *Fair American* lieutenant Luke Matthewman, ultimately made it out of the country with Thomas Wren's help, arriving in Philadelphia in mid-1781. The fate of the other successful escapee is unknown.

WHILE BEING A PRISONER at Mill or Forton was not pleasant and could be dismal, it was not uniformly so. Writing to his wife from Mill on March 4, 1781, privateersman William Russell, who had been imprisoned for more than fourteen months, painted a picture of prison life that was far cheerier than the typical inmate commentary but nevertheless is broadly reflective of the relatively decent treatment most prisoners received. "Notwithstanding my long confinement, I bless God that I have not experienced the want of any of the necessaries of life in this prison, for with my industry† and what I am allowed, I live comfortably for a prisoner. The usage we receive, if I am any judge, is very good, for we are allowed the liberty of the yard all day and an open market at the gate to buy and sell . . . besides we have comfortable lodgings. I have never been in the black hole once, for I have made it my study to behave as a prisoner ought."

After two and a half years at Mill, Russell was released in June 1782 in a prisoner exchange and sent back to Boston, arriving there in mid-August. His reprieve was short. A few days after being reunited with his family, he joined another privateer, which was captured by a British warship on September 16. Back to prison Russell went, but this time he wasn't sent to England. Instead, he was placed on the *Jersey*, one of the British prison ships in New York City. After just two months on board, he sent a letter to his wife, lamenting his situation. "I write with an aching heart to inform you of my miserable condition. I'm now in the worst of places and must suffer if confined here during the Winter, for I am short of clothing and the provisions is so scant that it is not enough to keep body and soul together. . . .

---

* On January 5, 1779, one hundred prisoners escaped from Mill, seventy-five of whom were captured the same day.

† Russell taught his fellow inmates in a makeshift school and received "tuition" in the form of monetary donations.

This is the awfullest place I ever saw, and I hope God will deliver me from it soon."

If anything, Russell's description understates the circumstances in which he found himself. Throughout the war there were many cases of cruelty and inhumanity on both sides. But by far the worst experience any combatant had to endure was a stay on one of the British prison ships in New York. Most of the inmates didn't make it out alive.

All told, there were seventeen prison ships in New York during the war, a few of which also served as hospitals.* The vessels were old naval warships and transports long past their prime. Stripped of their sails, rigging, spars, armaments, and most of their masts, they were transformed into floating hulks. The majority of the inmates were privateersmen, but the hulks also held naval seaman, soldiers, regular citizens, and French, Spanish, and Dutch combatants.

It was the sheer number of prisoners of war that created the need for prison ships in the first place. After the British took New York City in the summer of 1776, they placed the resulting mass of prisoners in makeshift jails throughout the city: in churches, government buildings, and sugarhouses (structures formerly used to refine and store sugar and molasses coming from the Caribbean). When these buildings filled up, inmates went to prison ships. The British treated this as a temporary solution, because they believed that the war would soon be over. But just like Mill and Forton Prisons in England, the prison ships in New York City would remain in use until nearly the end of the war.

As to how many prisoners were held on these ships, there is no definitive estimate. The extant records are poor, and some have disappeared. The late Edwin G. Burrows, the historian who delved most deeply into the data and contemporary reports, pointed to the total number most likely being between 15,700 and 22,000.

Most of the prison ships were moored in Wallabout Bay, a small, shallow inlet in the East River, located directly across the river from Manhattan, where the Brooklyn Navy Yard is today.

The relative distance from the city was a precaution against the spread

---

* At various times during the war, there were British prison ships in Philadelphia, Charleston, Newport, Savannah, Halifax, and off of Florida, but these are not covered here. Instead, the focus is on New York, because it had the largest concentration of prison ships, with the largest number of prisoners.

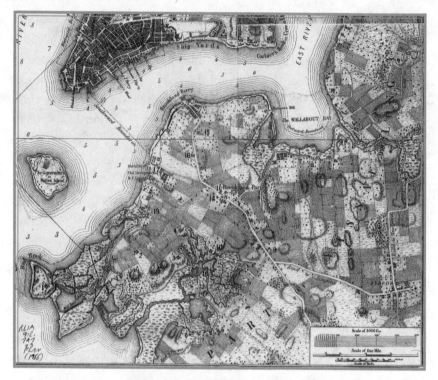

Brooklyn, circa 1766, showing Wallabout Bay toward
the upper right-hand corner of the map.

of disease, which was rampant on the ships. The land on the edge of Wallabout was sparsely inhabited, adding to the ships' isolation.

All of the prison ships were dreadful, but the *Jersey* was by far the worst. "Such an accumulation of horrors was not to be found in any other one [prison ship], or perhaps in all collectively," wrote a former prisoner after the war. "The very name of it struck terror into the sailor's heart, and caused him to fight more desperately, to avoid being made a captive." Nicknamed "Hell Afloat" by sailors who had the misfortune of being imprisoned on it, the *Jersey* had been a fourth-rate 64-gun British warship, launched in 1736. One hundred forty-four feet long and forty-two feet wide, its normal crew was four hundred. Before the start of the war, the *Jersey* had been transformed into a hospital ship and moored in the East River to serve the needs of the city. In late 1779, it was turned into a prison ship and towed to Wallabout Bay, where it was moored about a hundred yards from shore. The largest of the prison ships, the *Jersey* held at any one time between 850 and 1,200 prisoners. There is no consensus on exactly how many men, in total, languished on the *Jersey* during its more than three years as a prison, but it was most likely more than eleven thousand, and probably much more than that. As the early twentieth-century historian Danske Dandridge wrote, "Never before or since, in the dark annals of human sufferings, has so small a space enclosed such a heavy weight of misery."

Arriving at the *Jersey* for the first time was itself a harrowing experience. When the men of the Providence privateer *Chance* were brought into New York Harbor as prisoners on board a British warship, they were immediately transferred to boats that took them to the *Jersey*. According to Thomas Dring, master's mate on the *Chance*, seated in one of the boats was the "miscreant" David Sproat, who months earlier had assisted in the release of American privateersman John Greenwood. Now commissary general of naval prisoners, Sproat was "universally detested" for his cruelty. While the marine guards kept watch, the Americans rowed. They were harangued by Sproat, who yelled at them to pull harder. In no hurry, the Americans maintained their slow pace. This only enraged Sproat, who ominously said, "I'll soon fix you, my lads."

Nineteenth-century engraving depicting the interior of the prison ship *Jersey*.

As Wallabout Bay and the *Jersey* came into view, Sproat pointed, "then exultingly said 'There, rebels, there is a cage for you.'" While Sproat was gloating, Dring looked at the dreaded hulk, bathed in the dying light of day. "A multitude of moving men [were] upon her upper deck." Dring had spied the prisoners, who were being herded by armed guards from the main deck into the hold for the night. Seeing the boats coming nearer, a few of the prisoners "waved their hats and seemed to say 'approach us not,' at least we so construed it, and we afterwards found it verified."

When the boats pulled alongside the *Jersey*, Dring found himself right next to one of the "air ports" on the side of the ship. In transforming the warships into prison ships, all the gunports had been sealed. To provide ventilation for the prisoners, the British cut twenty-four-inch square openings into the hull above the waterline. These air ports were placed ten feet apart and covered over by iron grates to keep the men from escaping. With so many prisoners belowdecks, the relatively small openings were relatively ineffective at circulating fresh air, and the limited light they admitted did little to lift the gloom within.

From one of the air ports, Dring later recalled, "came a current of foul air." It brought back bad memories of the prison ship *Good Hope*, where he had spent four months in 1779 as an inmate before escaping. The smell precipitated an "accumulated nauseousness" that he found impossible to describe. While Dring was standing there waiting for orders to climb aboard, some of the *Jersey*'s inmates, speaking through the grates, addressed him. Given that night had fallen and there were no lights within the *Jersey*, Dring could not see his interlocutors; he could only hear their disembodied voices. They asked him what ship he had been on and how it had been captured. Upon receiving answers, one of the inmates replied that it was "a lamentable sight to them to see so many young men with health upon their countenances about to enter their infernal place of abode." The inmate then added "that death had no relish for their skeleton carcasses, and that he would now have a feast upon fresh comers."

And feast death did. Between six and twelve men died per day during the *Jersey*'s tenure as a prison. Every morning, as the sun rose, "there would be heard the loud, unfeeling and horrid cry" from the guards above: "Rebels, bring up your dead." Given the squalid conditions on the *Jersey*, it is surprising the death rate wasn't even higher. The hold was so

Silas Talbot, captain of the privateer *General Washington*, was captured by the HMS *Culloden* in the fall of 1780 and sent briefly to the *Jersey* before being transferred to Mill Prison. He left the following damning portrait of his time on the prison ship: "There were about 1,100 prisoners on board. There were no berths or seats, to lie down on, not a bench to sit on. Many were almost without clothes. The dysentery, fever, frenzy and despair prevailed among them, and filled the place with filth, disgust and horror. The scantiness of the allowance, the bad quality of the provisions, the brutality of the guards, and the sick, pining for comforts they could not obtain, altogether furnished continually one of the greatest scenes of human distress and misery ever beheld. It was now the middle of October, the weather was cool and clear, with frosty nights, so that the number of deaths per day was reduced to an average of ten, and this number was considered by the survivors a small one, when compared with the terrible mortality that had prevailed for three months before. The human bones and skulls, yet bleaching on the shore of Long Island, and daily exposed, by the falling down of the high bank on which the prisoners were buried, is a shocking sight, and manifestly demonstrates that the Jersey prison ship had been as destructive as a field of battle." Portrait painted in the uniform of a British officer, by Ralph Earl, 1785, courtesy of William R. Talbot Jr.

packed that the prisoners slept almost on top of one another, and it was not uncommon to go to sleep next to a living person and wake up next to a dead one. The floor was smeared with bodily secretions of all kinds. Because only two prisoners at a time were allowed on the main deck at night, many of the men who were unable to relieve themselves while waiting their turn went to the base of the ladder to do so. On most mornings a pile of excrement twelve feet in diameter lay around the ladder's bottom rung. Some men didn't even make it that far, and ended up defecating on their fellow inmates, covering them in "bloody and loathsome filth."

Legions of vermin infested the men's clothes, skin, and hair, causing an interminable itch that no amount of scratching could alleviate. Some men, driven by insatiable hunger, picked the lice and fleas from their body and ate them.* The air was thick and fetid. In the summer, the men broiled belowdecks in temperatures that soared past 100 degrees, while in the winter they huddled even closer together than normal to keep from freezing to death, which many of the weakest did.

The prisoners were fed an abominable and stingy diet of rancid food and water. The bread was "moldy and filled with worms," the peas "as indigestible as grape-shot," and the beef was so solid that it "would have set the keen edge of a broad-axe at defiance to cut across the grain"; if it had a "streak of fat," that "would have been a phenomenon." The pork, which was rarely served and always "unsavory," had "motley hues" and "the consistenc[y] and appearance of variegated fancy soap." The butter was not butter at all but a mystery oil that "was so rank and putrid that we could not endure even the smell of it," according to one prisoner. During New York City's periodic food shortages, when British forces and the

---

* In at least one instance, prisoners on the *Jersey* used vermin to have some fun. To pass the time, they picked insects off their bodies and placed them in a snuffbox "to deprive them of their liberty." When a very tall Irish officer went belowdecks to drum up recruits for the navy, he was forced to bend over at the waist to walk around, and that was all the opportunity the prisoners needed. One of them dumped the entire contents of the box on the officer's back, and then all the prisoners let out three cheers. When the officer emerged into the sunlight on the main deck, the Scottish captain of the ship, thinking that some practical joke of some sort might have been played, stepped forward to take a closer look and saw vermin "crawling" up the officer's "shoulders and aiming at his head." The captain yelled, "Hoot, mon, wha' is the matter with yer bock?" The officer looked down and, seeing the creeping menagerie, "flung off his coat in a paroxysm of rage," which caused the prisoners who were on the deck to let out some cheers of their own. This prank earned the prisoners involved a stretch of confinement and short rations. See Ebenezer Fox, *The Adventures of Ebenezer Fox, in the Revolutionary War* (London: Charles Fox, 1848), 143–46.

local population were placed on short rations, the prisoners' fare was further reduced.

It was not only that the meat was of poor quality and improperly cooked. The *Jersey* was so close to shore that its keel was permanently wedged into the mud, and the depth of the water around the ship was just a few feet at low tide. Into this shallow water the waste of roughly a thousand men was dumped daily, and because tidal flushing was weak in the bay, most of that waste accumulated, further decaying. That foul salt water was drawn onto the ship and placed in the large copper kettle where the meat was boiled. Not only did the salt water infect the meat with its putridity, but it also corroded the kettle, releasing copper and, in effect, dosing the men with high concentrations of the metal.

Cruelty Presiding Over the Prison Ship, an engraving accompanying Joel Barlow's poem *Columbiad*, circa 1807.

The drinking water, held in large barrels that were never cleaned, "was nauseous." Whenever the sediment at the bottom was disturbed, either by ladling out water or through the addition of new water, the noxious sludge became suspended in solution, rendering the water "most disgusting and poisonous in nature." The injustice of this situation was not lost on the prisoners, who could see the mill in Wallabout just a few hundred yards away on the shore, through which flowed "as fine water . . . as was perhaps ever drank."

Living on top of one another and with already weakened constitutions, the inmates were stalked by dysentery, yellow fever, smallpox, and other maladies. The cries of the afflicted rent the air. According to Thomas Andros, who had been captured on the New London privateer *Fair American* in 1781, "the whole ship, from her keel to the taffrail* . . . contained pestilence sufficient to desolate a world; disease and death were wrought into her very timbers. . . . It fell but little short of the Black Hole at Calcutta. Death was more lingering, but almost equally certain." Another prisoner later recalled that he found himself

> among a collection of the most wretched and disgusting looking objects that I ever beheld in human form. Here was a motley crew, covered with rags and filth; visages pallid with disease, emaciated with hunger and anxiety, and retaining hardly a trace of their original appearance. Here were men, who had once enjoyed life while riding over the mountain wave or roaming through pleasant fields, full of health and vigor, now shriveled by a scanty and unwholesome diet, ghastly with inhaling an impure atmosphere, exposed to contagion, in contact with disease, and surrounded with the horrors of sickness and death.

The sickest of prisoners were transported to the nearby hospital ships, which were really just way stations on the road to oblivion. Few men ever returned alive.

Disposing of the dead was a constant task. After the deceased were brought up to the main deck and laid out on the grating, the other prisoners sewed them into blankets if there were any to be found. Covered or not,

---

* The rail and ornamentation at the vessel's stern.

the dead were slid down a plank into a boat. Joining them were the prisoners chosen to dig the graves. Many volunteered for this duty, not out of reverence for the deceased but because it gave them a brief opportunity to leave the crowded ship, step on solid land, and breathe fresh air. Guards kept a watchful eye as the prisoners dug a shallow trench on the banks of Wallabout Bay, placed the bodies within, and quickly covered them with sand. The morbid act completed, the prisoners were marched back to the boat. Sometimes the gravediggers were allowed to bring a piece of turf back to the ship. When Dring did so, the offering was "sought after by" the other prisoners "with assiduity and passed around like a fragrant rose among them."

Because the graves were so shallow and close to the edge of the bay, storms and the tides would regularly uncover the dead. Thus exposed, the bodies decomposed, their bones bleaching in the sun. So many men were buried along the banks that their remains formed a grisly wrack line of death, which slowly washed into the water. The gruesome scene played out within sight of the *Jersey*, giving the prisoners a terrible glimpse of their possible fate, which must have seemed only slightly worse than their current predicament.

UNLIKE THEIR COUNTRYMEN across the Atlantic in Mill and Forton Prisons, the men on board the *Jersey* did not have distractions such as sports, crafts, or visits from the clergy and others who might have offered a reprieve. Nor did they have a daily market where they could supplement their meager fare or buy clothes. But they did enjoy the modest services of Dame Grant, at least for a while. She was, according to Dring, "a very corpulent old woman" who was rowed out to the *Jersey* by two boys every other day in her boat. Sitting in the stern with her box of goods, she offered a variety of articles for sale, including fruit, sugar, and tobacco. Only a few of the prisoners had ready cash, and those who did buy from Dame Grant often felt guilty because so many of their peers could only gawk at her wares. Still, she did a brisk business, and her arrival was eagerly anticipated by the men. In 1782, Dame Grant caught the "contagion" from the prisoners and died: "although not in the flower of [her] youth, it was in the time of usefulness to us prisoners, and we regretted her loss, which was never after supplied."

On prison ships, as at Mill and Forton, there were three main paths to freedom. One could voluntarily join the Royal Navy, although almost no inmates did. As Andros observed, "If there was any principle among the prisoners that could not be shaken, it was the love of their country. I knew no one to be seduced into the British service. They attempted to force one of our prize brig's crew into the navy, but he chose rather to die, than perform any duty, and he was again restored to the prison ship." Some prisoners who didn't volunteer were nevertheless conscripted through impressment, a practice that accelerated as British forces became severely depleted due to battlefield losses and disease.

Being placed on a cartel was another way out, but those were relatively rare events for prisoners kept in America, too, especially prior to the peace negotiations in 1782.* At most, cartels accounted for hundreds and perhaps a few thousand men held on prison ships being released. George Washington tried repeatedly to engineer prisoner swaps but was largely unsuccessful. Washington and Congress often couldn't agree on the terms of exchanges, causing negotiations to breakdown. A large number of British prisoners in America were not under Washington's or Congress's control but rather were spread out across the states, which were responsible

---

* Cartels were joyous affairs, including for an American named Nathaniel Fanning. Born in Stonington, Connecticut, in 1755, Fanning departed on his third privateering cruise at the end of May 1778, on board the brig *Angelica*, sailing from Boston with ninety-eight men and sixteen guns. Just a few days out, on Fanning's twenty-third birthday, the *Angelica* was captured by the HMS *Andromeda*, a 28-gun frigate, without a shot being fired. Sent to Forton, Fanning's day of deliverance came about a year later, on June 3, 1779, when he and 119 other Americans were told to assemble in the prison yard. "The rest of the American prisoners, amounting to about four hundred and eighty . . . were not permitted to mix with us, and not suffered to come out of their confinement till we began our march, which commenced about 10 o'clock, in company, or rather escorted by about forty British soldiers, and a number of black drummers and musicians, who beat up the tune of Yankee doodle, which they continued playing, till we arrived at the place of embarkation. . . . On our march through the town of Gosport, the streets became crowded with people; some wishing us safe to our desired homes; others crying out, that we were a set of rebels, and that if we had had our deserts we should have been hanged." The cartel ship took them to the small town of Paimboeuf on the Loire in France. "Here we disembarked, and as soon as we began to enter the town, great multitudes of the French came to welcome us; even the children appeared to rejoice at our landing; and to demonstrate this, they all joined by singing as they followed us along: '*Bon, bon, bon, cettez Boston rompez auce anglais aux des cannon.*' The substance of which in English is: 'Here are the good Bostonians who beat the English with their great guns.'" During the Revolution, the French tended to refer to all Americans as "Bostonians" because so many, privateersmen and others, hailed from Boston, or the French just assumed they came from there. See Nathaniel Fanning, *Fanning's Narrative: Being the Memoirs of Nathaniel Fanning, An Officer of the Revolutionary Navy, 1778–1783*, ed. John S. Barnes (New York: De Vinne Press, 1912), 19–21.

for them. Given that states, with a few exceptions, didn't have the capacity to hold the prisoners, many were allowed to melt into the general populace, hiring themselves out to local farms and businesses. Offering up such prisoners for a cartel was virtually impossible. Those states, like Connecticut, that held British prisoners in jails were often unwilling to provide them for cartels, and when they did, the exchanges were relatively insignificant. When there were trades to be made, strategic considerations often intervened. While the British were eager to trade American privateersmen for British soldiers or navy men, Washington balked at such proposals, unwilling to return trained fighters when his army might soon face them again.

British authorities, too, were ambivalent about cartels, further complicating negotiations. And when Washington and other American leaders urged their British counterparts to exchange prisoners for humanitarian reasons, officials including Admiral Howe and Commissary General Sproat often lied, claiming that inmates were treated quite well, despite clear evidence to the contrary. Their dissembling only made it that much more difficult to strike a deal.

Cartels didn't ensure that prisoners would survive the process of release. In early January 1777, after an eleven-day journey, a British ship with two hundred prisoners from the *Jersey* landed in Milford, Connecticut, and discharged its human cargo. According to the *Connecticut Gazette*, their "rueful countenances too well discovered the ill treatment they received in New York." Twenty prisoners died during the trip, and another twenty-six perished soon after arriving.

The final path to freedom was escape, the route chosen by Christopher Hawkins. In the summer of 1781, when he was seventeen, Hawkins left the Smithfield, Rhode Island, farm where he worked and joined the *Marianna*, a Providence privateer. A sinewy young man, five foot ten, with blue eyes, black hair, and a fair complexion, Hawkins's privateering career was brief. Within five days of sailing, the *Marianna* was captured by the frigate HMS *Medea*. Herded into the frigate's cable tier, Hawkins found himself among more than two hundred American privateersmen so tightly packed that they could neither lie down nor sit. For three days, as the frigate sailed to New York, the prisoners suffered mightily. Some died, but those who survived didn't lose their spirit. Often breaking out into song to annoy their captors, the Americans were particularly fond of a tune with a patriotic refrain: "For America and all her sons will forever shine." Guards repeatedly yelled at them to shut up and threatened to shoot them, though they never did. When the frigate reached New York, Hawkins and his fellow privateersmen were sent to the *Jersey*.

Not long after setting foot on board, Hawkins began plotting his escape. The consequences of failure were steep. A new regulation passed just months before the beginning of Hawkins's internment declared that anyone caught attempting to escape would be summarily shot. Fear of that outcome was only one of the impediments to breaking out. The *Jersey* had about sixty British soldiers on board, and the hospital ship and a guardship, both moored nearby, had armed sentinels as well. There were yet more guards stationed at the edge of the bay. To get ashore, one would have to swim and wade, all the while running the risk of being picked off. Then there was the cold. It was early October, and both the air and the water were chilly.

Aware of all of these obstacles, Hawkins and one of his shipmates, William Waterman, were yet determined to try. All they needed was a stormy night. When one came, they took an axe and a crowbar stolen from the cook's room and went to one of the gunports on the lower deck that was bolted shut with iron bars. Each time a peal of thunder rang out, they worked to dislodge the bolts and bars. After a few hours, they had wrenched the port open. They set the bolts and bars lightly back into place so as not to arouse the guards' attention. They also hung a few shirts over their handiwork to hide the cut marks.

Their plan was to leave late at night and swim to a distant point on the shore to avoid the land-based sentinels. They estimated that they would have to cover one and a half miles. When Hawkins and Waterman told the captain of their privateer, Christopher Whipple, about their plot, he was shocked. A mile and a half would be hard enough of a swim in the current conditions, but Whipple said they had misjudged the distance. The point they were aiming for was more like two and a half miles away. Even if they made it clear of the ship and avoided being shot, they would never survive the swim. But Hawkins and Waterman would not be deterred.

A few days later, on a particularly dark evening, they went into action. They removed the bolts and bars from the gunport and slung their makeshift knapsacks, filled with extra clothes, over their backs. Using a rope held by other prisoners, Waterman descended into the water first, followed by Hawkins. A few hundred feet from the *Jersey*, Hawkins softly called out for Waterman three times but got no reply. Assuming that his accomplice had drowned, Hawkins pressed on, using the lights of the prison ships and the twice-hourly calls of the sentinels—"All's well"—as guides to keep on course.* Two and a half hours later, having not only lost his knapsack but shed most of the clothes he had been wearing, Hawkins pulled himself ashore. Numb, cramped, nearly naked, and shivering, he stumbled into a nearby barn, entered, covered himself with hay, and fell into a fitful sleep.

The next morning was the start of his long journey home. Drinking from streams, scavenging rotten fallen fruit and rock-hard ears of corn, and sleeping in barns or out in the open, he traveled many miles. Just as he was becoming too weak to continue, he approached two boys in a field. They were shocked to see this almost naked, dirty, emaciated man before them and began to back away. Hawkins told them to not be afraid, and when they asked him where he had come from, he told them the truth and begged for clothes and food.

The boys, who were brothers, ran to tell their mother about the strange visitor and returned with pantaloons and buttered bread. They instructed Hawkins to go to the family barn. Soon their mother appeared and gave him a shirt and more food. Hawkins said he wanted to reach Sag Harbor, where he had contacts. The woman recommended that he go to Oyster Bay, where there was a man who would help him.

Skirting British sentinels on multiple occasions, Hawkins walked into Oyster Bay, where he was immediately accosted by Tory militiamen who thought he was a whaleboatman from Connecticut, come to steal from the locals. Exhibiting an astonishing lack of guile and imagination, Hawkins told them exactly who he was. His honesty got him placed under guard, as preparations were made send him back to the *Jersey*.

Supervision was lax, enabling Hawkins to escape once again. It was his remarkable luck a few days later to cross paths with Daniel Havens, the man he was trying to reach in Sag Harbor. Because Havens had business

---

* In fact, Waterman made it ashore and ultimately returned home.

to attend to first, he directed Hawkins to continue on alone and wait at his house. Even before Havens had returned, his family had helped Hawkins obtain a spot on a sloop heading for the Connecticut shore. He reached Mystic a day later and from there made his way to Providence. Having had his fill of seaborne adventure, the young Christopher Hawkins gladly returned to the farm he had left back in 1781.

AMERICANS WERE WELL AWARE of the suffering of their countrymen on prison ships. In 1777, the Continental Congress launched an investigation into widespread complaints about British brutality directed at "officers, soldiers, and [other] Americans" fighting for independence. An important thread of the investigation focused on conditions within prison ships. The resulting report concluded that the prisoners "were, in general, treated with the greatest barbarity," and that "multitudes died." Congress revisited the issue in 1781 and found that the situation had worsened, and "that notwithstanding every effort of Congress to obtain for our people, prisoners in the hands of the enemy, that treatment which humanity alone should have dictated, the British commanders . . . have persisted in treating our people, prisoners to them, with every species of insult, outrage and cruelty."

American leaders were under no illusions that these reports would change British behavior. They were intended to document an important side of the war, and to serve as propaganda, however sincere the intentions behind them. The reports were printed in newspapers throughout the states, along with heartrending letters from prisoners and stories of daring escapes. One of the most unusual, popular, and affecting published accounts of life on a prison ship was written by Philip Freneau, the man who would earn the moniker "Poet of the American Revolution."

Born in New York in 1752, Freneau graduated from the College of New Jersey (later Princeton University) in 1771, and in the lead-up to the Revolution he was writing satirical pieces for colonial newspapers lampooning the mother country. During the first few years of the war, he sailed on commercial ventures in the Caribbean and Bermuda, writing poetry on the side. By 1779 he was back in America—in Philadelphia, serving as editor of a political magazine. When it folded a few months later, Freneau decided to return to the Caribbean on board a letter of marque, the *Aurora*, and that's when things went terribly wrong.

The *Aurora* left Philadelphia on May 25, 1779, and just a day later was captured by the British frigate *Iris* and taken to New York as a prize. Freneau pleaded with the British authorities to let him go, pointing out that he was just a passenger on the ship, not a combatant, but they refused. Along with the crew of the *Aurora*, he was sent to the prison ship *Scorpion*. Of his first night in the hulk, packed tightly belowdecks with three hundred other prisoners, he later wrote, "I expected to die before morning, but human nature can bear more than one would at first suppose."

About a week later, thirty-five prisoners—Freneau not among them—decided to escape, taking advantage of the proximity of a small schooner that had moored right next to the *Scorpion*. On cue, they rushed the guards, disarmed them, and then shoved them into a cabin, barricading the door. Taking one of the *Scorpion*'s boats, the prisoners rowed over to the schooner and climbed aboard, easily beating back its crew, who attempted to defend their vessel with handspikes. By the time the *Scorpion*'s guards broke out of the cabin and regained control of their ship, the escapees had

Philip Freneau.

hoisted the schooner's sails and were out of sight. The guards' fury was now unleashed upon the prisoners who remained. Standing above the hatchways, they indiscriminately fired their cannons into the deck below. Somehow, only four men were wounded, though two later died.

Freneau survived the guards' retaliation, but on June 22 he came down with a fever and was transferred to the hospital ship *Hunter*. There he witnessed worse suffering than on the *Scorpion*. "Between decks," the sick lay "struggling in the agonies of death; dying with putrid and bilious fevers; lamenting their hard fate to die at such a fatal distance from their friends; others totally insensible, and yielding their last breath in all the horrors of light-headed frenzy." Freneau, however, would not die on this ship. Although details are scant, he was placed on a small cartel with thirty other prisoners and deposited in Elizabethtown, New Jersey, on July 12. Still sick and weak, he managed to walk to a friend's house, where he stayed the night, and then found transportation back to his family's home in Mount Pleasant (present-day Matawan).

Over the following months, Freneau wrote his most famous poem about the Revolution, titled "The British Prison Ship," which described his ordeal in more than fifty stanzas of verse, some of which are extracted here.*

> *The various horrors of these hulks to tell,*
> *These Prison Ships where pain and penance dwell,*
> *Where death in tenfold vengeance holds his reign,*
> *And injured ghosts, yet unavenged, complain;*
> *This be my task ungenerous Britons, you*
> *Conspire to murder whom you can't subdue.*

. . .

---

* Some historians believe that it is quite possible that Freneau was not a passenger on the *Aurora*, and that he never was on a prison ship, but instead took information from newspaper accounts and other documents relating to the ship to craft his famous poem. Others have not doubted that Freneau lived through the experiences he wrote about. Regardless, his poem did accurately describe the horrors of the prison ships, and it had significant influence on the way Americans viewed the war. See, for example, Edwin G. Burrows, *Forgotten Patriots: The Untold Story of American Prisoners During the Revolutionary War* (New York: Basic Books, 2008), 168–75; and Mary Weatherspoon Bowden, "In Search of Freneau's Prison Ships," *Early American Literature* 14, no. 2 (Fall 1979): 174–92.

Hail dark abode! what can with thee compare,
Heat, sickness, famine, death, and stagnant air,
Pandora's box, from whence all mischiefs flew,
Here real found, torments mankind anew!

. . .

Americans! a just resentment shew,
And glut revenge on this detested foe;
While the warm blood distends the glowing vein
Still shall resentment in your bosoms reign.

. . .

The years approach that may to ruin bring
Your lords, your chiefs, your desolating king,
Whose murderous deeds will stamp his name accursed,
And his last efforts more than damn the first.

The extensive newspaper coverage of the plight of inmates on prison ships, and to a much lesser extent at Mill and Forton Prisons, caused an uproar across the states. It also motivated many to fight even harder for independence. When John Adams sent the 1777 congressional report on Britain's cruel treatment of Americans to his wife, Abigail, he said that it would give her "some idea of the humanity of the present race of Britons." He thought that "the plainest relation of [the] facts" contained in the report "would convince every American that a nation, so great a part of which is thus deeply depraved, can never be again trusted with power over us."

Franklin echoed Adams's conclusions. "As to our submitting again to the government of Britain," he wrote to his friend David Hartley, a member of Parliament, in December 1777, "'tis vain to think of it. She has given us by her numberless barbarities, in the prosecution of the war, and in the treatment of prisoners . . . so deep an impression of her depravity, that we never again can trust her in the management of our affairs and interests." According to the historian Robert P. Watson, "The prison ships contin-

The nearly 150-foot granite-and-brick Prison Ship Martyrs Monument, topped by an eight-ton bronze brazier, is located in Fort Greene Park, Brooklyn. It was designed by the architectural firm of McKim, Mead and White and erected in 1908. There were earlier, small monuments and sepulchers built in the area, reaching back to the early 1800s, that gathered together and entombed the bones of hundreds of the victims of the prison ships, which were collected near the banks of Wallabout Bay. The 1908 monument is the final resting place for those collected bones. Image from the program dedicating the monument.

ued to serve as psychological weapons of terror, none more so than the *Jersey.*" Yet this may have backfired, because "for every colonial worried about the threat of imprisonment on the ghostly ship, several others were inspired by British cruelty to take up arms." As one contributor to the *Freeman's Journal* of Portsmouth, New Hampshire, commented in 1777,

"It is better to be slain in battle, than to be taken prisoner by British brutes, whose tender mercies are cruelty."

SUCH REACTIONS TO the barbaric treatment of imprisoned privateers-men helped shaped the broader American experience of the war. In other ways, too, privateering influenced the direction the war took. From 1775 to 1783, privateers played a central role in the states, and not just through their military exploits or by drawing violent reprisals from Britain; they were a serious irritant to the Continental navy and army, lightning rods for criticism, a source of confidence in the progress of the war, major employers, providers of critical supplies, and wealth generators.

The Home Front

John Langdon's Georgian mansion in Portsmouth, New Hampshire, built in 1784, which is today a National Historic Landmark. Langdon served as a New Hampshire delegate to the Second Continental Congress and, after the war, as a governor and senator of that state. Much of the money to build this lavish house came from his privateering activities during the war, which included investing in and owning privateers.

———

THROUGHOUT THE REVOLUTION, AS PRIVATEERS ATTACKED BRITish shipping and naval vessels, serving as a critical component of the American war effort, the debate in the new nation over their effectiveness, and their very existence, continued. Privateers were not just a threat to the British or a source of employment and adventure for many Americans. They were a significant source of controversy on the home front.

The American who had perhaps the most jaundiced view of privateersmen was William Whipple Jr., a fervent patriot devoted to the republican ideals of the Revolution. Whipple distinguished himself as a delegate of the Continental Congress representing New Hampshire and was a signer of the Declaration of Independence and a military officer at the critical Battle of Saratoga. In June 1778 he conveyed his beliefs about the evils of privateering in a letter to Josiah Bartlett, who had recently resigned his position as a congressional delegate to return to New Hampshire to tend to business affairs.

Whipple argued that the privateering business was "the most baneful to society of any that ever a civilized people were engaged in. The officers that command these vessels are generally the most profligate fellows that are to be met with, and if by chance a man of a fair moral character engages in the business, he very soon degenerates and falls into all the vices of his associates. . . . the sea is swarming with these, I had almost said freebooters—indeed they are but little better." His main concern was that privateers were draining the Continental navy of men, because so many chose privateering over naval service for financial reasons. Unless privateering was banned, Whipple argued, it would be impossible to fully man naval vessels, "for give what encouragement you will, those who are concerned in privateering will find means to prevent men from engaging in the public service. Your ships of war must lay by the walls, or perhaps some of them may get half manned." Whipple was also concerned about national reputation: "I am very apprehensive that unless some measure can be adopted to check the voracity of these people, they will exceedingly disgrace the American flag."

A few weeks later, Bartlett wrote back. While he agreed that there was value to having a stronger, better-manned navy, he had a different view when it came to privateers. "I cannot be fully of your opinion that it would be for the public service to put an entire stop to privateering, as I think experience has shown that privateers have done more towards distressing the trade of our enemies and furnishing these states with necessaries, than Continental ships of the same force." Bartlett's mild response precipitated another letter from Whipple, in which he picked up the cudgel again, this

William Whipple, a signatory of the Declaration of Independence and one of the heroes of the Battle of Saratoga, in 1777.

time with more vigor. "I agree with you that the privateers have much distressed the trade of our enemies, but had there been no privateers is it not probable there would have been a much larger number of public ships than has been fitted out, which might have distressed the enemy nearly as much and furnished these states with necessaries on much better terms than they have been supplied by privateers?" Whipple again claimed that privateersmen were depraved, writing, "No kind of business can so effectually introduce luxury, extravagance, and every kind of dissipation that tend to the destruction of the morals of a people. Those who are actually engaged in it, soon lose every idea of right and wrong; and for want of an opportunity of gratifying their insatiable avarice with the property of the enemies of their country, will, without the least compunction, seize that of her friends."

Whipple was acutely concerned about privateer owners luring away good officers who might otherwise serve on naval ships. As he put it, "officers that are worth employing will quit the service, and you'll have the navy (if you think it worthwhile to keep up that show) officered by tinkers,

Josiah Bartlett, mid-nineteenth-century engraving based on a painting by John Trumbull.

shoemakers and horsejockeys; no gentleman worth employing will accept a commission." Ending the debate in his reply, Bartlett said that he recognized the force of Whipple's arguments, and that there would be some benefit to restraining privateering a bit, but that still he could not agree to a total prohibition.

In retrospect, it is clear—as it was to many at the time—that Whipple was wrong on most counts. Privateers were not as a group akin to "freebooters"—pirates—either legally or in practice. Nor were they morally depraved individuals who, not content with British prizes, indiscriminately seized the vessels of America's allies and friends (France, Spain, and Holland). The vast majority of privateersmen acted honorably, carrying out their commissions, attacking only British vessels or vessels carrying British goods, and treating their prisoners well or at least civilly.

Of course, there were exceptions. As noted earlier, American privateer raids on towns in Nova Scotia provide a few notorious cases. There were also instances of privateersmen stripping prisoners captured at sea of their personal belongings or handling them roughly. And a few did claim as prizes vessels that were not fair game—for example, Spanish or French ships carrying neutral goods, which the American privateer would claim were British. That caused serious diplomatic tension with allies, and it happened often enough that Congress amended the privateering statute in 1780 with clear language stating that neutral vessels were not to be molested. But in the context of the war, the infractions were minor. Nearly every case was amicably, or at least legally, resolved, and those that weren't did not lead to diplomatic breaks, or to negative repercussions for the American war effort. Far from demonstrating that privateers were reckless in their actions, the infractions prove the opposite due to their relative rarity.

Although Whipple didn't mention it, there were examples of privateers capturing American vessels instead of British ones. In one notorious case, Nantucket whaling magnate William Rotch complained that one of Nicholas Brown's Providence privateers had "in a ruffian like manner [taken] possession" of a Nantucket merchant ship in which Rotch had a stake. In a blistering letter to Brown, Rotch, who didn't know the name of the vessel, said that Nantucketers—who had been bothered by this sloop before—christened it "Willful Murther" on account of its "atrocious villainy." Rotch begged Brown to intervene and to return the merchant ship, or at least let the ship unload and allow the vice admiralty court to decide if it was a lawful prize. Unfortunately, it is not known how Brown reacted. But what is clear is that, although there were other instances of privateers attacking American vessels, and even fellow privateers, they were few in number. And sometimes such attacks were initiated in good faith, with the aggressor thinking that the opposing vessel was British, only to be called off when its mistake became clear.*

As to their "insatiable avarice," privateers were no different from their peers in the navy and the army, motivated by money and not solely by republican ideals. And while some officers did leave the navy to serve on

---

* Another indication that the vast majority of privateers acted in a responsible manner is the relatively low number of appeals. When a prize was brought into port and libeled, the decision rendered by the court of the vice admiralty could be appealed to Congress if one of the parties (including America's allies or neutral nations) believed it to be in error. Of the many hundreds of prize cases tried in admiralty courts in the states, only 114 were appealed—and for a great variety of reasons, including disagreement over prize distribution and complaints about the illegality of the capture. See William James Morgan, "American Privateering in America's War for Independence, 1775–1783," *The American Neptune* 36, no. 2 (April 1976): 79n2.

John Paul Jones,
circa 1781.

privateers because of the prospect of more money, most did so because there were not enough spots on navy ships, and they could only fight the British by privateering until another position opened up. Rather than "tinkers, shoemakers and horsejockeys," most officers in the Continental navy were skilled mariners and respected leaders. Though it was also the case that precious few of them had any true naval experience on warships, many acquitted themselves quite well and remain among the most revered figures in the navy's long history.

Whipple, however, wasn't completely mistaken. Privateering was indeed in direct competition with both the Continental and state navies, and many men chose to become privateersmen instead of enlisting in military service in the first place. The ranks of privateers were also increased by navy men who deserted to go on a cruise.* As a result, many naval

---

* Although Americans had for many years prior to the Revolution railed at the British for impressing American mariners, during the Revolution there were a few instances of Continental navy captains impressing American privateersmen—even though the Continental Congress forbade it. Of course, these captains were frustrated over competition for men. As captain of the *Alfred*, John Paul Jones encountered the privateer *Eagle* in Tarpaulin Cove on Naushon Island, near Martha's Vineyard. He sent some of his marines onto the *Eagle* to look for deserters. They found two, whom they grabbed, and for good measure Jones took another twenty men to supplement his ranks. After his cruise ended, he found himself in Boston, where he was served with a lawsuit from the *Eagle*'s owner, claiming that he had engaged in piracy. Jones countersued, and the case was eventually

vessels were considerably delayed in getting to sea due to the inability to fill positions on board. The issue was widely acknowledged, and an easy solution was offered by none other than John Paul Jones. In October 1776, he wrote to Robert Morris from Providence, complaining that he was having great difficulty recruiting men for the naval ship *Alfred*—named after Alfred the Great, the ninth-century Anglo-Saxon king credited with founding the Royal Navy*—because "the privateers entice them away as fast as they receive their month's pay." Given that money was so persuasive to the average man, Jones believed that "unless the private emolument of individuals in our navy is made superior to that in privateers, it never can become respectable; it never will become formidable. And without a respectable navy—alas! America! In the present critical situation of affairs, human wisdom can suggest no more than one infallible expedient: enlist the seamen during pleasure, and give them all the prizes." In other words, allow navy men to benefit from captures more than privateersmen did. Jones's argument was shared with other members of Congress, but it did not become policy.

Privateers also competed with the navy for cannons and gunpowder, which were in limited supply. Because privateer owners had deep pockets, they were often able to outbid the government for these items. Some, such as the successful Providence merchant John Brown, also owned foundries that made cannons, and they favored their own privateers over naval ships when it came to selling them. When they did sell to the navy, the high prices drew accusations of price gouging. Beyond arms and powder, privateers also went head-to-head with the navy when procuring food, rope, and other supplies needed to go to sea.

The competition for men and materials was a serious problem for the navy, and it certainly hampered its operations. But does that mean that

---

thrown out of court. See Evan Thomas, *John Paul Jones: Sailor, Hero, Father of the American Navy* (New York: Simon & Schuster, 2003), 70–71, 75–76. For another example, see Martin I. J. Griffin, *The History of Commodore John Barry* (Philadelphia: Records of the American Catholic Historical Society, 1897), 47–49.

* Recent scholarship has cast doubt on Alfred's role, claiming that the creation of the Royal Navy actually predated him by twenty years. See Matthew Firth and Erin Sebo, "Kingship and Maritime Power in 10th-Century England," *International Journal of Nautical Archaeology* 49, no. 2 (September 2020): 329–40.

there is merit to Whipple's claim that "had there been no privateers is it not probable there would have been a much larger number of public ships than has been fitted out, which might have distressed the enemy nearly as much and furnished these states with necessaries on much better terms than they have been supplied by privateers?" There is clear reason to believe that the answer to Whipple's question was no. To see why, a closer look at the Continental navy is in order.

THERE WERE ROUGHLY sixty Continental navy warships operating in the Atlantic at various times during the Revolution.* Many had been built as warships, while others were converted merchantmen, leased from private owners, loaned by France, or captured vessels that were put into service. Building and assembling a navy from scratch would have overwhelmed a smoothly running government. For the relatively inexperienced, poorly staffed, and financially strapped Continental Congress, it was an almost insurmountable challenge.

The cost of fielding the fleet was between $12.5 and $13.5 million, or roughly 16 percent of all congressional expenditures during the war. Because Congress didn't have the power to levy taxes, relying instead on printing increasingly worthless money and on foreign loans as its primary sources of funds, it struggled to pay this staggering sum, and the fleet came to life haltingly. Developing schematic plans for new ships, hiring skilled shipwrights, obtaining materials, coordinating construction schedules, and paying bills each posed a myriad of difficulties. Given the speed with which the ships had to be built, there wasn't enough time to properly season the wood, and green timbers and planking were more susceptible to rotting and leaking, troubles that plagued many of the ships. As for the vessels that were chartered, leased, or captured, they were of varying quality, and they also required significant investments of materials and money to get them into fighting form.

---

*   Adding in all of the vessels in Washington's fleet, as well as the vessels that operated on Lake Champlain in the Battle of Valcour Island in 1776, the vessels operating on the Mississippi River, and various packets, the total number of ships in Continental service during the war was around one hundred. See Gardner W. Allen, *A Naval History of the American Revolution*, vol. 2 (Boston: Houghton Mifflin Company, 1913), 700–703.

Continental frigate *Alliance* (1778–1875), commanded by Captain
John Barry; the frigate is in the lower right-hand corner, and in
the background is Boston Lighthouse. Painting, circa 1780, by
naval captain Matthew Parke, who served on the *Alfred* and the
Ranger with John Paul Jones and the *Alliance* with John Barry.

The Continental navy was never meant to compete with the much
larger Royal Navy, which had bigger and faster ships, with more powerful cannons and larger, better-trained crews. Nevertheless, the navy
managed to capture twelve British warships, most of which were fairly
small, with fewer than twenty cannons—a record similar to that of privateers, which captured sixteen such vessels. The comparison with
privateers is apt, because naval ships often operated very much like privateers. While the navy performed important tasks such as shuttling
diplomats, convoying merchantmen, protecting state merchant vessels,
transporting specie, and raiding munitions depots, many naval ships
also raided commercial shipping. As William Ellery, congressional delegate from Rhode Island and signer of the Declaration of Independence,
wisely noted, "We cannot with all the naval force we collect be able to
cope with the Royal Navy. Our great aim should be to destroy the trade
of Britain."

The Continental navy's record in battle is not an enviable one.
Twenty-eight vessels were captured or destroyed, and many others were
lost at sea, sold, returned to France, or burned to keep them from being

taken by the enemy (as during the Penobscot Expedition). Only seven of the original thirteen frigates authorized by Congress actually made it to sea,* and none of those survived long enough to witness the victory at Yorktown in 1781, a year in which the entire naval fleet was comprised of only nine vessels, with a total of 164 cannons. The navy's only truly large ship, the 74-gun *America*, took six years to build, and by the time it was ready to sail, in November 1782, the war was essentially over. Instead of fighting for the American cause, *America* was given to the French as gift. At war's end just a few navy ships were left. These were sold, and the navy disbanded.

There were, however, some bright spots for the American navy. Raids on Caribbean munitions depots brought back much-needed gunpowder, and navy ships did an excellent job ferrying diplomats and diplomatic correspondence back and forth to Europe. Lambert Wickes, Gustavus Conyngham, John Barry, and other navy captains used their ships to inflict significant damage on British commerce, capturing roughly two hundred prizes. And of course there was the most celebrated naval victory of the war, the three-and-a-half-hour duel between John Paul Jones's *Bonhomme Richard* and the British frigate *Serapis* off Flamborough Head in England, during which Jones purportedly uttered the now immortal words "I have not yet begun to fight!"†

The navy also served an important symbolic role. As historian William James Morgan observed, "The Continental Navy did not represent private citizens or individual states, but it was an organ of the 13 United States, and in that capacity was a unifying factor. . . . On the ocean, in West Indian and European ports, the Continental Navy was material proof, for all to view, that England's revolting American colonies were determined to be a free and independent country." Like the army, the navy was one of the

---

* The other six frigates were either burned or sunk in port to keep them from being captured by the British, or they ran aground close to shore and were later captured or destroyed.

† It is not clear exactly what Jones said during the battle. The stirring phrase was first mentioned by his first lieutenant, Richard Dale, forty-five years later; Dale was talking to a writer preparing a biography of Jones. An account written down right after the battle has Jones saying, "I may sink, but I'll be damned if I strike." Whatever his exact remarks, he was clearly determined to fight on, and did. See Thomas, *John Paul Jones*, 192.

first truly American institutions, and it brought people from every state together in common purpose.

Still, the Continental navy's practical contribution to the war was limited. Even Jones's taking of the *Serapis* must be put into perspective. Although the victory did much to buoy morale in the new nation, the battle itself was a Pyrrhic victory: it ended with around 150 Americans dead or wounded and the *Bonhomme Richard* sinking to the bottom of the North Sea, forcing the Americans to transfer to the badly damaged *Serapis*. Furthermore, the convoy of British merchantmen that Jones had wanted to attack, and that the *Serapis* had been protecting, got away.

In July 1780, John Adams reflected on the fortunes of the Continental navy, which he had worked so hard to establish. In a letter to Samuel Huntington, president of the Continental Congress, he wrote, "In looking over the long list of vessels belonging to the United States taken and destroyed, and recollecting the whole history of the rise and progress of our navy, it is very difficult to avoid tears." There were still a few years more of naval misery to go. Historian William Fowler, who wrote one of the best books about the Continental navy, arrived at similar conclusions: "Despite a few glittering moments with captains like John Paul Jones, Lambert Wickes and John Barry, if the American Navy had never existed it is hard to see how the outcome of the Revolution would have been any different." While that is arguably too harsh of an assessment, it is not far off the mark. The American Revolution was the navy's first hour, but not its finest.

Contrary to Whipple, it is difficult to imagine a different record for the navy if privateering had been outlawed instead of embraced by Congress. If there had been no privateers, the navy would have had an easier time recruiting officers and sailors and obtaining cannons and ammunition. But the absence of privateers would not have meant a larger or significantly more effective navy. Congress would not somehow have had more money to spend on naval vessels. Indeed, given the great strain Congress was under in funding a navy of roughly sixty ships, it is virtually impossible to see how America could have fielded a larger navy even if it had wanted to.

It is in this light that the value of privateering becomes most evident. While many wished and preferred that America send forth a powerful navy to confront the British at sea, that was not a realistic option. In the absence of such a force, America relied heavily on its privateers to attack the enemy. Under the circumstances, that was the best strategy available, whatever the critics said.

WHIPPLE WAS FOCUSED on the navy, but privateering posed similar problems for the army. As with the navy, privateers competed with the army not only for munitions and general supplies but also for personnel. The direct competition for recruits is what concerned the army most. General Charles Lee, second-in-command to Washington, issued a warning and a request in a letter he sent to the New England governors in November 1776: "As the whole fate of America depends on the speedy completion of the new army; all considerations ought undoubtedly to be postponed to this object. The officers . . . are of [the] opinion, that nothing impedes the recruiting of the army so much as the present rage for privateering, that unless this is in some measure checked it is in vain to expect any success." Lee asked the governors to place an embargo on privateers until each state's regiments were filled. The governors complied, and starting around the beginning of the new year, privateers were forbidden from setting out on cruises.

Privateer owners—wealthy men with strong political connections—began complaining immediately. Some had already invested significant sums in vessels that were ready to sail; others argued that privateers, regardless of their effect on the army (or the navy), made valuable contributions to the war effort and should not be restrained. Many political leaders joined in the condemnation of the embargo. "I hope your embargo is off," John Adams wrote to James Warren, on April 6, 1777, so "that the privateers may have fair play. Indeed, I am sorry it was ever laid. I am against all shackles upon trade. Let the spirit of the people have its own way, and it will do something. I doubt much whether you have got a hundred soldiers the more for your embargo and perhaps you have missed opportunities of taking many prizes and several hundreds of seamen." Warren was in agreement: "The amazing damage we should have done them [the British], as well as the advantages derived to ourselves, make me execrate the policy of stopping our privateers. I always opposed it."

While some shipowners ignored the embargo and let their vessels sail, angering many local officials, most privateers stayed in port. During the late winter and spring of 1777, however, pressure mounted for repeal. At the end of March, for example, the Massachusetts General Court decided that its embargo should be partially lifted, allowing privateers to sail from those towns that had fulfilled their quota of soldiers. The change stemmed from the basic needs of the state's residents. With fewer prizes coming in due to the embargo, items such as rum, sugar, molasses, cocoa, cotton, wool, and salt were in increasingly short supply—which, ironically, affected the army itself. As the General Court explained in a letter to the other New England states, there was "the great necessity of opening a door for the admission either by capture or importation of many articles which we stand in great need of for the use of ourselves and the army."

Few towns in Massachusetts had met their army quotas, and privateer owners pleaded with the court to nevertheless let them sail. The state stood fast, but some privateers left anyway, making it to sea before authorities could stop them. In the summer, the Massachusetts embargo, as well as those in neighboring states, was lifted. Although the army had attracted nowhere near the number of recruits hoped for, the draw of privateering was only partly the cause. There were many other reasons why young men were reluctant to sign up for military service, among them the fear of dying in battle and the need to tend to matters at home.

EVEN AS IT WAS creating problems for the army and the navy—problems its critics, whether Whipple or General Lee or others, overstated—privateering was contributing materially to the American economy. Shipyards hummed with activity, with new vessels being built and existing merchantmen being reconfigured to make them more threatening and capable of carrying much larger crews. Merchants were kept busy outfitting privateers with food, munitions, and other supplies for their cruises. Meanwhile, the arrival of prizes kept the vice admiralty courts occupied, and newspapers benefited from advertisements purchased by shipowners and captains hoping to encourage men to join privateers and announcing prize auctions. Lawyers saw a rise in business due to increased demand for legal services related to privateering, such as drafting agreements among investors and representing owners at prize courts. In September 1776, merchant Thomas Cushing wrote to lawyer Robert Treat Paine: "Your brethren in the law have fine times of it. They are making money as fast almost as they can receive it. I suppose there never was a better chance for gentlemen of your profession getting money than the present. Privateering prevails so much and such a number of prizes are taken that it makes a vast deal of business in your way."

In short, privateering was a great economic boon for coastal towns and cities, keeping many businesses afloat during the war and creating new ones, and new fortunes, at the same time. Of course, the money that privateersmen earned helped them provide for their families and thereby give an additional jolt to their local economies.

An engaging and mostly reliable picture of the vibrancy that privateers brought to coastal communities is provided by two late nineteenth-century historians who described the streets of Salem in the late 1770s and early 1780s: "The town was full of sailors; every street swarmed with

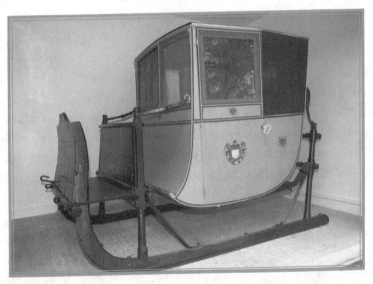

An elegant coach, circa 1777, that was taken from a British prize by the owners of the Newburyport privateer *Civil Usage* and presented to John Hancock in early 1778 "as a token of their respect for that gentleman, who has so nobly distinguished himself in the present contest with Great Britain." The coach originally had wheels, which at a later date were replaced by runners, transforming it into a sleigh. After receiving the chariot, Hancock had it repainted and added his family coat of arms on the door.

them, rolling and rollicking along, with their pockets full of money (hard money), singing songs, chewing tobacco, smoking cigars, drinking at all the public houses, playing tricks upon the country-men, and especially upon the country-women, who brought berries into town to sell; in any street could be seen sailors trying to navigate with horses, chaises and carts. But all this was in good nature; there was no quarrelling, no thieving, no rowdyism."

Goods brought in by privateers were central to privateering's economic impact as well. With many regular channels of trade cut off, the American states often suffered from shortages of both necessities and luxuries. Each prize auction delivered a new stream of commodities, including rum, beef, wool and cotton fabric, flour, sugar, tobacco, limes, oats, tin, lumber, coal, butter, cocoa, and salt. An example of the bounty brought can be seen in the cargo of a British prize sent into Marblehead in October 1776 by the Boston privateer *Speedwell*. On board were 57,000 pounds of bread, 8,000 pounds of pork, 16,000 pounds of beef, 12,000 pounds of flour, 4,200 pounds of rice, 4,00 pounds of raisins, 256 bushels of peas, 257 bushels of oatmeal, 540 gallons of whale oil, 540 gallons of vinegar, 3,500 gallons of rum, ¿,600 pounds of butter, and 5,500 candles. Because there was no consistency in the "imports" from privateers, it often happened that there would be a glut of one or more items, but in most cases the goods were easily and gratefully absorbed. In August 1779, a thankful Pennsylvanian who signed his letter *Duilius** told Congress that privateers have "rendered us the most essential services . . . and brought us many articles for public and private use, without which the war could hardly have been supported."

Yet here, too, privateers found critics. Some Americans railed against privateer owners for gouging the public—and the army and navy, for that matter—by charging exorbitant prices for goods. A letter to the *Continental Journal, and Weekly Advertiser* on November 21, 1776, offers an example of this perspective. "Money is now the grand object in view," argued the writer, who went by the initials B.M. He complained that "we are almost universally seeking to get as much money as we can," and that

---

* Duilius, or Gaius Duilius, was a Roman admiral who was victorious in a major naval battle during the First Punic War (264– 241 BC).

Sculpture/cenotaph of Nathaniel Bowditch, by R. Ball Hughes, at the Mount Auburn Cemetery, in Cambridge, Massachusetts. Bowditch, who was born in Salem, was a famed mathematician who produced *The New American Practical Navigator* (1802), referred to simply as the Bowditch by mariners. It revolutionized seafaring by setting forth accurate nautical and navigational information by which mariners could safely travel the world's oceans. As a young man, Bowditch had access to a particularly valuable resource: In 1781, the Beverly privateer *Pilgrim*, captained by Hugh Hill (*on the next page*), captured a British merchantman, the *Duke of Gloucester*, and on it was the library of the Irish geologist and chemist Richard Kirwan—more than one hundred books, many of them classics in the field of science, including works by Newton and Bernoulli. The library was donated to the newly formed Salem Philosophical Society, which later became the Salem Athenaeum. Bowditch had access to that library, and he credited it with giving him advantages that helped him develop his love for and knowledge of mathematics.

Hugh Hill, circa 1770.

this pursuit is "doing more to bring ruin on the country, than can be done by the enemy." He singled out not only privateer owners but all merchants: "These extortioners are the true source of that enormous rise upon everything that is bought and sold among us."

B.M. was correct about prices rising precipitously, a trend that continued for the remaining years of the Revolution. But the laws of supply and demand were also at play, as was massive inflation of U.S. currency—factors that were largely independent of the actions of privateer owners or privateersmen. Indeed, if it weren't for all the goods that privateers brought in, it is virtually certain that prices for many items would have risen even more sharply. Furthermore, public auctions in the various ports were not run by privateer owners, and the prices at public auctions were determined chiefly by what the market could bear. Still, it is true that privateer owners were often also bidders on the goods their ships brought in, and because they had deeper pockets, they could outbid others. And when that happened, they often turned around and sold those very same goods to the public or the military at even higher prices, thus leading to claims of extortion. One could wish, however, as B.M. did, that those who were selling goods might be less selfish—more driven by public spirit and public virtue and, as a result, more inclined to sell goods at greatly reduced prices to benefit the public good.

PRIVATEERING WAS A risky endeavor for all involved, and many owners and investors lost money when ships were captured or failed to bring in valuable prizes. One of the most prominent losers was Major General Nathanael Greene, who, along with his brothers and other relatives, invested in about twenty privateers. Some were lost to the enemy, and only a few managed to capture any prizes. Those prizes that were brought in were not particularly valuable. In a letter to Christopher Greene, his third cousin, Nathanael bemoaned these failures. "It seems that fortune is no friend of ours in the privateering business. Pray what affront have you given her ladyship? . . . It is almost immaterial from what quarter her displeasure originates[;] she is determined to be cruel."

Many other owners and investors grew quite rich, expanding the ranks of the nation's prosperous merchant class. A loyalist from Salem who fled to Bristol, England, soon after the war commenced wrote a letter to a friend in early 1780 lamenting the nouveau riche among the American rebels: "some are wallowing in undeserved wealth that plunder and rapine have thrown into their hands . . . Those who five years ago were the 'meaner people,' are now, by a strange revolution, become almost the only men of power, riches and influence. . . . The Cabots of Beverly, who, you know, had but five years ago a very moderate share of property, are now said to be by far the most wealthy in New England." In 1779, James Warren complained about this, writing to John Adams that while he was "still drudging at the Navy Board for a morsel of Bread . . . others, and among them fellows who would have cleaned my shoes five years ago, have amassed fortunes, and are riding in chariots [coaches]."

The Browns of Providence, who founded Rhode Island College (later Brown University), were already wealthy before the war from the carrying, slave, and whaling trades, and they viewed privateering as another means to enhance their fortunes. They outfitted their own ships and also supplied provisions and armaments, including cannons from their Hope Furnace, to many other privateers. In 1776, about sixty privateers were sent

Major General Nathanael Greene, circa 1786. He was considered by his close friend George Washington to be one of the most dependable and skilled officers and strategists in the war.

forth from Rhode Island, many of them by the Browns, and the returns were impressive indeed. Writing in his journal at the end of that year, Dr. Ezra Stiles, who later became the seventh president of Yale College, noted, "It has been computed that this war, by prizes, building ships of war, and the navy, has already within a year and a half brought into Providence near three hundred thousand sterling; which is double the property of the whole town, two years ago."

Similarly, when the Marquis de Chastellux, a staffer of General Jean-Baptiste Donatien de Vimeur, comte de Rochambeau, visited Philadelphia in 1782, he was amazed by Robert Morris's wealth.

It is scarcely to be credited, that amidst the disasters of America, Mr. Morris, the inhabitant of a town just emancipated from the hands of the English, should possess a fortune of eight million *livres* (between £300,000 and £400,000 sterling). It is, however, in the most critical times that great fortunes are acquired. The fortunate return of several ships, the still more successful cruises of his privateers, have increased his riches beyond his expectations, if not beyond his wishes. He is, in fact, so accustomed to the success of his privateers, that when he is observed on a Sunday to be more serious than usual, the conclusion is, that no prize has arrived in the preceding week.

Other privateer owners who became rich, or richer, included John Langdon, of Portsmouth; Joseph Peabody, of Salem; Blair McClenachan; and Israel Thorndike, of Beverly. One modern analysis of the Boston fortunes won and lost during the American Revolution concludes that "conspicuous among those who were most successful during and after the war were those invested in privateering." Of the nineteen merchants who were principal owners in three or more privateering ventures—and whose finances were tracked between 1771 and 1790—only one was less wealthy at the end of that period, while seven stayed at roughly the same level, and the remaining eleven saw their fortunes increase considerably. The money amassed by privateer owners was not merely a family concern. It was of critical importance to the new nation, because much of it was invested after the war in launching America's lucrative trading ventures to India, China, and other parts of the world that were by then open to Americans.

In addition to enriching themselves through the plunder of British vessels, a number of privateer owners also contributed more directly to the war effort. The patriotism evinced by the owners of the privateers *Chance* and *Congress*, who gladly provided Congress with more than $22,000 in desperately needed silver and gold coins in exchange for much less dependable Continental bills, was replicated by other owners who poured money into Congress's much-depleted coffers. Newburyport's Nathaniel Tracy, who owned 47 privateers, which captured 120 British prizes in total, donated $167,000 to the army and other public purposes. In 1780, when Congress was virtually bankrupt, leading citizens of Philadelphia banded together to create the Bank of Pennsylvania, whose main purpose was to purchase provisions for the army. Eighty-five subscribers contributed a total of £300,000, in gold and silver, to fund the venture, and many were privateer owners and investors. At the fore were owners Robert Morris and Blair McClenachan (each giving £10,000) and William Bingham (£5,000). In the public statement announcing the bank's creation, the subscribers said that they were taking action because "the greatest and most vigorous exertions are required for the successful management of the just and necessary war" against Great Britain. Hanging in the balance were the subscribers' "own freedom and that of our posterity, and the freedom and independence of the United States."

Privateering, beyond its material consequences, had a psychological effect on the home front. About thirty newspapers across the states chronicled the Revolution as it unfolded. Focusing on the most newsworthy events, the papers printed thousands of articles on privateers. Stories of dramatic battles were interspersed with accounts about captures made and goods brought back and sold at public auctions. There were also pieces that praised privateers in general, such as one that appeared in the *New-Jersey Gazette* on January 31, 1781, in which the author, one "Waterman," argued: "The easiest and most effectual way of distressing the enemy and relieving ourselves, would be to encourage privateering. The trade of Britain is her only strength. This can be no other way so effectually broken as by our privateers."

While some of the newspaper coverage, such as the piece by B.M., complained about privateering and its impact on the prices of goods, most of the articles during the conflict were positive. That coverage buoyed people's hopes and gave them confidence that the larger war might still be won, which was particularly important during those long stretches when almost all the news about the Continental army and navy was discouraging, if not disastrous.

The perspectives of key figures in the Revolution also offer some evidence of the psychological impact of privateering. Here a similar dichotomy can be seen. While many in the upper ranks of the Continental army and navy bemoaned privateering's impact on recruitment, and a number of congressional leaders and other elites denigrated privateers for supposedly pursuing profits with little regard for patriotism, they were counterbalanced by the many prominent individuals who supported privateering, including John Adams, Benjamin Franklin, Thomas Jefferson, Elbridge Gerry, Josiah Bartlett, John Langdon, James Warren, and Robert Morris. And just like the newspaper readers who found encouragement in the feats of privateers, so too did these illustrious supporters.

But it wasn't only positive news that shaped the nation's morale and sentiments. The tragic stories about the plight of prisoners, especially those held on ships off New York, enraged Americans no matter their station, and steeled their resolve to fight on.

THE UNITED STATES and Great Britain signed preliminary articles of peace on November 30, 1782. After more than seven years of fighting a bloody war, "His Britannic Majesty," King George III, finally recognized the thirteen colonies as "free sovereign and independent states." The articles became effective, but not final, on January 20, 1783, when Great Britain and France inked their own preliminary articles of peace. For all intents and purposes, the war was over.

As word spread, the few American privateers still at sea came home. For one ill-fated British ship, the news didn't travel fast enough. The 400-ton *Pompey*, sporting 20 cannons, had sailed from London to the West Indies on February 11, 1783, with a rich cargo of provisions. The *Pompey*'s captain, John Garrett, had learned that the preliminary articles of peace had been signed before he left. Thus when Garrett encountered the Salem privateer *Grand Turk* off St. Kitts on March 11, he put up no resistance when its captain, Joseph Pratt, ordered the *Pompey* to strike its colors and prepare to be boarded. Garrett assumed that because the preliminary articles had been signed, Pratt would let him go. Unfortunately for Garrett, Pratt had not heard about the signing and was reluctant to take Garrett at his word. Pratt put Garrett and his crew onto the *Pompey*'s boats and told them to row for nearby St. Kitts. Pratt then placed a prize crew on the *Pompey*, which sailed for Salem, arriving there on April 3. Now it was up to the Salem vice admiralty court to sort out the situation.

Because the United States issued its formal notice recalling all privateers on March 24, nearly two weeks after the capture, the court ruled that the *Pompey* was a legitimate prize. It was a mighty windfall for the

Oil sketch entitled *American Commissioners of the Preliminary Peace Agreement with Great Britain*, by Benjamin West, circa 1783. From left to right are John Jay, John Adams, Benjamin Franklin, Henry Laurens, and William Temple Franklin Jr. The agreement was signed on November 30, 1782. The British delegation refused to pose for the picture, leaving it unfinished.

Grand Turk's owners, given that the British merchantman was worth as much as the *Grand Turk* itself. For his part, after sending the *Pompey* back to Salem, Pratt had sailed for Martinique, where he learned that Garrett had been telling the truth about the peace. With the *Grand Turk*'s privateering days over, Pratt returned to Salem, dropping anchor on April 30.

A FEW WEEKS BEFORE the *Grand Turk* sailed into Salem Harbor, another chapter in the war closed, one in which privateersmen sadly had a starring role. On April 6, 1783, Commissary General David Sproat boarded the HMS *Amphion* in New York Harbor for a short sail to Wallabout Bay to visit the remaining prison ships. In his pocket was a proclamation from Rear Admiral Robert Digby, Britain's senior naval official in North Amer-

ica, stating that all prisoners on the ships were to be released three days
hence. To that end, on April 9 the prisoners were sent by ship to their
"respective places of abode to save them the expense and fatigue of long
marches." Only a few of the sickest men stayed on the prison ships, and
when they recovered, they were sent to Boston.

In truth, there were very few prisoners left to celebrate the news. British
authorities had started releasing them in 1782 after Britain finally recognized American combatants as prisoners of war on March 25 of that year.
That process sped up after the preliminary articles were signed. When
Sproat boarded the *Jersey* in April to read the proclamation, there were
only about two dozen prisoners there to hear him. They let out "three huzzahs" and began dreaming of home.

Exactly how many men died on the prison ships will never be known,
due to the fragmentary records. The number of deaths on the *Jersey*
alone is shocking. The best and most often cited contemporary estimates
point to its being roughly 11,500; the vast majority were Americans.
By comparison, in the entire war somewhere between 4,435 and 6,800
Americans were killed in action. The horrendous toll of the prison ships
led historians Henry Steele Commager and Richard B. Morris to claim
that "What Andersonville* was to the Civil War, the British prison ships
were to the Revolution."

Around the time that the ships were being emptied, so too were Mill and
Forton Prisons. As with the prison ships, most of the American prisoners
in England had already been released many months earlier. In April 1783,
when the gates of the two prisons were finally opened, only a few inmates
remained, and they finally arrived home in late spring or early summer.

THE FORMAL END OF the war came on September 3, 1783, when the
Treaty of Paris was signed. Surviving privateers that had been merchantmen before the war now reverted to form, while those vessels built for privateering were refitted as merchantmen. These ships now played their part
in transporting America's wares to near and distant ports, proudly flying

---

* Andersonville was the largest military prison in the Civil War. Forty-five thousand Union soldiers were held there, and roughly thirteen thousand of them perished.

the new nation's flag and announcing the arrival of the United States on the world stage. The men who owned and financed privateers, as well as those who had chosen to fight for their country on the decks of these vessels, looked back on their accomplishments with pride and wondered, as did all Americans, what the future would bring for themselves and their new country.

A Few More Rounds

On the evening of September 26, 1814, the American privateer brig *General Armstrong*, which was anchored in the harbor at Fayal, in the Azores, successfully repulsed the first attack of men from the HMS *Carnation*, *Plantagenet*, and *Rota*. But a second attack proved overwhelming, and the privateer's captain, Samuel Reid, ordered the brig to be scuttled to keep it from falling into the enemy's hands. This Nathaniel Currier print from the mid-1800s depicts the battle, which left one hundred twenty British and two American sailors dead.

———

BENJAMIN FRANKLIN HAD A CHANGE OF HEART. DURING THE WAR, as we have seen, he was a vocal proponent of privateering. But once the United States emerged victorious, he came to think of it as an abomination, or at least he professed to. The shift was a function of his general abhorrence of war. In early 1783, he wrote to British peace commissioner Richard Oswald with an idea that he hoped could be included in the treaty then being hammered out between the two countries. "It is for the interest of humanity in general," he argued, "that the occasions of war, and the inducements to it should be diminished." To that end, Franklin thought that if privateering were "abolished, one of the encouragements to war is taken away, and peace [is] therefore more likely to continue and be lasting." Using arguments that had been favored by critics during the Revolution, but which he had not deployed in those years, Franklin called privateering "the practice of robbing merchants on the high seas, a remnant of the ancient piracy," and said that "though it may be accidentally beneficial to particular persons, [it] is far from being profitable to all engaged in it, or to the nation that authorizes it." He went into detail about the evils of privateering, describing "the national loss of all the labor of so many men during the time they have been employed in robbing; who besides spend what they get in riot, drunkenness, and debauchery, lose their habits of industry, are rarely fit for any sober business after a peace, and serve only to increase the number of highwaymen and housebreakers. Even the undertakers, who have been fortunate, are by sudden wealth led into expensive living, the habit of which continues when the means of supporting it ceases, and finally ruins them."

A few months later Franklin reiterated his plea, this time with even more passion, in a letter to Oswald's successor, David Hartley. Even though Franklin knew that wartime privateering could again be crucial to the United States—which still had no real navy, and whose targets of opportunity included heavily laden European merchant ships—he wanted to put an end to it, for the betterment of humankind. He feared that America's "privateering success in the two last wars"—he was including the Seven Years' War—might have already "given our people too strong a relish for that most mischievous kind of gaming mixed with blood"; but he still thought it possible to put a stop to the practice, if only Britain would consent. "Try, my friend, what you can do, in procuring for your nation the glory of being, though the greatest naval power, the first who voluntarily relinquished the advantage that power seems to give them, of plundering others, and thereby impeding the mutual communication among men of the gifts of God, and rendering miserable multitudes of merchants

Painting of Solomon Drowne (1753–1834) by Charles Cromwell Ingham, 1863. Drowne went on one privateering cruise, as a surgeon, on board the *Hope*, which sailed from Providence. This exposure caused him to develop a rather unfavorable view of privateering, which echoes some of Franklin's misgivings. Drowne wrote, "If virtue is the doing good to others, privateering cannot be justified upon the principles of virtue; though I know it is not repugnant to The Laws of Nations, but rather deemed policy amongst warring powers thus to distress each other, regardless of the suffering individual. But however agreeable to, and supportable by the rights of war; yet, when individuals come thus to despoil individuals of their property, 'tis hard: the cruelty then appears, however, political."

and their families, artisans and cultivators of the earth, the most useful, peaceable and innocent part of the human species."

Franklin failed to persuade the British, who still viewed privateers as a valuable adjunct to traditional naval forces, and there was no mention of privateering in the final peace treaty. He had more luck with Prussia. Using similar arguments, he convinced Thomas Jefferson and other American leaders to include a clause abolishing privateering in the Treaty of Amity and Commerce with the kingdom of Prussia, which Jefferson negotiated and George Washington signed on September 10, 1785. Under the treaty's terms, if the two countries ever went to war with each other, they both agreed not to engage in privateering.

That was as far as Franklin's dream of ending privateering went. On June 21, 1788, about two years before he died, the Constitution was ratified. Article I, section 8, gave Congress the power "to declare war, grant letters of marque and reprisal, and make rules concerning captures on land and water." When the War of 1812 began, Americans invoked this clause as they turned again to privateering. Embroiled in another conflict with Britain, the United States set aside any qualms about privateering in favor of expediency—the same force that had compelled Franklin to embrace privateering during the Revolution. And why should the nation not revert to privateering? The situation was similar to that during the Revolution. America had a puny navy—just a handful of frigates, sloops, and gunboats—to send out against the Royal Navy, still the largest and most powerful in the world, albeit now preoccupied with the Napoleonic Wars. Jefferson, who had supported Franklin's opposition to privateering in the negotiations with Prussia, now balked at the notion of not sending out privateers. On June 28, 1812, about a week after President James Madison declared war on Britain, Jefferson wrote a letter to Tadeusz Kościuszko, the Polish-Lithuanian military engineer who had fought alongside Americans during the Revolution. Jefferson shared his thoughts about the nature of the war to come: "I hope we shall confine ourselves to the conquest of their possessions, and defense of our harbors, leaving the war on the ocean to our privateers. These will immediately swarm in every sea, and do more injury to British commerce than the regular fleets of all Europe would do."

Around a month later, Hezekiah Niles, editor of Baltimore's *Weekly Register*, penned a full-throated defense of privateering, capturing the rationale used during the Revolution and revived during the War of 1812.*

What is war? Mr. Jefferson has happily described it as a contest of trying who can do the other the most harm. Who carries on the war? Armies are formed and navies manned by individuals. How is

---

* Niles's essay has incorrectly been attributed to Thomas Jefferson, but it was not written by Jefferson, though he is mentioned. Personal communication of April 26, 2021, with Lisa A. Francavilla, PhD, senior managing editor, Papers of Thomas Jefferson: Retirement Series and Jefferson Quotes & Family Letters, International Center for Jefferson Studies, Charlottesville, VA.

a battle gained? By the death of individuals. What produces peace? The distress of individuals. What difference to the sufferer is it that his property is taken by a national or private armed vessel? . . . One man fights for wages paid him by the government, or a patriotic zeal for the defense of his country—another, duly authorized, and giving the proper pledges for his good conduct, undertakes to pay himself at the expense of the foe, and serve his country as effectually as the former[.] . . . In the United States, every possible encouragement should be given to privateering in time of war with a commercial nation. We have tens of thousands of seamen that without it would be destitute of the means of support, and useless to their country.— Our national ships are too few in number to give employment to a twentieth part of them, or retaliate the acts of the enemy. But by licensing private armed vessels, the whole naval force of the nation is truly brought to bear on the foe, and while the contest lasts, that it may have the speedier termination, let every individual contribute his mite, in the best way he can, to distress and harass the enemy, and compel him to peace.

Despite Jefferson's dream of a privately waged war on the seas, the U.S. Navy, small though it was, had some notable and heroic engagements that burnished its reputation, contributed much to America's success, and won the respect of the British. But, again, it was privateers that did most of the fighting and capturing of British prizes at sea. On June 26, 1812, Congress authorized privateering, and soon the letters of marque started to flow. Ultimately, Madison issued 526 privateering commissions, with most of the applicants coming from Massachusetts, Maryland, and New York. As with the Revolution, estimates of the number of privateer prizes varied, with Lloyd's of London claiming that the Americans captured 1,175 British vessels, of which 373 were recaptured or ransomed. On the other end of the spectrum was the *Weekly Register*, which put the number as just north of 2,300. In contrast, the U.S. Navy captured about 250 British vessels. Theodore Roosevelt, in his magisterial book on the war, published in 1882, recognized privateers' outsized role, claiming that they "were of incalculable benefit to us, and inflicted enormous damage on" Britain. Indeed, the vociferous complaints from British merchants about the depredations of American privateers fed Britain's desire to end the war, a desire realized when the Treaty of Ghent was signed, on December 24, 1814.

In the decades following the War of 1812, a number of high-profile American politicians, including John Quincy Adams and Presidents Franklin Pierce and James Buchanan, came out in favor of eliminating privateering as an acceptable means of waging war. But when the United States had a chance to outlaw the practice in 1856, it demurred. In April of that year, at the end of the Crimean War, fifty-five countries, including England and France, signed the Paris Declaration Respecting Maritime Law. Its main purpose was to abolish privateering. The United States declined to become a signatory, in large part because it still had a relatively small navy and wanted to retain the ability to use privateers in future wars. The country was not ready to abandon a tool of war that had helped bring it into being in the first place.

A few years later, privateering sprang back to life during the Civil War, though this time European nations would not suffer as a result. On April 17, 1861, less than a week after Confederate forces fired on Charleston's Fort Sumter, Confederate president Jefferson Davis issued a proclamation inviting Southerners to apply for letters of marque. In so doing, he used the very same arguments that the United States had employed in the Revolution and the War of 1812. Because the Confederacy had no navy at the outset of the conflict and the Union had a fleet of forty-two warships, privateers offered the quickest and best chance of damaging the North's maritime commerce. To justify their support of privateering and to defend its legality, Southern politicians pointed to the fact that the United States had not signed the Paris Declaration. Davis ultimately issued nearly one hundred letters of marque, mainly to small vessels, including former slavers and revenue cutters.*

Ironically, the Union viewed Confederate privateersmen just as Britain had viewed American privateersmen during the Revolution: as pirates who ought to be hanged. Recognizing the legitimacy of Confederate privateers would have been tantamount to recognizing the South as a sovereign nation instead of as a rebellious faction within the country. The Union saw

---

* These privateers were separate, and quite different, from the Confederate raiders the South sent forth as part of the official Confederate States Navy. Confederate States Navy ships such as the *Alabama*, the *Shenandoah*, and the *Merrimack* were naval ships, not privateers.

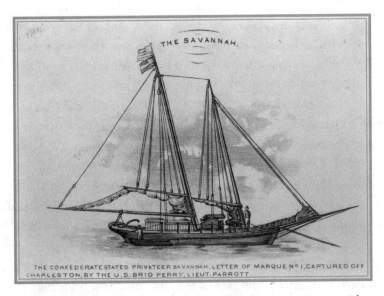

THE SAVANNAH.

THE CONFEDERATE STATES PRIVATEER SAVANNAH, LETTER OF MARQUE N° I, CAPTURED OFF CHARLESTON, BY THE U.S. BRIG PERRY, LIEUT. PARROTT.

Engraving of the Confederate privateer *Savannah*, circa 1861.

Confederate privateers as pirates but did not treat them as such. The case of the *Savannah* made sure of that.

The *Savannah*, a former Charleston pilot boat, was the first vessel to receive a Confederate letter of marque and also the first Confederate privateer to be captured. On June 3, 1861, it surrendered to the U.S. brig *Perry* after a brief fight. Thirteen Confederate sailors were taken to New York City, where they were paraded in chains through the streets in front of jeering crowds, placed in the Tombs, and put on trial for piracy. When Davis learned of the men's imprisonment, poor treatment, and impending trial, he exploded in rage and issued a threat. If any Confederate privateersmen captured by the North were hanged for piracy, the South would retaliate and hang an equal number of its Union prisoners. The threat worked: the privateersmen imprisoned in New York City were treated as prisoners of war instead of pirates, and were exchanged via cartel for Union prisoners. That precedent held. Just as Britain didn't hang any American privateersmen during the Revolution, neither did the North hang any Southern ones during the Civil War.*

---

* Despite the North's negative view of privateering, in March 1863 the Union authorized privateering. On the surface, the rationale for this act was to send out privateers to harass Confederate shipping and aid the blockade of Southern ports; but the real target was Britain, which had not only supplied the Confederacy with ships, such as the *Alabama* and the *Shenandoah*, but had also

Many Confederate privateers were captured, sunk, or burned, and only a few met with any notable success. Among the last group was the 230-ton brig *Jefferson Davis*, a former slaver and merchantman that captured nine prizes in two months during the summer of 1861. However, those achievements were soon followed by disaster. The *Jefferson Davis* wrecked in a gale off St. Augustine, Florida, and seven of its nine prizes never made it to port, because they were released, torched, or recaptured. Given the poor record of Southern privateers and the growing fear, among would-be privateersmen, of being captured, the Confederacy's enthusiasm for privateering quickly cooled, and after 1861, few letters of marque were issued. In the end, although Confederate privateers spread fear throughout Northern ports, they had very little influence on the course of the Civil War.

Since the Civil War, the United States has agreed to abide by the terms of the Paris Declaration and refrain from privateering, despite its refusal to become a signatory. Although the Constitution still allows the United States to employ privateers in wartime, there is no reasonable expectation that it will do so. After all, America now has the most powerful navy in the world.*

----

run the Union blockade, delivering goods to the South. The Union hoped that its privateers would punish Britain by capturing its merchant ships. In the end, the law had no impact, because the North never issued any letters of marque. See Nicholas Parrillo, "The De-Privatization of American Warfare: How the U.S. Government Used, Regulated, and Ultimately Abandoned Privateering in the Nineteenth Century," *Yale Journal of Law and the Humanities* 19, no. 1 (2007): 72–73.

* In recent decades, the idea of bringing back privateering in the United States has been floated— to deal with terrorists or other nonstate belligerents, even to counter China's growing military power, by attacking their large merchant fleet, thereby threatening the country's economy and destabilizing the Communist Party. The merits or demerits of such arguments are well beyond the scope of this book. See, for example, Mark Cancian and Brandon Schwarz, "Unleash the Privateers!," *U.S. Naval Institute Proceedings* 146, no. 4 (April 2020), https://www.usni.org/magazines/proceedings/2020/april/unleash-privateers, accessed May 27, 2021; and Robert P. DeWitte, "Let Privateers Marque Terrorism: A Proposal for a Reawakening," *Indiana Law Journal* 82, no. 1 (2007): 131–58.

ACKNOWLEDGMENTS

=

WHEN I GAVE LECTURES ON MY EARLIER BOOK—
Black Flags, Blue Waters: The Epic History of America's Most Notorious Pirates—many attendees would ask me if the book covered privateering. No, I responded, it focuses on pirates, who were different from privateersmen—at least different from privateersmen who acted legally, within the constraints of their letters of marque, as opposed to privateersmen who were privateersmen in name only and who acted just like pirates and therefore were indeed pirates. That oft-repeated question, however, made me more interested in privateering. So when my editor at Liveright, my agent, and I were discussing what my next book might be, the subject was on my mind. And when I started reading about privateering in the American Revolution, I quickly concluded that I would like to write a book on it. Fortunately, Liveright agreed.

I would like to thank Dan Gerstle, my main editor at Liveright, and Bob Weil, editor in chief, for championing this book. Dan is a maestro with the pen, cutting the unnecessary, enlivening what remained, and offering numerous suggestions that made the book much better. He was a real pleasure to work with, although it took me a while to get used to his concise manner of communicating, especially since I am prone to writing multiparagraph emails. Zeba Arora, Dan's assistant, was very helpful in getting the manuscript through the process and patiently and graciously answering my many questions.

The rest of the crew at Liveright and W. W. Norton—Steve Attardo, Haley Bracken, Cordelia Calvert, Nick Curley, Rebecca Homiski, Gina Iaquinta, Peter Miller, Anna Oler, Don Rifkin, and Bill Rusin—did their typical excellent job of creating a gorgeous book and giving it a wonderful launch into the world.

Janet Byrne, my copyeditor, was a joy to work with. Her eye for detail is amazing. (I only wish I hadn't given her so many things that needed modification or improvement!) Her grammatical, stylistic, and substantive suggestions made the book much better—the clearest sign of a great copyeditor—and for that I am very appreciative.

I owe a special thanks to the external reviewers of the manuscript, whose excellent feedback also greatly improved the book. They include Donald G. Shomette, James L. Nelson, Bethany Groff Dorau, and Christian McBurney.

Other people who were quite helpful include Alex Cain, Alex Cranmer, Leon Doucette, Daniel Finamore, Scarlett Faro, Lisa A. Francavilla, Michelle M. Frauenberger, Stephanie Hall, Suzanne Inge, Sherri Jackson, Tracie Logan, Erin Luckett, Valeri-Anne Lutz, Lauren McCormack, John Millar, Martha Curtis O'Connell, Matthew Rowe, Mike Rutstein, Christopher Stepler, and Andrew Williams.

If you read the dedication, you will know of my great respect for librarians. Let me be a bit more specific. The staff and librarians at the Phillips Library of the Peabody Essex Museum, the Widener Library at Harvard University, and the Abbot Public Library, in my hometown of Marblehead, were wonderful to work with and quite helpful. I owe a special thanks to the librarians at the Abbot, who were always welcoming and never got annoyed by the flood of books on privateering and American history I ordered through interlibrary loan.

I also want to thank the Widener Library for a most unusual reason. I use the Widener extensively, especially to obtain rare books and search through the many historical databases the library subscribes to. In early March 2020, just when things were becoming really scary with COVID-19 and just a few days before a national emergency was declared, I decided to spend a few days visiting the Widener, scanning sections from scores of books and downloading hundreds of articles and other documents, most of them primary sources. A week or two later, the lockdown began and the Widener closed (as did all the other libraries I typically use). Since I was still heavily into the research phase of writing this book, I desperately needed all the sources I had obtained pre-lockdown. Had I not made those multiple trips to the Widener and obtained those critical documents before the library shut down, I don't think I would have been able to finish the book during COVID, or at least write the book I wanted to.

Russell Galen, my longtime agent, continues to be indispensable in helping me build my writing career and navigate my way through the often bewildering world of publishing. Equal parts tactician, sounding board, cheerleader, and therapist, Russ is truly an agent's agent.

Of all who deserve thanks, none are more important than the members of my immediate and extended family, whose unwavering support is the main reason I have had the amazing and much-appreciated opportunity to be a full-time writer, far and away the best and most difficult job I have ever had. My daughter, Lily, and mother-in-law, Ruth, each read the manuscript and offered valuable suggestions. My mom, Ruth, expressed keen interest in the progress of the book and has encouraged my writing from the start. My father-in-law, George, has also been a great fan of my writing, and has offered sage advice at critical moments in my career. But my wife, Jennifer, as is always the case, deserves the biggest and most heartfelt thanks. Her comments on the manuscript were invaluable. She is the person I most respect and love, and my partner in everything. I would not be a writer without her.

NOTES

ABBREVIATIONS USED IN THE NOTES

FONA   *Founders Online, National Archive* (https://founders.archives.gov/about)

NDAR   *Naval Documents of the American Revolution* (the Naval History and Heritage Command has prepared twelve volumes to date, ranging from December 6, 1774, to August 15, 1778. These volumes have a variety of editors.

NRAR   Library of Congress, *Naval Records of the American Revolution: 1775–1788* (Washington, DC: Government Printing Office, 1906)

INTRODUCTION

xi   **A tall, angular:** Background for this section on Haraden comes from "Memoir of Elias Hasket Derby, Merchant of Salem, Mass.," *Hunt's Merchants' Magazine and Commercial Review*, February 1857; Israel Thorndike, "Biographical Memoir of the Late Captain J. Haraden, Extracted from the *Centinel* of 1824," Miscellaneous non-Derby Papers, B23 F8, Phillips Library, Peabody Essex Museum; "Mr. Willis," *Independent Chronicle*, August 17, 1780; "Boston, August 10," *Connecticut Journal*, August 17, 1780; Sidney G. Morse, "New England Privateering in the American Revolution" (PhD diss., Harvard University, 1941), 430–55; Joseph B. Felt, January 1, 1857, "Accounts of Capt. Haraden's Action with the *Achilles* by Israel Thorndike, Robert Cowan, Charles W. Upham, Stephen Haraden, Samuel Newhall, and William Pynchon of Salem," Miscellaneous Papers, Excerpts from Derby Manuscripts (B22 F2), Phillips Library, Peabody Essex Museum; William Pynchon, *The Diary of William Pynchon of Salem*, ed. Fitch Edward Oliver (Boston: Houghton, Mifflin and Company, 1890), 37; Joseph B. Felt, *The Annals of Salem: From Its First Settlement* (Salem, MA: W. & S. B. Ives, 1827), 508, 516; Frank A. Gardner, "Captain Jonathan Haraden," *The Massachusetts Magazine*, October 1909; Samuel H. Batchelder, "Jonathan Haraden," *Sketches About Salem People* (Salem, MA: The Club, 1930), 1–15; and George Atkinson Ward, *The Journal and Letters of Samuel Curwen, An American in England, from 1775 to 1783* (Boston: Little, Brown and Company, 1864), 234, 556–58.

xii   **"I shan't run":** "Memoir of Elias Hasket Derby," 157.

xii   **"brave officer":** Gardner, "Captain Jonathan Haraden," 195.

xiii **"the militia":** William P. Sheffield, *An Address Delivered by William P. Sheffield Before the Rhode Island Historical Society, in Providence, February 7, A. D. 1882* (Newport, RI: John P. Sanborn, 1883), 5.

xiv   **Privateers brought:** Morse, "New England Privateering," 390.

xiv   **A particularly spectacular:** Thomas Clark, *Naval History of the United States*, vol. 1 (Philadelphia: M. Carey, 1814), 111; and Morse, "New England Privateering," 440.

xiv   **"though a brave . . . his duty":** "Mr. Willis."

xiv   **"go alongside":** Morse, "New England Privateering," 438.

xv   **"was the largest":** "Mr. Willis."

xv **"calmly rose ... their fire":** Thorndike, "Biographical Memoir of the Late Captain J. Haraden."

xvi **"looked like a longboat":** Charles W. Upham, *Oration, Delivered at the Request of the City Authorities of Salem, July 4, 1842* (Salem, MA: Chapman and Palfray, 1842), 30–31.

xvi **"If you knew":** Ibid.

xvi **"could have walked":** "Memoir of Elias Hasket Derby," 158.

xvii **"one of the most":** Gardner, "Captain Jonathan Haraden," 199.

xviii **"desperate actions":** Charles S. Osgood and H. M. Batchelder, *Historical Sketch of Salem, 1626–1879* (Salem, MA: Essex Institute, 1879), 218.

xviii **"He was a perfect":** Thorndike, "Biographical Memoir of the Late Captain J. Haraden."

xviii **Privateeering has long:** See, for example, Robert Middlekauff, *The Glorious Cause: The American Revolution: 1763–1789* (New York: Oxford University Press, 2005); Benson Bobrick, *Angel in the Whirlwind: The Triumph of the American Revolution* (New York: Simon & Schuster, 1997); John Ferling, *Whirlwind: The American Revolution and the War That Won It* (New York: Bloomsbury, 2015); John Ferling, *Almost a Miracle: The American Victory in the War of Independence* (New York: Oxford University Press, 2007); Alan Taylor, *American Revolutions: A Continental History, 1750–1804* (New York: W. W. Norton, 2016); and Rick Atkinson, *The British Are Coming: The War for America, Lexington to Princeton, 1775–1777* (New York: Henry Holt and Company, 2019).

xviii **The coverage in:** See, for example, Nathan Miller, *Sea of Glory: A Naval History of the American Revolution* (Charleston, SC: The Naval & Aviation Publishing Company of America, 1974); James M. Volo, *Blue Water Patriots: The American Revolution Afloat* (Westport, CT: Praeger, 2007); and Sam Willis, *The Struggle for Sea Power: A Naval History of the American Revolution* (New York: W. W. Norton, 2015).

xviii **"From the beginning ... virtually ignores":** John Lehman, *On Seas of Glory: Heroic Men, Great Ships, and Epic Battles of the American Navy* (New York: The Free Press, 2001), 41–42.

xviii **The relatively small:** See, for example, Donald Grady Shomette, *Privateers of the Revolution: War on the New Jersey Coast, 1775–1783* (Atglen, PA: Schiffer Publishing, 2016); Robert H. Patton, *Patriot Pirates: The Privateer War for Freedom and Fortune in the American Revolution* (New York: Vintage Books, 2008); Edgar Stanton Maclay, *A History of American Privateers* (London: Sampson, Low, Marston & Co., 1900); Wick Griswold, *Connecticut Pirates & Privateers: Treasure and Treachery in the Constitution State* (Charleston, SC: The History Press, 2015); Leonard Szaltis, Chesapeake Bay Privateers in the Revolution (Charleston, SC: The History Press, 2019); Jackson Kuhl, *Samuel Smedley: Connecticut Privateer* (Charleston, SC: The History Press, 2011); William and Virginia Packwood, *Two Revolutionary War Privateers: William and Joseph Packwood of Connecticut* (St. Paul, MN: Two Trees Roots, 2019); William Bell Clark, *Ben Franklin's Privateers: A Naval Epic of the American Revolution* (Baton Rouge: Louisiana State University Press, 1956); and J. P. Hand and Daniel P. Stites, *The Cape May Navy: Delaware Bay Privateers in the American Revolution* (Charleston, SC: The History Press, 2018).

xix **"a rich and powerful":** William Moultrie, *Memoirs of the American Revolution*, vol. 1 (New York: David Longworth, 1802), 63–64.

xix **"was little short of":** George Washington, "Farewell Address to the Armies of the United States," November 2, 1783, *The Writings of George Washington*, vol. 8, ed. Jared Sparks (Boston: Russell, Odiorne, and Metcalf, 1835), 492.

xx **The best single:** *NRAR,* ed. Charles Henry Lincoln (Washington, DC: Government Printing Office, 1906). See also Gardner W. Allen, *A Naval History of the American Revolution*, vol. 2 (Boston: Houghton Mifflin Company, 1913), 716–17.

xx **Even as they ... as one thousand:** Morse, "New England Privateering," 549–62; Richard

E. Winslow III, *"Wealth and Honour": Portsmouth During the Golden Age of Privateering, 1775-1815* (Portsmouth, NH: Portsmouth Marine Society, 1988), 18; and Gardner W. Allen, *A Naval History of the American Revolution*, vol. 1 (Boston: Houghton Mifflin Company, 1913), 45-46.

xxi   **"assumed such":** John Franklin Jameson, *Privateering and Piracy in the Colonial Period* (New York: The Macmillan Company, 1923), viii.

xxi   **Privateers were not . . . commission any privateers:** These numbers are based primarily on calculations done by historian Donald Grady Shomette, whose sources included not only the *Naval Records of the American Revolution* but letters to delegates of Congress, American and British newspapers, and contemporary accounts in journals. Personal communication with Donald G. Shomette, May 25, 2021. Also see Shomette, *Privateers of the Revolution*, 365. See also Winslow, *"Wealth and Honour": Portsmouth During the Golden Age of Privateering, 1775-1815*, 18; and Alexander Boyd Hawes, *Off Soundings: Aspects of the Maritime History of Rhode Island* (Chevy Chase, MD: Posterity Press, 1999), 97. With respect to New Jersey, the relatively low number is due to the location of the commission issuing authority. As historian J. P. Hand points out, many privateers listed as coming from Pennsylvania were actually New Jersey vessels; they are listed as being from Pennsylvania because they received their letters of marque in Philadelphia. See Hand and Stites, *The Cape May Navy*, 14.

xxi   **enemies of all mankind:** For background on piracy, and why pirates were referred to as the enemies of all mankind, see Eric Jay Dolin, *Black Flags, Blue Waters: The Epic History of America's Most Notorious Pirates* (New York: Liveright, 2018), xxvii.

xxi   **"licensed":** See, for example, William Barton, *A Dissertation on the Freedom of Navigation and Maritime Commerce and Such Rights of States, Relative Thereto, as Are Founded on the Law of Nations* (Philadelphia: John Conrad, 1802), 294; "Privateers and Prizes," in Malachy Postlethwayt, *The Universal Dictionary of Trade and Commerce*, vol. 2 (London: W. Strahan et al. 1774); and James Kirby Martin and Mark Edward Lender, *A Respectable Army: The Military Origins of the Republic, 1763-1789* (Wheeling, IL: Harlan Davidson, 1982), 143.

xxi   **"legalized":** "Art. VI.—Privateering," De Bow's *The Commercial Review of the South and West,* June 1846, 519n.

xxi   **The first recorded:** William Laird Clowes, *The Royal Navy: A History from the Earliest Times to the Present*, vol. 1 (London: Sampson, Low, Marston and Company, 1897), 126.

xxi   **For example, in the sixteenth century:** For background on Drake see William Wood, *Elizabethan Sea-Dogs: A Chronicle of Drake and His Companions* (New Haven, CT: Yale University Press, 1921); Harry Kelsey, *Sir Francis Drake: The Queen's Pirate* (New Haven, CT: Yale University Press, 1998), 11-39, 75-82, 137-70, 207-19; Charles Wye Kendall, *Private Men-of-War* (New York: R. M. McBride & Company, 1932), 40-41.

xxii   **"no man is a *pirate*":** Samuel Taylor Coleridge, *Specimens of the Table Talk of the Late Samuel Taylor Coleridge*, vol. 2 (New York: Harper & Brothers, 1835), 16.

xxii   **Another egregious:** For background on the Red Sea Men see Dolin, *Black Flags, Blue Waters*, 49-69.

xxiii   **This happened after:** Ibid., 145-46, 175-301.

xxiii   **"privateers were essentially":** Barbara W. Tuchman, *The First Salute* (New York: Alfred A. Knopf, 1988), 47.

xxiii   **As we will see:** See, for example, William James Morgan, "American Privateering in America's War for Independence, 1775-1783," *The American Neptune* 36, no. 2 (April 1976): 79; George Friedrich Martens, *An Essay on Privateers, Captures, and Particularly on Recaptures, According to the Laws, Treaties, and Usages of the Maritime Powers of Europe*, trans. Thomas Hartwell Horne (London: E. and R. Brooke, 1801), 1-3; Michael J. Crawford, "The Privateering Debate in Revolutionary America," *The Northern Mariner* 21, no. 3 (July 2011): 221-22; and C. Kevin Marshall, "Putting Privateers in Their Place: The Applicability of the

Marque and Reprisal Clause to Undeclared Wars," *University of Chicago Law Review* 64, no. 3 (1997): 971.

CHAPTER 1: MASSACHUSETTS FIRST

2 **"prepare for a vigorous"**: John Adams to Moses Gill, June 10, 1775, *FONA*, https://founders .archives.gov/documents/Adams/06-03-02-0014, accessed May 11, 2021.

3 **In every war:** See, for example, Howard M. Chapin, *Privateer Ships and Sailors: The First Century of American Colonial Privateering, 1625-1725* (Toulon, France: Imprimerie G. Moulton, 1926); James G. Lydon, *Pirates, Privateers, and Profits* (Upper Saddle River, NJ: The Gregg Press, 1970); Howard M. Chapin, *Privateering in King George's War 1739-1748* (Providence, RI: E. A. Johnson, 1928); and Jameson, *Privateering and Piracy.*

3 **In these wars:** See, for example, Lydon, *Pirates, Privateers, and Profits*, 154–59; Howard M. Chapin, *Privateering in King George's War 1739-1748* (Providence, RI: E. A. Johnson, 1928); Edwin G. Burrows and Mike Wallace, *Gotham: A History of New York City to 1898* (New York: Oxford University Press, 1999), 169; and Carl E. Swanson, "American Privateering and Imperial Warfare, 1739–1748," *William and Mary Quarterly* 42, no. 3 (July 1985): 362, 379.

3 **"the metropolis":** Rick Atkinson, *The British Are Coming: The War for America, Lexington to Princeton, 1775-1777* (New York: Henry Holt, 2019), 13.

4 **"all those persons":** Louis De Loménie, *Beaumarchais and His Times*, vol. 3, trans. Henry S. Edwards (London: Addy and Co., 1856), 110.

5 **For more than one hundred:** Christopher P. Magra, "Anti-Impressment Riots and the Origins of the Age of Revolution," *International Review of Social History* 58, no. S21 (December 2013): 131–51.

5 **"lords of the":** James Macpherson, *History of Great Britain, from the Restoration, to the Accession of the House of Hanover*, vol. 1 (Dublin: J. Exshaw et al., 1775), 88.

5 **The most famous:** John Adams, "Adams' Minutes of the Trial: Special Court of Admiralty, Boston, June 1769," *FONA*, https://founders.archives.gov/documents/ Adams/05-02-02-0008-0002-0006, accessed December 16, 2020; Christopher P. Magra, "'Soldiers . . . Bred to the Sea': Maritime Marblehead, Massachusetts, and the Origins and Progress of the American Revolution," *New England Quarterly* 77, no. 4 (December 2004): 531–62; and Magra, "Anti-Impressment Riots," 131–51.

6 **"they wanted . . . man of war":** Adams, "Adams' Minutes of the Trial."

6 **"If you step . . . fellow before now":** John Adams to Joseph Bradley Varnum, January 9, 1809, *FONA*, https://founders.archives.gov/documents/Adams/99-02-02-5289. (This is an Early Access document from the Adams Papers. It is not an authoritative final version.)

6 **In that telling:** Adams, "Adams' Minutes of the Trial." See also "Editorial Note," *FONA*, https://founders.archives.gov/documents/Adams/05-02-02-0008-0002-0001, accessed May 11, 2021.

6 **"in law, truth":** John Adams to Dr. J. Morse, January 20, 1816, *The Works of John Adams, Second President of the United States: with a Life of the Author, Notes and Illustrations, by his Grandson Charles Francis Adams* (Boston: Little, Brown and Co., 1856), vol. 10, 205.

7 **"contributed largely":** Ibid., 204.

7 **One of the most:** For background on the Machias affair, see James L. Nelson, "Taking the Fight to Sea: Machias and the First Sea Fight of the American Revolution," *Sea History*, Summer 2008, 24–27; Machias Committee to Massachusetts Congress, June 14, 1775, *American Archives: Fourth Series, Containing a Documentary History of the English Colonies in North America*, vol. 2, ed. Peter Force (Washington, DC: M. St. Clair Clarke and Peter

Force, 1839), 988–90; and "Pilot Nathaniel Godfrey's Report of Action Between the Schooner Margueritta and the Rebels at Machias," June 11, 1775, *NDAR*, vol. 1, 655–56.

7 **They were there:** James L. Nelson, *George Washington's Secret Navy: How the American Revolution Went to Sea* (New York: McGraw Hill, 2008), 21–22.

9 **"determined to":** Machias Committee to Massachusetts Congress, 989.

9 **"he preferred":** Ibid., 656.

9 **As for Jones:** James Warren to John Adams, August 9, 1775, 2n, *FONA*, https://founders.archives.gov/documents/Adams/06-03-02-0065#PJA03d068n2, accessed July 31, 2021; "Cambridge, August 10," *New England Chronicle*, August 10, 1775, *NDAR*, vol. 1, 1108; and "Journal of the Massachusetts House of Representatives" August 21, 1775, *NDAR*, vol. 1, 1195.

9 **"the Lexington":** James Fenimore Cooper, *History of the Navy of the United States of America*, vol. 1 (Cooperstown, NY: H. & E. Phinney, 1846), 45.

10 **"The New Englanders":** Thomas Jefferson to George Gilmer, July 5, 1775, *FONA*, https://founders.archives.gov/documents/Jefferson/01-01-02-0112, accessed May 11, 2021.

10 **"impatient . . . appeared off":** "Narrative of Vice Admiral Samuel Graves," September 1, 1775, *NDAR*, vol. 1, 1282.

10 **"schooner for a":** Gardner Weld Allen, *Massachusetts Privateers of the Revolution* (Boston: Massachusetts Historical Society, 1927), 23.

10 **"as a privateer":** Ibid., 32–33.

10 **"the expediency":** Ibid. See also "Journal of the House of Representatives," August 22, 1775, *NDAR*, vol. 1, 1200.

11 **"carried eleven sail":** William Tudor to John Adams, September 30, 1775, *NDAR*, vol. 2, 248.

11 **On October 9:** "Oct. 9, 1775, The Report of the Committee Appointed to Consider the Expediency of Fitting Out Armed Vessels," *The Acts and Resolves, Public and Private, of the Province of the Massachusetts Bay*, vol. 5 (Boston: Wright & Potter, 1886), 516.

11 **"My attention is":** Elbridge Gerry to Samuel Adams, October 9, 1775, in James T. Austin, *The Life of Elbridge Gerry*, vol. 1 (Boston: Wells and Lilly, 1828), 116.

12 **"being divested of . . . said inhabitants":** "Massachusetts Act Authorizing Privateers and Creating Courts of Admiralty," *NDAR*, vol. 2, 834.

13 **"I grounded . . . political curiosity":** Austin, *The Life of Elbridge Gerry*, 94–95n.

14 **"I want to know":** John Adams to James Warren, November 5, 1775), *Warren-Adam Letters, Being Chiefly a Correspondence Among John Adams, Samuel Adams, and James Warren*, vol. 1 (Boston: Massachusetts Historical Society, 1917), 174.

14 **"What numbers might":** To John Adams from James Warren, November 14, 1775, *FONA*, https://founders.archives.gov/documents/Adams/06-03-02-0162, accessed May 11, 2021.

14 **The first letter of:** "Bond of Owner and Sureties of the Massachusetts Privateer Schooner Boston Revenge," December 7, 1775, *NDAR*, vol. 2, 1316; and Allen, *Massachusetts Privateers*, 87.

14 **Through early 1776:** Morse, "New England Privateering," 36.

14 **Among them was:** Thomas Jones and Others to Benjamin Greenleaf, December 8, 1775, *NDAR*, vol. 3, 4.

14 **That morning:** Background for the *Washington*'s two captures comes from E. Vale Smith, *History of Newburyport: From the Earliest Settlement of the Country to the Present Time* (Newburyport, MA: Damrell and Moore, 1854), 107–8; John J. Currier, *History of Newburyport, Mass., 1764–1905* (Newburyport, MA: Published by the author, 1906), 614–19.

15 **"We are from":** Smith, *History of Newburyport*, 108.

16 **"The good success":** To John Adams from Joseph Ward, December 3, 1775, *FONA*, https://founders.archives.gov/documents/Adams/06-03-02-0178, accessed May 11, 2021.

16 **In due course:** Winslow, *"Wealth and Honour": Portsmouth During the Golden Age of Privateering, 1775–1815*, 15–16; An Act for Encouraging the Fixing Out, and Authorizing Armed vessels, to defend the Sea-Coast of America; and for Erecting a Court to Try and Condemn All Vessels That Shall Be Found Infesting the Same, *Records of the Colony of Rhode Island and Providence Plantations in New England*, vol. 7 (Providence, RI: A. Crawford Greene, 1862), 481–88; and Morse, "New England Privateering," 51.

16 **"is one of the most":** John Adams to Elbridge Gerry, April 14, 1813, *The Works of John Adams*, vol. 10, 37.

CHAPTER 2: EXPANDING THE FIGHT AT SEA

18 **"their harbors and":** July 18, 1775, *Journals of the Continental Congress, 1774–1789*, ed. Worthington C. Ford et al. (Washington, DC: Government Printing Office, 1904–37), vol. 2, 189.

18 **That anger had:** Background for the *Gaspee* affair comes from John Russell Bartlett, *A History of the Destruction of His Britannic Majesty's Schooner Gaspee, in Narragansett Bay, on the 10th June, 1772* (Providence, RI: A. Crawford Greene, 1861), 22–28, 34–35; Ephraim Bowen, "An Account of the Capture and Burning of the British Schooner 'Gaspee,'" *The Family Magazine; or Monthly Abstract General Knowledge*, 1840 (Cincinnati: J. A. James & Co., 1840), 280—all the quotes come from this source; Steven Park, *The Burning of His Majesty's Schooner Gaspee: An Attack on Crown Rule Before the American Revolution* (Yardley, PA: Westholme, 2016), 15–27; and Nelson, *George Washington's Secret Navy*, 65–75.

18 **"haughty, insolent":** Anonymous letter, *Providence Gazette*, January 9, 1773.

19 **Leading the operation:** Sheldon S. Cohen, *Commodore Whipple of the Continental Navy* (Tallahassee: University Press of Florida, 2010), 10–17.

20 **Within the coming . . . valuable British prizes:** Charles O. Paullin, *The Navy of the American Revolution: Its Administration, Its Policy and Its Achievements* (Chicago: The Burrows Brothers Company, 1906), 80, 315–477; Willis, *The Struggle for Sea Power*, 84; William M. Fowler Jr., *Rebels Under Sail: The American Navy During the Revolution* (New York: Charles Scribner's Sons, 1976), 46; and Martin and Lender, *A Respectable Army*, 143.

21 **His only maritime:** Jack D. Warren Jr., "Washington's Journey to Barbados," George Washington's Mount Vernon, https://www.mountvernon.org/george-washington/washingtons-youth/journey-to-barbados/#:~:text=George%20Washington%20traveled%20widely%20in,an%20indelible%20imprint%20on%20him, accessed December 21, 2020.

21 **In early August:** Background for Washington's creation of his own navy comes from Nelson, *George Washington's Secret Navy*; and Fowler, *Rebels Under Sail*, 15–38.

21 **"As to the furnishing":** George Washington to a Committee of the General Court of Massachusetts Bay, August 11, 1775, *The Writings of George Washington*, vol. 3, ed. Jared Sparks (Boston: Hilliard, Gray, and Company, 1833), 58–59.

22 **It is not exactly:** Nelson, *George Washington's Secret Navy*, 77–79.

22 **While Congress had:** "Commission from the Continental Congress," June 19, 1775, *FONA*, https://founders.archives.gov/documents/Washington/03-01-02-0004, accessed May 11, 2021.

22 **Washington told him:** "Instructions to Captain Nicholson Broughton," September 2, 1775, *FONA*, https://founders.archives.gov/documents/Washington/03-01-02-0292, accessed May 11, 2021.

23 **Washington's little navy:** William Bell Clark, *George Washington's Navy: Being an Account of His Excellency's Fleet in New England Waters* (Baton Rouge: Louisiana State University, 1960), 229–36.

23 **But as soon as:** "Dec. 29, 1775," *The Remembrancer, or Impartial Repository of Public Events. Part I for the Year 1776* (London: J. Almon, 1776), 340.

23 **There were 2,000:** Nelson, *George Washington's Secret Navy*, 214–15; Clark, *George Washington's Navy*, 70; and "The following is an American account of the taking the above transport. Worcester, Nov. 15," *The Remembrancer, or Impartial Repository of Public Events. Part I for the Year 1776*, 340.

23 **"was pronounced to be":** "Watertown, Dec. 11," *Boston Gazette*, December 11, 1775.

23 **"instance of divine":** From George Washington to Lieutenant Colonel Joseph Reed, November 30, 1775, *FONA*, https://founders.archives.gov/documents/Washington/03-02-02-0419, accessed May 11, 2021.

24 **"Such universal joy":** Richard Frothingham, *History of the Siege of Boston, and of the Battles of Lexington, Concord, and Bunker Hill* (Boston: Charles C. Little, 1851), 270.

24 **"BRAVE MANLEY":** "Manley, a Favorite New Song," *NDAR*, vol. 3, 47.

24 **About five months:** Background for Mugford's exploits comes from the *Pennsylvania Evening Post* (Philadelphia), June 1, 1776, in Frank Moore, *The Diary of the Revolution* (Hartford, CT: The J. B. Burr Publishing Company, 1876), 244–46; "Exeter, May 27th, 1776," *New-Hampshire Gazette*, January 9, 1776; "Exeter, May 27th, 1776," *New-Hampshire Gazette*, January 9, 1776; Chester G. Hearn, *George Washington's Schooners: The First American Navy* (Annapolis, MD: Naval Institute Press, 1995), 162–69.

25 **"went on deck":** Joshua Davis, *A Narrative of Joshua Davis, An American Citizen, Who was Pressed and Served on Board Six Ships of the British Navy* (Boston: B. True, 1811), 12; and Stephen Taylor, *Sons of the Waves: The Common Seaman in the Heroic Age of Sail* (New Haven, CT: Yale University, 2020), 99.

27 **"The brave Captain Mugford":** *Pennsylvania Evening Post*, May 28, 1776, in Moore, *The Diary of the Revolution*, 246n.

27 **"left this honor":** *New-England Chronicle*, May 30, 1776, *NDAR*, vol. 5, 304.

27 **Although Rhode Island's:** Nelson, *George Washington's Secret Navy*, 73–75.

28 **"that the building and equipping":** "Journal of the Rhode Island General Assembly," August 26, 1775, *NDAR*, vol. 1, 1236.

28 **On October 5:** *The Works of John Adams*, vol. 3, 6; and Fowler, *Rebels Under Sail*, 50.

28 **Congress appointed a committee:** *The Works of John Adams*, vol. 3, 7–8.

28 **"very loud . . . by his horns":** Ibid.

28 **"The winds and seas":** James Thomson, *Prospect: Being the Fifth Part of Liberty. A Poem* (London: A. Millar, 1736), 34.

28 **"that the monarchs":** *The Seaman's Vade-Mecum, and Defensive War by Sea* (London: W. and J. Mount, 1756), preface.

28 **With 270 warships:** Allen, *A Naval History of the American Revolution*, vol. 1, 53, 181.

29 **"on the continental risk":** Thursday, October 5, 1775, *Journals of the Continental Congress, 1774–1789*, vol. 3, 279.

29 **"it is the maddest":** "[Notes of Debates, Continued] Octr. 7.," *FONA*, https://founders.archives.gov/documents/Adams/01-02-02-0005-0004-0004, accessed May 11, 2021.

29 **Since this was:** "Navy Birthday," Naval History and Heritage Command, https://www.history.navy.mil/browse-by-topic/commemorations-toolkits/navy-birthday.html, accessed December 26, 2020.

29 **Over the next few . . . independence was declared:** *Journals of the American Congress, from 1774 to 1778*, vol. 1 (Washington, DC: Way and Gideon, 1823), 147–50, 153–54, 159–61, 183–92; Paullin, *The Navy of the American Revolution*, 40–47, 125–27; *The Works of John Adams*, vol. 3, 8–12; and Fowler, *Rebels Under Sail*, 5–65.

30 **From that point forward:** "Resolved," October 30, 1776, *Journals of the Continental Congress, 1774–1789*, vol. 6, 913.

31 **"open and avowed . . . traitors to justice":** King George III, "No. 79. Proclamation of Rebellion," *Select Charters and Other Documents Illustrative of American History, 1606–1775*, ed. William Macdonald (New York: The Macmillan Company, 1899), 390.

31 **"I am desired":** Simeon Deane to Silas Deane, November 27, 1775, *Collections of the Connecticut Historical Society*, vol. 2 (Hartford: Published for the Society, 1870), 326.

31 **"Is a sea coast":** "William Cooper to John Adams, December 5, 1775, *NDAR*, vol. 2, 1287.

CHAPTER 3: ALL IN

33 **"a complete dismemberment":** John Adams to Brigadier General Horatio Gates, March 23, 1776, *NDAR*, vol. 4, 481.

34 **The Prohibitory Act completely:** An Act to Prohibit All Trade and Intercourse with the Colonies . . . , *A Collection of All the Statutes Now in Force, Relating to the Revenue of Officers of the Customs in Great Britain and the Plantations*, vol. 2 (London: Charles Eyre and William Strahan, 1780), 1459–74.

34 **"fit out privateers . . . the minds of":** Josiah Bartlett to John Langdon, February 21, 1776, *NDAR*, vol. 4, 31; and Wednesday, March 13, 1776, *Journals of the Continental Congress, 1774–1789*, vol. 4, 200.

34 **"it behooves us":** Oliver Wolcott to Lyman, March 16, 1776, *NDAR*, vol. 4, 397.

34 **The privateering debate soon:** "Richard Smith Diary," March 13, 1776, *Letters of Members of the Continental Congress*, ed. Edmund C. Burnett, vol. 1 (Washington, DC: Carnegie Institution of Washington, 1921), 386; Oliver Wolcott to Lyman, March 16, 1776, *NDAR*, vol. 4, 397; "Richard Smith Diary," March 18, 1776, *Letters of Members of the Continental Congress*, ed. Burnett, vol. 1, 398; "Richard Smith Diary," March 22, 1776, *Letters of Members of the Continental Congress*, ed. Burnett, vol. 1, 404; and *Journals of the Continental Congress, 1774–1789*, vol. 4, 201–25.

34 **"wherein the King":** "Proposed Preamble to a Congressional Resolution," FONA, https://founders.archives.gov/documents/Franklin/01-22-02-0193, accessed July 15, 2021.

34 **"was effectually severing":** "Richard Smith Diary," March 22, 1776, *Letters of Members of the Continental Congress*, ed. Burnett, vol. 1, 404.

35 **The very next day:** *Journals of the Continental Congress, 1774–1789*, vol. 4, 229–32.

35 **"an unjust war . . . pertinaciously pursued":** Ibid., 229–30.

35 **Privateers were free:** Ibid., 230–31.

35 **Later, neutral ships:** Morse, "New England Privateering," 64–68.

35 **About the same time, Congress:** *Journals of the Continental Congress, 1774–1789*, vol. 5, 605–6.

37 **If it was a lawful prize, the privateer:** *Journals of the Continental Congress, 1774–1789*, vol. 4, 231.

37 **"We have hitherto":** John Adams to Brigadier General Horatio Gates, March 23, 1776, *NDAR*, vol. 4, 481.

37 **Although the privateering system:** Background for the content of privateering regulations and the quote come from Wednesday, April 3, 1776, *Journals of the Continental Congress, 1774–1789*, vol. 4, 251–55.

37 **In May 1780:** "The Form of the Bond," *Journals of the American Congress, from 1774 to 1788*, vol. 3 (Washington, DC: Way and Gideon, 1823), 453.

38 **"It is necessary":** "Philadelphia, April 10, 1776," *American Archives: Fourth Series, Containing a Documentary History of the English Colonies in North America*, vol. 5, ed. Peter Force (Washington, DC: M. St. Clair Clarke and Peter Force, 1844), 1443.

38 **John Adams had been:** Middlekauff, *The Glorious Cause*, 318–19.

38 **"This is not"**: John Adams to Brigadier General Horatio Gates, March 23, 1776, *NDAR*, vol. 4, 481.

38 **Privateering might have:** Background for Paine's experience with privateering comes from Thomas Paine, *Rights of Man, Being an Answer to Mr. Burke's Attack on the French Revolution, Part 1* (London: R. Carlisle, 1819), 68; Alyce Barry, "Thomas Paine, Privateersman," *The Pennsylvania Magazine of History and Biography* 101 (October 1977): 451–61; Samuel Stokes, *A Narrative of the Many Hardships, and Cruel Sufferings, While in France; of the Crew of the Terrible Privateer, Commanded by Captain William Death* (London: J. Towers, 1757), 3–15; and Jett Conner, "Thomas Paine Goes to Sea: A Pre-Revolutionary Tale," *Journal of the American Revolution*, November 6, 2018, https://allthingsliberty.com/2018/11/thomas-paine-goes-to-sea-a-pre-revolutionary-tale/, accessed January 2, 2021.

39 **"were smothered to"**: Stokes, *A Narrative of the Many Hardships*, 14.

40 **"reconciliation . . . at hand"**: Thomas Paine, *Common Sense* (Philadelphia: W. and T. Bradford, 1776), 18, 32–33, 43, 45, 87–88.

40 **"now openly avow"**: "The King's Speech Opening the Session," October 26, 1775, *The Parliamentary History of England, from the Earliest Period to the Year 1803*, vol. 18 (London: T. C. Hansard, 1813), 695–96.

40 **Many of the arguments:** Middlekauff, *The Glorious Cause*, 324–35.

40 **twenty-five editions:** Gordon S. Wood, *The American Revolution: A History* (New York: A Modern Library Chronicles Book, 2003), 55.

40 **On April 6:** "Saturday, April 6, 1776," *Journals of the Continental Congress, 1774–1789*, vol. 4, 257–58.

41 **"that these United"**: "Friday, June 7, 1776," *Journals of the Continental Congress, 1774–1789*, vol. 5, 425.

41 **"objects of the most"**: John Adams to William Cushing, June 9, 1776, *FONA*, https://founders.archives.gov/documents/Adams/06-04-02-0109, accessed May 11, 2021.

41 **Still hesitant:** "Tuesday, July 2, 1776," *Journals of the Continental Congress, 1774–1789*, vol. 5, 506–7.

41 **"the second day of"**: John Adams to Abigail Adams, July 3, 1776, *FONA*, https://founders.archives.gov/documents/Adams/04-02-02-0016, accessed May 11, 2021.

41 **It wasn't until:** *Journals of the Continental Congress, 1774–1789*, vol. 5, 431, 491–502, 509–16.

42 **"the lives of our . . . of right do"**: Ibid., 511–14.

43 **Philadelphia's *Chance* and *Congress*:** Background for this section on the two privateers comes from Shomette, *Privateers of the Revolution*, 59–61; Elbridge Gerry to James Warren, June 6, 1776, *Letters of Delegates to Congress, 1774–1789*, vol. 4, ed. Paul H. Smith et al. (Washington, DC: Library of Congress, 1979), 152; John Hancock to George Washington, June 5, 1776, *Letters of Delegates to Congress, 1774–1789*, vol. 4, 145; and Eugene S. Ferguson, *Truxtun of the Constellation: The Life of Commodore Thomas Truxtun, U.S. Navy, 1755–1822* (Baltimore: Johns Hopkins University Press, 2000), 23–27.

43 **With gunpowder:** *Journals of the Continental Congress, 1774–1789*, vol. 4, 250.

43 **"The West Indian"**: Eric Williams, *Capitalism and Slavery* (Chapel Hill: University of North Carolina Press, 1994; orig. 1944), 52.

43 **The ships' cargoes:** Robert Morris to Silas Deane, June 5, 1776, *Letters of Delegates to Congress, 1774–1789*, vol. 4, 148.

44 **"I fancy many"**: Ibid.

44 **"first truly global"**: Niall Ferguson, *The Ascent of Money: A Financial History of the World* (New York: Penguin Press, 2008), 25–26.

44 **"great occasion . . . essential service"**: John Hancock to James Athearn, June 22, 1776,

Letters of Delegates to Congress, 1774–1789, vol. 4, 293. See also John Hancock to George Washington, June 5, 1776, *Letters of Delegates to Congress, 1774–1789*, vol. 4, 145; and "Wednesday, June 12, 1776," *Journals of the Continental Congress, 1774–1789*, vol. 5, 432.

44 **To put such numbers:** U.S. Census Bureau, *Bicentennial Edition: Historical Statistics of the United States, Colonial Times to 1970* (Washington, DC: Government Printing Office, 1975), 1196; Bureau of Labor Statistics, *History of Wages in the United States from Colonial Times to 1928* (Washington, DC: Government Printing Office, 1934), 53; and Alice Hanson Jones, *Wealth of a Nation to Be: The American Colonies on the Eve of the Revolution* (New York: Columbia University Press, 1980), 251–52.

44 **As for mariners:** Bureau of Labor Statistics, *History of Wages*, 97.

44 **By one calculation:** MeasuringWorth.com, https://www.measuringworth.com/index.php, accessed January 4, 2021.

45 **"privateers will":** John Adams to John Winthrop, June 23, 1776, *FONA*, https://founders .archives.gov/documents/Adams/06-04-02-0134, accessed May 11, 2021.

45 **"Thousands of schemes":** John Adams to Abigail Adams, August 12, 1776, *FONA*, https:// founders.archives.gov/documents/Adams/04-02-02-0054, accessed May 11, 2021.

45 **"The rage for":** Abigail Adams to John Adams, September 7, 1776, *FONA*, https://founders .archives.gov/documents/Adams/04-02-02-0079, accessed May 11, 2021.

45 **"The spirit of":** James Warren to Samuel Adams, August 15, 1776, *NDAR*, vol. 6, 191. See also David Cobb to Robert Treat Paine, September 9, 1776, *NDAR*, vol. 6, 775.

45 **"In the eastern":** Robert Morris to the Commissioners, December 21, 1776, *The Diplomatic Correspondence of the American Revolution*, vol. 1, ed. Jared Sparks (Boston: Nathan Hale and Gray & Bowen, 1829), 243.

45 **"privateering was never":** "Extract of a letter from a seaport-town, in Massachusetts Bay, dated May 16, 1779," *Pennsylvania Packet*, June 8, 1779.

45 **"Privateering still":** Morse, "New England Privateering," 277.

45 **The demand for:** See, for example, John Avery to the President of Congress, June 16, 1777, *NDAR*, vol. 9, 123; and Peter E. Jones, "Grant Us Commissions to Make Reprisals upon any Enemies of Shipping," *Rhode Island History*, November 1975, 105–6.

45 **"for want of":** Thomas Jefferson to John Jay, June 19, 1779, *FONA*, https://founders.archives .gov/documents/Jefferson/01-03-02-0004, accessed May 11, 2021.

CHAPTER 4: A PRIVATEERSMAN'S LIFE

46 **"during the gay":** John Adams to Abigail Adams, April 23, 1777, *FONA*, https://founders .archives.gov/documents/Adams/04-02-02-0166, accessed May 11, 2021.

47 **"sprightly":** John Adams to Abigail Adams, April 23, 1776, *FONA*, https://founders .archives.gov/documents/Adams/04-01-02-0255, accessed May 11, 2021.

47 **"that a privateer...enjoy it":** John Adams to Abigail Adams, April 23, 1777, *FONA*, https://founders.archives.gov/documents/Adams/04-02-02-0166, accessed May 11, 2021.

48 **"The stagnation":** "Voted, That the following INSTRUCTIONS be given to the Gentlemen who represent the Town in the General Court, viz.," December 11, 1781, *Proceedings of the Massachusetts Historical Society*, vol. 4 (Boston: Published by the Society, 1889), 51.

48 **"those who have":** Robert Morris to Silas Deane, September 12, 1776, *NDAR*, vol. 6, 794.

49 **"You must know":** Robert Morris to William Bingham, December 4, 1776, *NDAR*, vol. 7, 368.

49 **Morris proceeded:** Charles Rappleye, *Robert Morris: Financier of the Revolution* (New York: Simon & Schuster, 2010), 105.

49 **"My scruples":** Robert Morris to William Bingham, April 25, 1777, *NDAR*, vol. 8, 429.

50 **Of the 158:** Robert E. Peabody, "The Derbys of Salem, Mass.," *Historical Collections of the Essex Institute,* July 1908, 215; and "Memoir of Elias Hasket Derby," 163–64.

50 **Another privateering . . . "The Millionaire Maker":** Shomette, *Privateers of the Revolution,* 132–33 (including quotes).

50 **Privateering spurred:** *Bulletin of the Business Historical Society* 7, no. 3 (May 1933): 9.

51 **Among the more . . . multiple ventures:** To George Washington from John Parke Custis, October 1777, *FONA,* https://founders.archives.gov/documents/Washington/03-12-02-0068, accessed May 11, 2021; George Washington to John Parke Custis, November 14, 1777, *FONA,* https://founders.archives.gov/documents/Washington/03-12-02-0235, accessed May 11, 2021; Erna Risch, "The Logistical Problems of the Continental Army," *United States Army Logistics, 1775–1992: An Anthology,* ed. Charles R. Shrader, vol. 1 (Washington, DC: Center of Military History, 1997), 67–69; Phillip Hamilton, *The Revolutionary War Lives and Letters of Lucy and Henry Knox* (Baltimore: Johns Hopkins University Press, 2017), 189n58; Patton, *Patriot Pirates,* 85–87, 105–8; and Crawford, "The Privateering Debate," 234.

51 **Other noted personages:** To George Washington from Samuel Allyne Otis, December 24, 1777, *FONA,* https://founders.archives.gov/documents/Washington/03-12-02-0642, accessed May 11, 2021; John Bradford to John Hancock, September 30, 1776, *NDAR,* vol. 6, 1053; *NRAR,* 230, 308, 323; Benson J. Lossing, *Our Countrymen: Or Brief Memoirs of Eminent Americans* (New York: Ensign, Bridgman & Fanning, 1855), 251; and Michael M. Greenburg, *The Court-Martial of Paul Revere: A Son of Liberty & America's Forgotten Disaster* (Lebanon, NH: University Press of New England, 2014), 217.

51 **One could bet:** Ralph D. Paine, *The Ships and Sailors of Old Salem* (Chicago: A. C. McClurg & Co., 1912), 64–65.

51 **When Andrew Sherburne:** Andrew Sherburne, *Memoirs of Andrew Sherburne: A Pensioner of the Navy of the Revolution* (Providence, RI: M. M. Brown, 1831), 34.

51 **"It is well":** Willing, Morris & Co. to William Bingham, October 20, 1776, *NDAR,* vol. 6, 1339.

52 **It was common:** *The Freeman's Journal, or, The New-Hampshire Gazette,* June 9, 1778.

52 **"An Invitation to all":** Sidney G. Morse, "The Yankee Privateersman of 1776," *New England Quarterly* 17, no. 1 (March 1944): 71–72; and *Independent Ledger and the American Advertiser,* November 20, 1780.

53 **Those who responded:** Paine, *The Ships and Sailors of Old Salem,* 68.

53 **"At this period":** Sherburne, *Memoirs of Andrew Sherburne,* 19.

53 **The agreement for:** Background and all the quotes pertaining to the *Hibernia*'s articles come from Louis F. Middlebrook, *History of Maritime Connecticut During the American Revolution, 1775–1783,* vol. 2 (Salem, MA: Essex Institute, 1925), 123–30.

54 **"Her love for":** Maclay, *A History of American Privateers,* 8.

55 **The average age:** Michael Schellhammer, *George Washington and the Final British Campaign for the Hudson River, 1779* (Jefferson: McFarland & Company, 2012), 74; Charles Patrick Neimeyer, *America Goes to War: A Social History of the Continental Army* (New York: New York University Press, 1996), 16; and Harold E. Selesky, *A Demographic Survey of the Continental Army That Wintered at Valley Forge, Pennsylvania, 1777–1778* (New Haven, CT: Privately published, 1987), 17.

55 **Lending further support:** Paul A. Gilje, *Liberty on the Waterfront: American Maritime Culture in the Age of Revolution* (Philadelphia: University of Pennsylvania Press, 2004), 27.

55 **Many privateers had:** Christopher Prince, *The Autobiography of a Yankee Mariner: Christopher Prince and the American Revolution,* ed. Michael J. Crawford (Washington, DC: Brassey's Inc., 2002), xxi.

55 **An extreme example:** William Arthur Baller, "Military Mobilization During the Ameri-

can Revolution in Marblehead and Worcester, Massachusetts" (PhD diss., Clark University, 1994), 181–84.

56 **By one account:** Maclay, *A History of American Privateers*, vii.

56 **These men include:** Louis Arthur Norton, *Captains Contentious: The Dysfunctional Sons of the Brine* (Columbia: University of South Carolina Press, 2009), 46–63; Amos Blanchard, *American Military and Naval Biography* (Cincinnati: A. Salisbury, 1832), 454; William Barry Meany, *Commodore John Barry: The Father of the American Navy* (New York: Harper & Brothers Publishers, 1911); and Ferguson, *Truxtun of the Constellation*.

57 **"no consideration":** Lieutenant James Campbell to Daniel of St. Thomas Jenifer, May 1, 1776, *NDAR*, vol. 4, 1369.

57 **"in order to be":** Captain James Smith to the Maryland Council of Safety, May 1, 1776, *NDAR*, vol. 4, 1369.

57 **Black men served:** Benjamin Quarles, *The Negro in the American Revolution* (Chapel Hill: University of North Carolina Press, 1996), 92–93.

57 **Slave owners seeking:** See, for example, *Pennsylvania Gazette* (Philadelphia), December 12, 1776; Advertisement, *Newport (RI) Mercury*, July 15, 1780; *Pennsylvania Gazette*, January 12, 1777; and Advertisement, *Connecticut Gazette* (New London), October 13, 1779.

57 **"To be SOLD":** Winslow, *"Wealth and Honour": Portsmouth During the Golden Age of Privateering, 1775–1815*, 26.

58 **Joshua Barney . . . the *Hyder Ally*:** Joshua Barney, *A Biographical Memoir of the Late Joshua Barney: From Autographical Notes and Journals,* ed. Mary Barney (Boston: Gray and Bowen, 1832), 112–22, 303–4; Shomette, *Privateers of the Revolution*, 216–30, 408; Hulbert Footner, *Sailor of Fortune: The Life and Adventures of Commodore Barney, U.S.N.* (New York: Harper & Brothers, 1940), 101–15; and "Philadelphia, April 16," *Pennsylvania Evening Post*, April 16, 1782.

59 **American privateers captured:** Christian McBurney, *Dark Voyage: An American Privateer's War on Britain's African Slave Trade* (Yardley, PA: Westholme, 2022), in press.

59 **"The unintended":** Ibid.

59 **Providence merchant . . . Brown's pockets:** McBurney, *Dark Voyage*.

60 **Babcock met with:** "Providence, June 13," *Massachusetts Spy*, June 25, 1778.

60 **In Cape May . . . human cargo:** Hand and Stites, *The Cape May Navy*, 94–96.

60 **"presumed that":** Charles R. Foy, "Eighteenth Century 'Prize Negroes': From Britain to America," *Slavery and Abolition* 31, no. 3 (September 2010): 388.

60 **"Titus cares not":** Pynchon, *The Diary of William Pynchon of Salem*, 103. See also L. Vernon Briggs, *History and Genealogy of the Cabot Family, 1475–1927*, vol. 2 (Boston: Charles E. Goodspeed & Co., 1927), 799.

61 **The financial reward . . . among all comers:** Morse, "New England Privateering," 175–76.

61 **The role of money:** See, for example, Jay F. Feyerabend, "For Prize or Patriotism: The Understood Role of Privateers in the American Revolution," *James Blair Historical Review* 9, no. 1 (2019), https://scholarworks.wm.edu/jbhr/vol9/iss1/3, accessed May 7, 2021; Crawford, "The Privateering Debate," 226–34; and Paul A. Gilje, "Loyalty and Liberty: The Ambiguous Patriotism of Jack Tar in the American Revolution," *Pennsylvania History: A Journal of Mid-Atlantic Studies* 67, no. 2 (Spring 2000): 165–93.

62 **"the common class":** John Henry Sherburne, *The Life and Character of the Chevalier John Paul Jones, a Captain in the Navy of the United States* (New York: Vanderpool & Cole, 1825), 21.

62 **"were unlike any":** Francis Raymond Stark, *The Abolition of Privateering and the Declaration of Paris* (New York: Columbia University, 1897), 121.

62 **"Thousands of men":** Gilje, "Loyalty and Liberty," 166.

62 **"had a tendency:"** Mercy Warren, *History of the Rise, Progress and Termination of the American Revolution*, vol. 1 (Boston: Manning and Loring, 1805), 366.

62 **Many of the Founding Fathers:** Gordon S. Wood, "Classical Republicanism and the American Revolution," *Chicago-Kent Law Review* 66, no. 1 (April 1990): 13–38.

63 **Had Congress deemed:** Crawford, "The Privateering Debate," 233–34.

63 **The argument that . . . than they were:** John Ferling, "Myths of the American Revolution," *Smithsonian Magazine*, January 2010; Alan Taylor, *American Revolutions: A Continental History, 1750–1804* (New York: W. W. Norton, 2016), 194–96; Gilje, "Loyalty and Liberty," 165; and Stuart D. Brandes, *Warhogs: A History of War Profits in America* (Lexington: University Press of Kentucky, 1997), 35–37.

63 **"It really gives me":** Thomas Egleston, *The Life of John Paterson, Major-General in the Revolutionary Army* (New York: G. P. Putnam's Sons, 1898), 215. See also Ray Raphael, *A People's History of the American Revolution: How Common People Shaped the Fight for Independence* (New York: Perennial, 2001), 76–83.

64 **"men who could":** "May 16. 1776. Thursday," *FONA*, https://founders.archives.gov/documents/Adams/01-03-02-0016-0121, accessed May 11, 2021.

64 **"Great Encouragement":** "Great Encouragement for Seaman," Danvers: Facsimile of broadside printed by E. Russell at the House late the Bell-Tavern, 1777, https://www.loc.gov/item/rbpe.0400020a/, accessed January 16, 2021.

66 **"Men may speculate":** George Washington to John Banister, April 21, 1778, *FONA*, https://founders.archives.gov/documents/Washington/03-14-02-0525, accessed May 11, 2021.

66 **"who act upon":** George Washington to John Hancock, September 25, 1776, *FONA*, https://founders.archives.gov/documents/Washington/03-06-02-0305, accessed May 11, 2021.

67 **"Through the whole":** Prince, *The Autobiography of a Yankee Mariner*, 210.

67 **"I have ever":** Wilkins Updike, *History of the Episcopal Church in Narragansett, Rhode-Island* (New York: Henry M. Onderdonk, 1847), 123.

67 **"I hope our long":** Charles Herbert, *A Relic of the Revolution* (Boston: Charles H. Pierce, 1847), 104.

67 **"We must all hang":** Personal communication with Valerie-Anne Lutz, Head of Manuscripts Processing at the American Philosophical Association, February 26, 2021.

68 **On the eve of the Revolution, Americans were arguably:** Peter A. Coclanis, "The Wealth of British America on the Eve of the Revolution," *Journal of Interdisciplinary History* 21, no. 2 (Autumn 1990): 245; and John J. McCusker, "Colonial Statistics," in *Historical Statistics of the United States: Earliest Times to the Present, Millennial Edition*, vol. 5, part E, ed. Susan B. Carter et al. (Cambridge: Cambridge University Press, 216), 5-627-36.

69 **most privateers were former:** *NRAR*.

69 **Later in the war:** Robert Peabody, *The Log of the Grand Turks* (Boston: Houghton Mifflin Company, 1926), 11–13, 31.

69 **"The great American":** Howard I. Chapelle, *The History of American Sailing Ships* (New York: W. W. Norton, 1935), 130.

70 **This usually required:** For background on the types of arms on board privateers, see William Gilkerson, *Boarders Away II* (Lincoln, RI: Andrew Mowbray, 1993), 45–88, 190–94, 225–59.

70 **For cannon rounds:** "Application for a Privateering Commission for the Connecticut Sloop *Gamecock*," May 1776, *NDAR*, vol. 5, 76–77.

70 **In addition to:** "Petition of John Mercer and Others," October 18, 1776, *American Archives: Fifth Series, Containing a Documentary History of the United States of America*, vol. 3, ed. Peter Force (Washington, DC: M. St. Clair Clarke and Peter Force, 1853), 397.

70 **When the New London:** Packwood, *Two Revolutionary War Privateers*, 111–15.

72 **The names of:** *NRAR*, 217–495.

72 **revered figure for:** Katherine Harper, "Cato, Roman Stoicism, and the American 'Revolution'" (PhD diss., University of Sydney, 2014), 75–92.

72 **"in the working . . . brought to action":** Charles Biddle, *Autobiography of Charles Biddle, Vice-President of the Supreme Executive Council of Pennsylvania, 1745–1821* (Philadelphia: E. Claxton and Company, 1883), 113–14.

73 **Most of the time, privateers hunted alone:** See, for example, Griswold, *Connecticut Pirates & Privateers*, 98–100.

73 **In the late spring:** Background for this section on the *Hancock* and all the quotes come from Prince, *The Autobiography of a Yankee Mariner*, 174, 181–84.

74 **Despite Fosdick's:** Middlebrook, *History of Maritime Connecticut*, vol. 2, 180–83.

74 **On the privateer *Porus*:** Morse, "The Yankee Privateersman," 76–77.

75 **herring-hog:** Solomon Drowne, *Journal of a Cruise in the Fall of 1780 in the Private-Sloop of War*, Hope, with notes by Henry Thayer Drowne (New York: Charles L. Moreau, 1872), 10.

77 **These drawings of the Philadelphia privateer:** Shomette, *Privateers of the Revolution*, 171–77.

78 **"A momentary . . . for your lives!":** John W. Barber and Henry Howe, *Historical Collections of the State of New Jersey* (New York: S. Tuttle, 1847), 134.

78 **"the captain of the":** "*New-England Chronicle*, Thursday, August 15, 1776," *NDAR*, vol. 6, 193.

80 **"two of her":** Smith, *History of Newburyport*, 117.

80 **In October it engaged:** "The American Privateer *Vengeance*," *The Pennsylvania Magazine of History and Biography* 14 (1890): 93.

80 **On June 7, 1776:** Background for the *Yankee Hero* comes from "The Public Having Been Only Transiently Informed of the Capture of the Privateer Brig Yankee-Hero, of This Port, of Which James Tracy . . . ," *Essex Journal*, August 9, 1776—all the quotes from this source; Thomas Cahill, *The Famous Tracys of Newburyport, Massachusetts* (Somerville: Captain Jeremiah O'Brien's Memorial Associates, 1942), 10–13; "Colony Bond for the Massachusetts Brig *Yankee Hero*," *NDAR*, vol. 4, 19; "Master's Log of the HMS Milford," *NDAR*, vol. 5, 391–92; and *NRAR*, 333.

82 **The privateer *Hampden*'s:** Background and all the quotes for this section on the *Hampden* come from Winslow, *"Wealth and Honour": Portsmouth During the Golden Age of Privateering, 1775–1815*, 44–45.

83 **"this [fight] was one":** Cooper, *History of the Navy of the United States of America*, vol. 1, 98.

83 **On the night of May 3:** Background and all quotes for the *Fame* come from Pynchon, *The Diary of William Pynchon of Salem*, 72–83. See also Morse, "The Yankee Privateersman," 85–86.

84 **The British privateer sloop *Tartar*:** "New-York, June 19," *Connecticut Gazette*, July 1, 1779.

84 **The sloop *Eagle*:** "New-London, May 13," *The Remembrancer, or Impartial Repository of Public Events for the Year 1779* (London: J. Almon, 1779), 129.

85 **Once a ship was:** See, for example, "By Virtue of a Decree of the Hon. Court of Admiralty of This States Will be Sold at Public Vendue for Ready Money on Monday," *Maryland Journal*, October 9, 1776; Advertisement, *New-England Chronicle*, August 15, 1776; Advertisement, *Virginia Gazette*, November 15, 1776; Advertisement, *Pennsylvania Packet*, July 24, 1781; "Mr. Gill. Be Pleased to Give the following Lines a Place in Your Next Journal," *Continental Journal, and Weekly Advertiser*, November 21, 1776; "To the Printer," *Freeman's Journal*, January 21, 1777; and "This Evening," *Pennsylvania Packet*, December 9, 1780.

85 **In the later:** Chapelle, *The History of American Sailing Ships*, 131; and Robert A. Becker,

"Currency, Taxation, and Finance, 1775–1787," *The Companion to the American Revolution*, ed. Jack P. Greene and J. R. Pole (Oxford: Blackwell Publishers, 2000), 390.

85 **"what I had":** Christopher Hawkins, *The Adventures of Christopher Hawkins*, ed. Charles I. Bushnell (New York: Privately printed, 1864), 37.

86 **"Boston Harbor swarms":** *The Remembrancer, or, Impartial Repository of Public Events for the Year 1777* (London: J. Almon, 1778), 173.

86 **"Well Jack!":** "Mr. Edes," *Boston Gazette*, January 4, 1779.

86 **"Whereas Elizabeth":** Morse, "The Yankee Privateersman," 84.

86 **Few, if any:** Philip Besom, "Captain Besom's Narrative," *Proceedings of the Massachusetts Historical Society*, vol. 5, 1860–1862 (Boston: Printed for the Society, 1862), 357–60.

CHAPTER 5: THE FRENCH CONNECTION

88 **William Bingham:** Background for this section on Bingham comes from Robert C. Alberts, *The Golden Voyage: The Life and Times of William Bingham, 1752–1804* (Boston: Houghton Mifflin Company, 1969), 10–82.

88 **"to feel the pulse":** Andrew Jackson O'Shaughnessy, *An Empire Divided: The American Revolution and the British Caribbean* (Philadelphia: University of Pennsylvania Press, 2000), 155.

88 **"encourage as many":** "The Committee of Secret Correspondence: Instructions to William Bingham," June 3, 1776, *FONA*, https://founders.archives.gov/documents/Franklin/01-22-02-0267, accessed May 11, 2021; Margaret L. Brown, "William Bingham, Agent of the Continental Congress," *The Pennsylvania Magazine of History and Biography* 61 (January 1937): 54-87.

90 **"To give all possible":** Josiah Bartlet to William Whipple, August 27, 1776, *NDAR*, vol. 6, 325.

90 **"treated with as":** "Extract of a Letter from Grenada," April 29, 1777, *The Remembrancer, or Impartial Repository of Public Events for the Year 1777*, 199.

90 **Britain and France had been intermittent enemies:** Middlekauff, *The Glorious Cause*, 402–3; James Pritchard, "French Strategy and the American Revolution: A Reappraisal," *Naval War College Review* 47, no. 4 (Autumn 1994): 87; Edward S. Corwin, "The French Objective in the American Revolution," *The American Historical Review* 21, no. 1 (October 1915): 59–60; and Helen Augur, *The Secret War of Independence* (Westport, CT: Greenwood Press, 1955), 15–17.

90 **"the two powers":** Alberts, *The Golden Voyage*, 456.

90 **Instead of being:** "Extract of a Letter from William Bingham," March 15, 1777, *FONA*, https://founders.archives.gov/documents/Adams/06-05-02-0060, accessed May 11, 2021; Vice Admiral James Young to Philip Stephens, March 9, 1777, *NDAR*, vol. 8, 69; and Lord Stormont to Lord Weymouth, June 11, 1777, *NDAR*, vol. 9, 392.

90 **Europeans were . . . from American imports:** Thomas Fleming, *The Perils of Peace: America's Struggle or Survival After Yorktown* (Washington, DC: Smithsonian Books, 2007), 5.

92 **"is a matter of":** Governor Thomas Shirley to Count d'Argout, January 8, 1777, *NDAR*, vol. 7, 902.

92 **"Everything continues":** "Extract of a Letter from Grenada," April 18, 1777, *NDAR*, vol. 8, 372.

92 **"within the space":** "Extract of a letter from Jamaica by the Grenville Packet, May 2," *The Remembrancer, or Impartial Repository of Public Events for the Year 1777*, 169.

92 **According to a British spy:** Rappleye, *Robert Morris*, 105.

92 **"for the arrival of":** James Richard Wills, "'In Behalf of the Continent': Privateering and Irregular Naval Warfare in Early Revolutionary America, 1775-1777" (master's thesis, East Carolina University, 2012), 80.

92 **"with the greatest":** *Public Advertiser*, Monday, July 29, 1776, *NDAR*, vol. 6, 512.

92 **Early in 1777:** American Commissioners in France to the Secret Committee of the Continental Congress, February 6, 1777, *NDAR*, vol. 8, 571; and "London, April 5," *The Remembrancer, or Impartial Repository of Public Events for the Year 1777*, 76; and "London, March 15," *Connecticut Gazette*, June 20, 1777.

92 **A year later . . . West Indian products:** "Proceedings in the Lords Respecting the Commercial Losses Occasioned by the American War," February 6, 1778, *The Parliamentary History of England, from the Earliest Period to the Year 1803*, vol. 19 (London: T. C. Hansard, 1814), 708–16; The American Commissioners to the Committee for Foreign Affairs, May 26, 1777, *FONA*, https://founders.archives.gov/documents/Franklin/01-24-02-0055, accessed May 11, 2021; and "London, March 15," *Connecticut Gazette*, June 20, 1777.

93 **It was estimated:** Stark, *The Abolition of Privateering*, 123.

93 **If there was no:** Clark, *Naval History of the United States*, vol. 1, 43l; *Public Advertiser*, Monday, July 29, 1776, *NDAR*, vol. 6, 512; and David Syrett, *Shipping and the American War, 1775–83* (London: The Athlone Press, 1970), 1n, 131.

93 **"impropriety of":** "Proceedings in the Lords Respecting the Commercial Losses Occasioned by the American War," February 6, 1778, *The Parliamentary History of England, from the Earliest Period to the Year 1803*, vol. 19, 718.

93 **It specifically . . . as possible:** Casimir Freschot, *The Compleat History of the Treaty of Utrecht*, vol. 2 (London: A. Roper and S. Butler, 1715), 130, 139–40. See also "Proceedings in the Lords Respecting the Commercial Losses Occasioned by the American War," February 6, 1778, 19, 130.

93 **On November 16:** Tuchman, *The First Salute*, 5–6.

94 **Like Bingham:** "The Committee of Secret Correspondence: Instructions to Silas Deane," March 2, 1776, *FONA*, https://founders.archives.gov/documents/Franklin/01-22-02-0222, accessed May 11, 2021.

94 **"blank commissions":** Silas Deane to John Jay, December 3, 1776, *NDAR*, vol. 7, 776–77.

95 **"It is certainly":** Silas Deane to the Committee of Secret Correspondence, October 1, 1776, *The Revolutionary Diplomatic Correspondence of the United States*, vol. 2, ed. Francis Wharton (Washington, DC: Government Printing Office, 1889), 155.

96 **Deane was soon:** "The Continental Congress: Instructions to Franklin, Silas Deane, and Arthur Lee as Commissioners to France," September 24–October 22, 1776, *FONA*, https://founders.archives.gov/documents/Franklin/01-22-02-0371, accessed May 11, 2021.

97 **"all conspire to":** *American Archives: Fifth Series*, vol. 3, 1327.

97 **In addition to seeking:** Committee of Secret Correspondence to the American Commissioners in France, October 24, 1776, *NDAR*, vol. 6, 1406.

97 **Thus began an intricate:** The background for the following section on American privateering from French ports on the continent comes from Ruth Y. Johnston, "American Privateers in French Ports 1776–1778," *The Pennsylvania Magazine of History and Biography* 53 (December 1929), 357–74; Allen, *A Naval History of the American Revolution*, vol. 1, 252–86; Morse, "New England Privateering," 253–75; Michael J. Crawford, "The *Hawke* and the *Dove*, a Cautionary Tale: Neutral Ports and Prizes of War During the American Revolution," *The Northern Mariner* 18, nos. 3–4 (July–October 2008): 51–66; Joel Barlow, *The History of England, from The Year 1765, to the Year 1795*, vol. 2 (London: J. Parsons, 1795), 387–89; Stacy Schiff, *A Great Improvisation: Franklin, France, and the Birth of America* (New York: Henry Holt and Company, 2005), 24–25, 30–32, 42–43, 59–61, 94–100, 112–15; Paullin, *The Navy of the American Revolution*, 254–67, 281–93; John Andrews, *An History of the War with American, France, Spain, and Holland Begun in the Year 1775, and Ended in 1783* (London, 1787), 219–20, 277–78; Henri Malo, "American Privateers at Dunkerque," *United States Naval Institute Proceedings*, vol. 37 (Annapolis, MD: U.S. Naval Institute,

1911), 933–48; William Lee to the American Commissioners, August 18, 1777, *FONA*, https://
founders.archives.gov/documents/Franklin/01-24-02-0340, accessed May 11, 2021; Lord
Stormont to Lord Weymouth, April 16, 1777, *NDAR*, vol. 8, 772; and Vergennes to the Marquis de Noailles, March 22, 1777, *NDAR*, vol. 8, 701.

97 **"I have intelligence from":** Lord Stormont to Lord Weymouth, January 8, 1777, *NDAR*,
vol. 8, 514.

99 **"Distress, of course":** Stark, *The Abolition of Privateering*, 123.

101 **at one point threatened:** David Ramsay, *The History of the American Revolution*, vol. 2
(Philadelphia: Aitken & Son, 1789), 24. See also Lord Stormont to Lord Weymouth, April
16, 1777, *NDAR*, vol. 8, 772–73.

101 **"The views of the rebels":** Lord Weymouth to Lord Stormont, July 4, 1777, *NDAR*, vol. 9,
462.

102 **"That which makes":** Benjamin Franklin, Silas Deane, and Arthur Lee to the Committee
of Secret Correspondence, February 6, 1777, *The Diplomatic Correspondence of the American Revolution*, vol. 1, 192.

102 **"England is extremely":** American Commissioners in France to the Committee for Foreign
Affairs, September 8, 1777, *NDAR*, vol. 9, 633.

102 **"been of infinite":** Silas Deane to Robert Morris, August 23, 1777, *NDAR*, vol. 9, 597–98.

102 **"that resistance was . . . small a boat":** Carmichael to Dumas, June 13, 1777, *The Revolutionary Diplomatic Correspondence of the United States*, vol. 2, 338–39.

103 **"It is our business":** William Carmichael to William Bingham, June 25–July 6, 1777, *The
Revolutionary Diplomatic Correspondence of the United States*, vol. 2, 347.

103 **"that the coasts":** *The Revolutionary Diplomatic Correspondence of the United States*,
vol. 2, 168n. See also George Jackson to Wakefield, Pratt & Myers, London, May 20, 1777,
NDAR, vol. 8, 854n1; and Andrews, *An History of the War with American, France, Spain,
and Holland Begun in the Year 1775, and Ended in 1783*, 277.

103 **"that the greatest":** *Public Advertiser*, Thursday, May 15, 1777, *NDAR*, vol. 8, 847. See also
The General Advertiser, Liverpool, Friday, May 16, 1777, *NDAR*, vol. 8, 836, and *Public
Advertiser*, Wednesday, May 14, 1777, *NDAR*, vol. 8 , 846.

103 **"an immediate":** *Public Advertiser*, Wednesday, May 14, 1777, *NDAR*, vol. 8, 846.

103 **On a cruise:** Morse, "New England Privateering," 249.

103 **"Let England's boasted":** Ibid., 219.

104 **"A council":** "Copy of a letter from an English Gentleman at Paris, dated July 28, 1777," *The
Remembrancer, or Impartial Repository of Public Events for the Year 1777*, 203.

104 **"We were permitted":** Captain William Day and Others to the Public, November 29, 1777,
NDAR, vol. 10, 629.

104 **The cruises of:** Allen, *A Naval History of the American Revolution*, vol. 1, 264–72, 285.

105 **Simply put . . . welcome in France:** Augur, *The Secret War of Independence*, 230–34, 250–
61; "Verbal Instructions Given to Jean Holker," November 25, 1777, *NDAR*, vol. 10, 1028;
"Memorial of the Merchants, Traders, and Ship Owners of London to Lord Wentworth,"
November 24, 1777, *NDAR*, vol. 10, 1023; William Clark, *Lambert Wickes, Sea Raider and
Diplomat: The Story of a Naval Captain of the Revolution* (New Haven, CT: Yale University
Press, 1932), 294–310; and Morse, "New England Privateering," 268–75.

105 **Eighteenth-century engraving of Gustavus Conyngham:** Erin Weinman, "Gustavus
Conyngham: American Privateer," September 18, 2019, "From the Stacks," New-York
Historical Society, https://blog.nyhistory.org/gustavus-conyngham-american-privateer/,
accessed April 30, 2021.

106 **"We have lately":** Lord George Germain to Lord Howe, August 4, 1777, *Report on the Manuscripts of Mrs. Stopford-Sackville, of Drayton House, Northamptonshire*, vol. 2 (Boston:
The Gregg Press, 1972), 73.

106 **"to forbear"**: Commissioners in France to the Committee of Foreign Affairs, November 30, 1777, *The Diplomatic Correspondence of the American Revolution*, vol. 1, 344.

107 **"Before he had"**: *The Revolutionary Diplomatic Correspondence of the United States*, vol. 1, ed. Francis Wharton (Washington, DC: Government Printing Office, 1889), 630–31.

107 **The northern . . . other munitions**: Middlekauff, *The Glorious Cause*, 387–91.

107 **"Thus ended all"**: "Journal of Lieutenant William Digby of the Shropshire Regiment," October 17, 1778, *The Spirit of 'Seventy-Six: The Story of the American Revolution as Told by Participants*, ed. Henry Steele Commager and Richard B. Morris (Edison, NJ: Castle Books, 1958), 604.

107 **"The power that will"**: *The Spirit of 'Seventy-Six*, 676.

107 **"You cannot"**: Walter Isaacson, *Benjamin Franklin: An American Life* (New York: Simon & Schuster, 2003), 349.

107 **The Treaty of Amity and Commerce granted**: The Franco-American Treaty of Amity and Commerce, February 6, 1778, *FONA*, https://founders.archives.gov/documents/Franklin/01-25-02-0477, accessed May 11, 2021.

108 **"were not a major"**: Alan G. Jamieson, "American Privateers in the Leeward Islands, 1776–1778," *The American Neptune* 43, no. 1 (January 1983): 30.

108 **"part of a broader"**: Willis, *The Struggle for Sea Power*, 192.

108 **"Oh God"**: Benjamin Terry, *A History of England from the Earliest Times to the Death of Queen Victoria*, 4th ed. (Chicago: Scott, Foresman and Company, 1908), 939.

108 **The French, too**: Malo, "American Privateers at Dunkerque," 935.

109 **In 1776, 34**: *NRAR*, 217–496; and Jack Coggins, *Ships and Seamen of the American Revolution* (Mineola, NY: Dover Publications, 1969), 74.

CHAPTER 6: PRIVATEERING TRIUMPHS AND TRAGEDIES

111 **The Newburyport *General Arnold***: Background for this section on the *General Arnold* comes from Smith, *History of Newburyport*, 105–14; and Edgar Stanton Maclay, *Moses Brown, Captain U.S.N.* (New York: The Baker and Taylor Company, 1904), 40–44, 69–97.

111 **Between 1775 . . . astonishing $3,950,000**: Smith, *History of Newburyport*, 106–7.

112 **"but a single"**: Maclay, *Moses Brown*, 44.

112 **"killed or wounded . . . though a prisoner"**: Smith, *History of Newburyport*, 110–13.

116 **"I arrived home"**: Maclay, *Moses Brown*, 97.

116 **The other *General Arnold***: Background for this section on the *General Arnold* comes from Barnabas Downs, *A Brief and Remarkable Narrative of the Life and Sufferings of Barnabas Downs, Jun[ior]* (Boston: E. Russell, 1786)—all of the quotes are from this source; C. F. Swift, *Genealogical Notes of Barnstable Families, Being a Reprint of the Amos Otis Papers*, vol. 1 (Barnstable: F. B. & F. P. Goss, 1888), 351–57; and *NRAR*, 308.

116 **Captain James Magee, an experienced**: Cornelius Marchant, "A Sketch of the Number of Cruises," *Proceedings of the Massachusetts Historical Society*, vol. 12 (Boston: John Wilson and Son, 1899), 198.

119 **As for Captain Magee**: Henry Lee, "The Magee Family and the Origins of the China Trade," *Proceedings of the Massachusetts Historical Society* 81 (1969): 105–12.

119 **When the storm**: Charles Edward Banks, *The History of Martha's Vineyard, Dukes County, Massachusetts*, vol. 1 (Boston: George H. Dean, 1911), 410.

119 **At the age of thirteen**: Background for this section on John Greenwood and all the quotes come from John Greenwood, *The Revolutionary Services of John Greenwood of Boston and New York, 1775–1783*, ed. Isaac J. Greenwood (New York: De Vinne Press, 1922).

124 **After the war, he became a dentist**: John Miller, "John Greenwood (1760–1819)," George Washington's Mount Vernon, https://www.mountvernon.org/library/digitalhistory/digital

-encyclopedia/article/john-greenwood-1760-1819/, accessed February 26, 2021); George Washington to John Greenwood, February 16, 1791, *FONA*, https://founders.archives.gov/documents/Washington/05-07-02-0210, accessed May 11, 2021; J. A. Taylor, *History of Dentistry* (Philadelphia: Lea & Febiger, 1922), 68; and Esther Forbes, *Paul Revere and the World He Lived In* (Boston: Houghton Mifflin Company, 1999; orig. 1942), 131–33.

125 **"Washington's favorite":** Miller, "John Greenwood."

125 **Everyone expected:** Background for this section on the Penobscot Expedition comes from James S. Leamon, *Revolution Downeast: The War for American Independence in Maine* (Amherst: University of Massachusetts Press, 1995), 104–19; John Calef, *The Siege of Penobscot by the Rebels* (London: G. Kearsley, 1781); Gilbert Nash, *The Original Journal of General Solomon Lovell* (Weymouth, MA: Weymouth Historical Society, 1881), 52–83; William D. Williamson, *The History of the State of Maine: From Its First Discovery, A.D. 1602, to the Separation, A. D. 1820, Inclusive*, vol. 2 (Hallowell, ME: Glazier, Masters & Smith, 1839), 468–78; Jon M. Nielson, "Penobscot: From the Jaws of Victory—Our Navy's Worse Defeat," *The American Neptune* 37, no. 4 (October 1977): 288–305; "Intelligence from Penobscot," *Massachusetts Spy*, August 12, 1779; "Sir George Collier; Embellishments; British," *Pennsylvania Journal*, September 22, 1779; Clark, *Naval History of the United States*, vol. 1, 97–104; and James Sullivan to John Sullivan, August 30, 1779, in Thomas C. Amory, *Life of James Sullivan*, vol. 2 (Boston: Phillips, Sampson and Company, 1859), 376–78.

126 **The fort would serve:** Henry Clinton, *The American Rebellion: Sir Henry Clinton's Narrative of His Campaigns, 1775–1782, with an Appendix of Original Documents* (New Haven, CT: Yale University Press, 1954), 423–24.

126 **Despite these sweeteners:** Allen, *Massachusetts Privateers*, 52.

126 **"Some part":** Nash, *The Original Journal of General Solomon Lovell*, 58.

127 **"willful & unaccommodating":** Leamon, *Revolution Downeast*, 109.

127 **"behaved towards":** Samuel Eliot Morison, *John Paul Jones: A Sailor's Biography* (Boston: Northeastern University, 1959), 52.

127 **"a true old":** Williamson, *The History of the State of Maine*, vol. 2, 471.

127 **"endeavoring to capture":** State of Massachusetts Bay to Solomon Lovell, July 2, 1779, *Documentary History of the State of Maine*, vol. 16, ed. James Phinney Baxter (Portland, ME: Lefavor-Tower Company, 1910), 321; and Nielson, "Penobscot: From the Jaws of Victory," 295.

127 **"We can't but flatter":** William Frost to War Office, July 7, 1779, *Documentary History of the State of Maine*, 330.

127 **"bid high":** "Extract of a letter from Penobscot, dated 22d August, 1779," *The Boston and Country Gazette, The Journal*, September 27, 1779.

128 **"take oaths":** Calef, *The Siege of Penobscot*, 28.

128 **In fact, the Massachusetts:** James Sullivan to John Sullivan, August 30, 1779, *Life of James Sullivan*, vol. 2, 377.

129 **"I was in no":** George Augustus Wheeler, *History of Castine, Penobscot, and Brooksville, Maine* (Bangor, ME: Burr & Robinson, 1875), 332.

129 **"The transports then":** Nash, *The Original Journal of General Solomon Lovell*, 78.

130 **How many Americans:** Leamon, *Revolution Downeast*, 117; and Calef, *The Siege of Penobscot*, 25.

130 **"want of proper . . . reduced the enemy":** Acts and Resolves, Public and Private, of the Province of the Massachusetts Bay, chapter 459, "Resolves requesting the council to make strict inquiry into the detaching 1,500 men for the Penobscot expedition, to send a copy of the report on the failure of said expedition, and the papers accompanying the same, to Congress, and directing the secretary to publish the report in a Boston newspaper as soon as

the court-martial of the Commodore is over," vol. 21 (Boston: Wright & Potter Printing Co., 1922), 216–17.

130 **Some have argued:** To George Washington from Henry Babcock, November 20, 1779, *FONA*, https://founders.archives.gov/documents/Washington/03-23-02-0288, accessed May 11, 2021.

131 **"the dishonorable":** "Report of J. H. Allan," September 10, 1779, *Documentary History of the State of Maine*, 108.

131 **"A prodigious wreck":** Williamson, *The History of the State of Maine*, vol. 2, 476.

131 **"The severe blow":** Clinton, *The American Rebellion: Sir Henry Clinton's Narrative of His Campaigns, 1775–1782*, 424–23.

132 **"the attack on":** James P. Baxter, "A Lost Manuscript," Collections and Proceedings of the Maine Historical Society, second series, vol. 2 (Portland, ME: Published by the Society, 1891), 365.

133 **"We have lost":** James Duncan Phillips, *Salem in the Eighteenth Century* (Salem, MA: Essex Institute, 1969), 417.

133 **Robert Wormsted's:** Background for this section on Wormsted and the quote come from Timothy Alden, *A Collection of American Epitaphs and Inscription, with Occasional Notes* (New York: S. Marks, 1814), 122–29.

134 **Luke Ryan, a pale:** Background for this section on Luke Ryan comes from Clark, *Ben Franklin's Privateers*; Donald A. Petrie, "The Piracy Trial of Luke Ryan," *The American Neptune* 55, no. 3 (1995): 185–204; and Joseph Shiels, "Captain Luke Ryan of Rush," *Dublin Historical Record* 24, no. 2 (March 1971): 25–40.

136 **"The King's":** Jared Sparks, *The Works of Benjamin Franklin*, vol. 1 (Boston: Charles Tappan, 1844), 426.

136 **Not long before:** Catherine M. Prelinger, "Benjamin Franklin and the American Prisoners of War in England during the American Revolution," *William and Mary Quarterly* 32, no. 2 (April 1975): 272–76.

137 **"We are all in":** Clark, *Ben Franklin's Privateers*, 53.

138 **"Being much":** Ibid., 96.

138 **"We continue to":** Benjamin Franklin to John Jay, October 4, 1779, *The Private Correspondence of Benjamin Franklin*, vol. 1, ed. William Temple Franklin (London: Henry Colburn, 1818), 430.

138 **"Complaints are very":** Clark, *Ben Franklin's Privateers*, 115.

138 **From March through:** "Extract of a Letter from Glasgow, April 15," *The New-York Gazette: and The Weekly Mercury* (New York, NY), August 14, 1780.

138 **"on the west coast":** Petrie, "The Piracy Trial of Luke Ryan," 193.

139 **The cruises were . . . as a ruse:** Clark, *Ben Franklin's Privateers*, 129–30.

140 **"Despite all Franklin's":** Ibid., 173.

140 **Luke Ryan's luck:** Donald Petrie, "The Piracy Trial of Luke Ryan," 185; and Shiels, "Captain Luke Ryan of Rush," 34.

140 **Realizing the enormity:** "Extract of a Letter from Edinburgh, April 18," *Royal Georgia Gazette* (Savannah, GA), July 12, 1781.

140 **"to be struck":** Shiels, "Captain Luke Ryan of Rush," 35.

141 **Ryan was put:** "The Trial of Captain Luke Ryan and Thomas Coppinger, for Piracy, with a Striking Likeness of Captain Ryan," *The Hibernian Magazine*, April 1782, 169–70; and *The New-York Gazette: and The Weekly Mercury*, May 27, 1782.

141 **"captured more":** *The Gentlemen's Magazine*, June 1789, 578.

141 **Adams begged Genet:** Background for the battles of the *Thorn* comes from Allen, *A Naval History of the American Revolution*, vol. 2, 415–17—all the quotes are from this source; and Clark, *Naval History of the United States*, vol. 1, 81–82.

141   **"glorious combat . . . from New York":** John Adams to Edmé Jacques Genet, May 3, 1780, *FONA*, https://founders.archives.gov/documents/Adams/06-09-02-0156, accessed May 11, 2021.

143   **The Pennsylvania privateer brig:** Background for this section on the *Holker* and the *Admiral Rodney* is from William Bell Clark, "That Mischievous *Holker*: The Story of a Privateer," *The Pennsylvania Magazine of History and Biography* 79 (January 1955): 38–39; "July 10," *Diary of the American Revolution from Newspapers and Original Documents*, vol. 2, ed. Frank Moore (New York: Privately printed, 1865), 298–99; "New-York, July 10," *Documents Relating to the Revolutionary History of the State of New Jersey*, vol. 4, ed. William Nelson (Trenton, NJ: State Gazette Publishing Co., 1914), 491; "Philadelphia, July 12," *New-Jersey Gazette* (Burlington), July 19, 1780; and *NRAR*, 218, 339.

143   **"a very close":** "July 10," *Diary of the American Revolution from Newspapers and Original Documents*, vol. 2, 298–99. See also "New-York, July 10," *Documents Relating to the Revolutionary History of the State of New Jersey*, vol. 4, 491.

143   **"So much justice":** "July 10," *Diary of the American Revolution*, 298.

143   **"the enemy sheared":** Clark, "That Mischievous *Holker*," 39.

144   **Owned by Blair:** Ibid., 27–62.

144   **In one of . . . Washington's troops:** Ibid., 45–46.

144   **"could hear the screeches":** Jacob Nagle, *The Nagle Journal: A Diary of the Life of Jacob Nagle, Sailor, from the Year 1775 to 1841*, ed. John C. Dann (New York: Weidenfeld & Nicolson, 1988), 19.

145   **The only other . . . was hanged:** Clark, "That Mischievous *Holker*," 47–48 (quote from this); and Nagle, *The Nagle Journal*, 23.

146   **"He acknowledged":** Clark, "That Mischievous *Holker*," 32.

146   **The brig arrived:** "Holker, on a cruise, September 1, 1779," *Pennsylvania Packet*, September 11, 1779.

146   **Its cargo included:** Clark, "That Mischievous *Holker*," 31.

146   **"pair of very":** George Washington to George Geddes, September 30, 1779, *FONA*, https://founders.archives.gov/documents/Washington/03-22-02-0468, accessed May 11, 2021.

146   **An article from:** "From Rivington's Royal Gazette, New-York, May 5," *Pennsylvania Gazette*, May 9, 1781.

147   **"after a successful":** Clark, "That Mischievous *Holker*," 51. See also "Philadelphia, June 6," *New-Jersey Gazette*, June 13, 1781.

147   **The end finally . . . run was over:** Clark, "That Mischievous *Holker*," 60–61.

147   **During the Revolution, Connecticut governor:** Background for this section on whaleboat privateers comes from Jackson Kuhl, "The Whale-Boat Men of Long Island Sound," *Journal of the American Revolution*, November 1, 2013, https://allthingsliberty.com/2013/11/whale-boat-men-long-island-sound/, accessed March 14, 2021; Wallace Evan Davies, "Privateering Around Long Island During the Revolution," *New York History* 20, no. 3 (July 1939): 291–93; James F. Collins, "Whaleboat Warfare on Long Island Sound," *New York History* 25, no. 2 (April 1944): 195–201; Griswold, *Connecticut Pirates & Privateers*, 68–75; and Alexander Rose, *Washington's Spies: The Story of America's First Spy Ring* (New York: Bantam, 2006), 226–33.

147   **One of the most enterprising:** Middlebrook, *History of Maritime Connecticut*, vol. 2, 189–90; "Stamford's Three-Gun Armada," Connecticuthistory.org, https://connecticuthistory.org/stamfords-one-gun-armada/, accessed March 13, 2021; and Elijah B. Huntington, *History of Stamford, Connecticut, from Its Settlement in 1641, to the Present Time* (Stamford, CT: Published by the author, 1868), 217.

148   **"it has been lately":** "Governor Trumbull Notified That Depredators from Connecticut Plunder Long Islanders," *Public Papers of George Clinton, First Governor of New York*, vol. 6 (Albany, NY: J. B. Lyon Company, 1902), 778.

148 **"many evils":** "At a Meeting of the Governor and Council of Safety at Lebanon, Tuesday, 23d January, 1781," *The Public Records of the State of Connecticut*, vol. 3, ed. Charles J. Hoadly (Hartford, CT: Press of the Case, Lockwood & Brainard Co., 1922), 292–93.

148 **"that in some . . . may be obtained":** "Governor Trumbull Points Out the Mode of Redress for Persons Plundered on Long Island," *Public Papers of George Clinton*, vol. 6, 803.

149 **"One of the party . . . they are robbed":** Caleb Brewster to George Clinton, August 20, 1781, *Public Papers of George Clinton, First Governor of New York*, vol. 7 (Albany, NY: J. B. Lyon Company, 1902), 233–34.

150 **Brewster's alarming:** "Governor Clinton Suggests to Governor Trumbull the Necessity for the Revocation of Certain Commissions," ibid., 234–36.

150 **"landing or going":** "At a Meeting of the Governor and Council of Safety Holden at Hartford on the 15th Day of September, 1781," *The Public Records of the State of Connecticut*, vol. 3, 513.

150 **Hoping to finally:** "At a Meeting of the Governor and Council of Safety at Lebanon, Friday 23d November, 1781," *The Public Records of the State of Connecticut*, vol. 3, 553.

150 **"After this, complaints":** Kuhl, "The Whale-Boat Men of Long Island Sound."

151 **"that when the General":** " 'Burnt All Their Houses': The Log of HMS *Savage* During a Raid up the Potomac River, Spring 1781," ed. Fritz Hirschfeld, *Virginia Magazine of History and Biography* 99, no. 4 (October 1991): 516–17.

152 **"It would have been":** "To Lund Washington, Mount Vernon," April 30, 1781, *The Life of General Washington*, vol. 2, ed. C. W. Upham (London: Office of the National Illustrated Library, 1851), 21–22.

152 **"You cannot conceive":** From the Marquis de Lafayette to General Washington, April 23, 1781, *The Life of General Washington*, vol. 2, 23.

152 **After leaving the Potomac:** Background for this section on the battle between the *Savage* and the *Congress* comes from "An Account of the Action betwixt the *Savage* Sloop of War of 16 Guns, Capt. Stirling, and the *Congress*, an American Frigate of 20 Guns, Capt. Geddis; from a Letter of Capt. Stirling's to Rear-Admiral Graves," September 23, 1781, *The Annual Register, Or a View of the History, Politics, and Literature, for the Year 1781* (London: J. Dodsley, 1791), 251–53—all quotes from this source; and Arthur D. Pierce, *Smuggler's Woods: Jaunts and Journeys in Colonial and Revolutionary New Jersey* (New Brunswick, NJ: Rutgers University Press, 1992), 76–77.

153 **As the Americans were sailing the *Savage*:** "Notice Is Hereby Given," *The London Gazette*, December 15, 1789.

154 **He heard the:** Julie Winch, *A Gentleman of Color: The Life of James Forten* (New York: Oxford University Press, 2002), 30–31.

154 **James Forten was nearly ten:** Ibid., 3–51; and Robert Purvis, *Remarks on the Life and Character of James Forten, Delivered at the Bethel Church, March 30, 1842* (Philadelphia: Merrihew and Thompson, 1842), 4–8.

154 **"My great-grandfather":** Sidney Kaplan, *The Black Presence in the Era of the American Revolution, 1770–1800* (Washington, DC: Smithsonian Institution Press, 1973), 47.

154 **"was marked for":** Purvis, *Remarks on the Life*, 4. For "disinterested," see Gordon S. Wood, *Revolutionary Characters: What Made the Founders Different* (New York: Penguin Press, 2006), 16.

154 **An Act for the Gradual:** An Act for the Gradual Abolition of Slavery, March 1, 1780, Pennsylvania Historical & Museum Commission, http://www.phmc.state.pa.us/portal/communities/documents/1776-1865/abolition-slavery.html, accessed February 15, 2021.

155 **"What the quality":** Winch, *A Gentleman of Color*, 36.

155 **Royal Louis:** *NRAR*, 449; and John A. McManemin, *Captains of the Privateers During the Revolutionary War* (Spring Lake, NJ: Ho-Ho-Kus Publishing Company, 1985), 307–8.

155 **"fired with the":** Purvis, *Remarks on the Life*, 4.

155 **Most gave up:** Winch, *A Gentleman of Color*, 39–40; and Stephen H. Gloucester, "A Discourse Delivered on the Occasion of the Death of Mr. James Forten Sr.," April 17, 1842, University of Detroit Mercy Black Abolitionist Archives, Doc. No. 006615, 10, https://www.logcollegepress.com/stephen-henry-gloucester-18021850, accessed February 15, 2021.

155 **"loud huzzas":** Purvis, *Remarks on the Life*, 5.

155 **"His mind was":** Ibid.

156 **"patronage":** Ibid., 6.

156 **"I am here":** Ibid.

157 **And a very successful:** Winch, *A Gentleman of Color*, 333.

157 **even giving his:** Ibid., 239–42.

157 **"received a wound . . . up the vessel":** "Salem, July 11," *Salem Gazette*, July 11, 1782.

158 **"the relief . . . our lives":** "From the Nova Scotia Gazette, June 4. to the Printer," *Independent Ledger*, July 22, 1782.

CHAPTER 7: THE LION ROARS

161 **"nothing had given":** Oliver Wolcott to George Wyllys, April 17, 1777, *Letters of Delegates to Congress, 1774 to 1789*, vol. 6, ed. Paul H. Smith (Washington, DC: Library of Congress, 1980), 608.

161 **"Naval captures":** David Ramsay, *The History of the American Revolution*, vol. 1 (Trenton, NJ: James J. Wilson, 1811; orig. 1789), 289.

161 **Even if it were:** Morse, "New England Privateering," 564–65; and Morgan, "American Privateering in America's War," 84–85.

161 **One of the most oft-mentioned:** Maclay, *A History of American Privateers*, viii.

161 **Bennett concluded:** Charles Wright and C. Ernest Fayle, *A History of Lloyd's: From the Founding of Lloyd's Coffee House to the Present Day* (London: Macmillan and Company, 1928), 156.

162 **However, because American:** Historian Sidney Morse concludes that privateers from Massachusetts, Connecticut, Rhode Island, New Hampshire, Pennsylvania, and New Jersey—and excluding New York, North Carolina, Maryland, Virginia, and South Carolina—brought in a total of 2,106 prizes. He bases this on newspaper and prize court notices but admits that "a high degree of accuracy cannot be claimed for [these numbers]. . . . In compiling them there are innumerable difficulties to solve, all of which would be an enormous research task in itself." To this author, such numbers seem too high, especially given Lloyd's of London records on captures. See Morse, "New England Privateering," 566–67.

162 **In February 1778:** "Proceedings in the Lords Respecting the Commercial Losses Occasioned by the American War," February 6, 1778, *The Parliamentary History of England, from the Earliest Period to the Year 1803*, vol. 19, 709.

162 **There are many records of American prizes:** See, for example, "Boston, June 19," *Pennsylvania Evening Post*, July 1, 1777; and "Auction Sales in Salem, of Shipping and Merchandise, During the Revolution," *Historical Collections of the Essex Institute*, April 1913, 99–111.

162 **"When the merchants of this country":** "Proceedings in the Lords Respecting the Commercial Losses Occasioned by the American War," February 6, 1778, *The Parliamentary History of England, from the Earliest Period to the Year 1803*, vol. 19, 717–18.

163 **At war's end, the tally:** Starkey, *British Privateering in the Eighteenth Century*, 217–18.

163 **If we add to that:** George E. E. Nichols, "Notes on Nova Scotian Privateers," *Collections of*

the Nova Scotia Historical Society 13 (1908): 122; and Oscar Theodore Barck, *New York City During the War for Independence* (Port Washington, NY: Ira J. Friedman, 1931), 131.

163 **"the value of":** *Public Advertiser*, Monday, July 15, 1776, *NDAR*, vol. 6, 476.

163 **"it is a proof":** Cooper, *History of the Navy of the United States of America*, vol. 1, 136.

163 **According to Lloyd's:** Wright and Fayle, *A History of Lloyd's*, 156–57.

163 **"From London, we":** Winslow, *"Wealth and Honour": Portsmouth During the Golden Age of Privateering, 1775–1815*, 36.

164 **"The widespread":** Thomas G. Frothingham, "The Military Test of the Spontaneous American Revolution," *Proceedings of the Massachusetts Historical Society*, October 1924– June 1925 (Boston: Published by the Society, 1925), 116.

164 **While the Royal Navy . . . were in fighting form:** Allen, *A Naval History of the American Revolution*, vol. 1, 53, 181.

164 **First, reacting:** See, for example, George Jackson to Wakefield, Pratt, & Myers, London, May 20, 1777, *NDAR*, vol. 8, 854; Lords Commissioners, Admiralty, to Captain Robert Linzee, R.N., January 2, 1777, *NDAR*, vol. 8, 504; "London, May 10," *Pennsylvania Evening Post*, August 19, 1777; and J. Campbell, *Lives of the British Admirals*, vol. 4 (London: Alexander Donaldson, 1779), 394.

165 **"use your best":** Lords Commissioners, Admiralty, to Captain Robert Linzee, R.N., January 2, 1777, NDAR, vol. 8, 504. See also Lords Commissioners, Admiralty, to Captain John Elphinston, R.N., October 16, 1777, *NDAR*, vol. 10, 998.

165 **One captain who:** Background for this battle comes from "Journal of the H.M.S. *Brune*, Captain James Ferguson," September 1777, *NDAR*, vol. 9, 940; and *The Gazette of the State of South-Carolina*, Tuesday, December 2, 1777, *NDAR*, vol. 10, 655—all of the quotes are from this source.

166 **An even greater:** Background for this section on the *Terrible* and the *Rising States* comes from "Journal of the H.M.S. *Terrible*, Captain Sir Richard Bickerton," *NDAR*, vol. 7, 768; "Journal of Timothy Connor, Massachusetts Privateer Brigantine *Rising States*," *NDAR*, vol. 7, 768–69; and "*Rising States* Massachusetts Brigantine [Thompson]," American War of Independence—At Sea, The American Privateers, https://www.awiatsea.com/Privateers/ Privateers_R.html, accessed March 18, 2021.

166 **"vegetating in":** Rear Admiral James Gambier to the Earl of Sandwich, July 19, 1778, *NDAR*, vol. 13, 466.

166 **"rebels could muster":** "Rear Admiral James Gambier to the Earl of Sandwich, July 6, 1778, *NDAR*, vol. 13, 283.

167 **In early September 1778:** Background on this expedition comes from Daniel Ricketson, *The History of New Bedford* (New Bedford: Published by the author, 1858), 278–87; Clinton, *The American Rebellion: Sir Henry Clinton's Narrative of His Campaigns, 1775–1782*, 103– 4; and Sir Charles Grey, "Memoirs of General Sir Charles Grey, K.B.," February 1799, *The British Military Library*, vol. 1 (London: J. Carpenter and Co., 1804), 166–67.

167 **"to exterminate":** Thomas Jones, *History of New York During the Revolutionary War*, vol. 1, ed. Edward Floyd DeLancey (New York: New-York Historical Society, 1879), 278.

167 **"the stores destroyed":** Daniel Ricketson, *The History of New Bedford, Bristol County, Massachusetts* (New Bedford, MA: Published by the author, 1858), 279.

168 **Then it was on:** Charles Edward Banks, *The History of Martha's Vineyard*, vol. 1 (Boston: George H. Dean, 1911), 380–81.

168 **"The keeping the":** George Washington, *The Writings of George Washington from the Original Manuscript Sources, 1745–1799*, vol. 14, ed. John C. Fitzpatrick (Washington, DC: Government Printing Office, 1936), 49n, 306.

168 **Soon after the fleet:** Background for the attack on Little Egg Harbor comes from William S. Stryker, *The Affair at Egg Harbor, New Jersey, October 15, 1778* (Trenton, NJ: Naar, Day

& Naar, 1894); Shomette, *Privateers of the Revolution*, 147–57; and Richard J. Koke, "War, Profit, and Privateers Along the New Jersey Coast," *The New-York Historical Society Quarterly* 41 (July 1957): 290–93.

169 **"skulking banditti":** Stryker, *The Affair at Egg Harbor*, 28.

170 **In subsequent years, the British:** Clinton, *The American Rebellion: Sir Henry Clinton's Narrative of His Campaigns, 1775–1782*, 130.

170 **But the deadliest:** Background for this section on the raid on New London comes from Walter L. Powell, *Murder or Mayhem? Benedict Arnold's New London, Connecticut Raid, 1781* (Gettysburg, PA: Thomas Publications, 2000); Eric D. Lehman, *Homegrown Terror: Benedict Arnold and the Burning of New London* (Middletown, CT: Wesleyan University Press, 2014); Charles Allyn, *The Battle of Groton Heights: A Collection of Narratives, Official Reports, Records, Etc.* (New London, CT: Charles Allyn, 1882); and Clinton, *The American Rebellion: Sir Henry Clinton's Narrative of His Campaigns, 1775–1782*, 331, 565–67.

170 **Most recently, in July:** Middlebrook, *History of Maritime Connecticut*, vol. 2, 163–64.

170 **"annoy the enemy's":** Clinton, *The American Rebellion: Sir Henry Clinton's Narrative of His Campaigns, 1775–1782*, 330–31.

172 **"We will not":** Powell, *Murder or Mayhem?*, 46.

173 **"more formidable":** Ibid.

173 **"Who commands this":** Rufus Avery and Stephen Hempstead, *Narrative of Jonathan Rathbun, with Accurate Accounts of the Capture of Groton Fort, the Massacre That Follows, and the Sacking and Burning of New London* (New London, CT: Privately published, 1840), 27.

173 **"was bayoneted":** Powell, *Murder or Mayhem?*, 65.

174 **"wantonly went to":** 51.

174 **"the attack was":** Clinton, *The American Rebellion: Sir Henry Clinton's Narrative of His Campaigns, 1775–1782*, 566.

174 **"The Battle of Groton Heights":** Lehman, *Homegrown Terror*, 160.

174 **"the rebellious colonies":** *Public Advertiser*, Tuesday, March 11, 1777, *NDAR*, vol. 8, 662–63.

174 **Adding privateers:** David J. Starkey, *British Privateering Enterprise in the Eighteenth Century* (Exeter, UK: University of Exeter Press, 1990), 193–94.

175 **Between 1777 and 1783:** Ibid., 197.

175 **But these figures:** Ibid., 199.

175 **Between August 1778:** Gomer Williams, *History of the Liverpool Privateers and Letters of Marque* (London: William Heinemann, 1897), 183.

175 **"the privateering trade":** David Lester, "Privateering in the Colonial Chesapeake" (master's thesis, College of William and Mary, 1989), 17.

175 **The most spectacular battle:** Background for the fight between the *Watt* and the *Trumbull* comes from Williams, *History of the Liverpool Privateers*, 272–74; "The Story of the Vessels Built in Connecticut for the Continental Navy, the *Trumbull*," *Records and Papers of the New London County Historical Society*, part 1, vol. 1 (New London, CT: Published by the Society, 1890), 51–56; and "Account of James Nicholson, Captain of the *Trumbull*," June 20, 1780, *The Spirit of 'Seventy-Six*, 956–59.

176 **"instantly gave her":** "Account of John Coulthard, Captain of the *Watt*," June 14, 1780, *The Spirit of 'Seventy-Six*, 958.

176 **"yardarm to yardarm":** Williams, *History of the Liverpool Privateers*, 273.

176 **"It is beyond my power":** "The Story of the Vessels Built in Connecticut for the Continental Navy, the *Trumbull*," 51.

176 **"I give you my":** "Account of James Nicholson, Captain of the *Trumbull*," June 20, 1780, *The Spirit of 'Seventy-Six*, 958.

177 **On August 5:** Lord George Germain to Governors in North America, August 5, 1778, in John Romeyn Brodhead, *Documents Relative to the Colonial History of the State of New York*, vol. 8 (Albany, NY: Weed, Parson and Company, 1857), 748.

177 **For a brief moment:** Background for this section on Nova Scotian privateers comes from John Dewar Faibisy, "Privateering and Piracy: The Effects of New England Raiding Upon Nova Scotia During the American Revolution, 1775–1783" (PhD diss., University of Massachusetts, 1972); John Dewar Faibisy, "A Compilation of Nova Scotia Vessels Seized During the American Revolution and Libeled in the New England Prize Courts," *NDAR*, vol. 10, 1201–10; and Emily P. Weaver, "Nova Scotia and New England During the Revolution," *The American Historical Review* 10, no. 1 (October 1904): 52–71.

177 **"robbing poor":** John Hanc, "When Nova Scotia Almost Joined the American Revolution," Smithsonianmag.com, June 5, 2017, https://www.smithsonianmag.com/history/when-nova-scotia-almost-joined-american-revolution-180963564/, accessed March 22, 2021.

178 **Between 1779 and 1781:** Nichols, "Notes on Nova Scotian Privateers,"122.

178 **"hot engagement":** Beamish Murdoch, *A History of Nova Scotia or Acadie*, vol. 2 (Halifax: James Barnes, 1866), 608.

179 **Nobody pushed . . . were American privateers:** Barck, *New York City During the War for Independence*, 131.

179 **"all those who are":** "New-York, March 10, by His Excellency William Tryon, Esq.," *Royal Gazette* (New York, NY), March 10, 1779.

179 **"never exhausted":** Claude Halstead Van Tyne, *The Loyalists of the American Revolution* (New York: The Macmillan Company, 1902), 180.

179 **"to any person who":** "Ardent, off New-York, 16th Dec. 1778," *Royal Gazette*, January 16, 1779.

180 **"death by the sentence":** "By Sir George Collier," *Royal Gazette*, May 12, 1779.

180 **The most remarkable:** "New-York, March 6," *Royal Gazette*, March 6, 1779.

180 **"loyal ladies . . . gentleness and benevolence":** "Extract of a Letter from an Officer on Board Admiral Keppel's Fleet, to His Friend in London," *Royal Gazette*, January 6, 1779.

180 **"Brave loyal tars":** "Long-Island, January 10, 1779," *Royal Gazette*, January 16, 1779.

180 **The *Royal Charlotte* had:** "Prizes sent in since our last," *The New-York Gazette: and The Weekly Mercury*, May 3, 1779; and "Prizes sent in since our last," *The New-York Gazette: and The Weekly Mercury*, July 26, 1779.

180 **"choice Tenerife":** "Public Auction," *The New-York Gazette: and The Weekly Mercury*, July 19, 1779.

181 **"she is a fast-sailing":** "To Be Sold at Public Auction," *Royal Gazette*, November 13, 1779.

CHAPTER 8: "HELL AFLOAT"

182 **Britain had a problem:** Background for this section on how to legally deal with American prisoners comes from T. Cole Jones, "'The Dreadful Effects of British Cruilty': The Treatment of British Maritime Prisoners and the Radicalization of the Revolutionary War at Sea," *Journal of the Early Republic* 36, no. 3 (Fall 2016): 435–37; and William R. Lindsey, "Treatment of American Prisoners of War During the Revolution," *The Emporia State Research Studies* 22, no. 1 (Summer 1973): 5.

183 **"secure and detain":** "*London Chronicle*, Saturday, February 8 to Tuesday, February 11, 1777," *NDAR*, vol. 8, 581; and "America: Bill to Detain Suspected Persons," *Journals of the House of Commons, from October the 31st, 1776, to October the 1st, 1778* (London: House of Commons, 1803), 192.

183 **"great bulwark":** Samuel Curwen to Judge Sewall, February 13, 1777, *The Journal and Let-*

ters of Samuel Curwen, An American in England, from 1775 to 1783, 107. See also Sheldon S. Cohen, *Yankee Sailors in British Gaols: Prisoners of War at Forton and Mill, 1777–1783* (Newark: University of Delaware Press, 1995), 27–29.

184   **The two main:** Cohen, *Yankee Sailors in British Gaols*, 18; and Jesse Lemisch, "Listening to the 'Inarticulate': William Widger's Dream and the Loyalties of American Revolutionary Seamen in British Prisons," *Journal of Social History* 3, no. 1 (Autumn, 1969): 7n15.

184   **"you are supposed":** Herbert, *A Relic*, 44.

184   **"What sort of people":** Ibid., 19–20.

185   **Herbert was sent:** Background for Mill Prison comes from Howard Lewis Applegate, "American Privateersmen in the Mill Prison," *Historical Collections of the Essex Institute*, October 1961), 303–20.

185   **Forton Prison was in Gosport:** Background information about Forton Prison comes from John K. Alexander, "Forton Prison During the American Revolution: A Case Study of British Prisoner of War Policy and the American Prisoner Response to That Policy," *Historical Collections of the Essex Institute*, October 1967, 365–89.

185   **As at Mill, the Americans were thrown:** Ibid., 369–70.

185   **Upon entering either:** Cohen, *Yankee Sailors in British Gaols*, 56–59.

186   **"thick with":** Applegate, "American Privateersmen in the Mill Prison," 311.

186   **"stinking beef":** Timothy Connor, "A Yankee Privateersman in Prison in England, 1777–1779," *The New-England Historical and Genealogical Register*, vol. 30 (Boston: Published at the Society's House, 1876), 352.

186   **Captured rats:** Applegate, "American Privateersmen in the Mill Prison," 309.

186   **The worst example:** Nathaniel Fanning, *Fanning's Narrative: Being the Memoirs of Nathaniel Fanning, An Officer of the Revolutionary Navy, 1778–1783*, ed. John S. Barnes (New York: De Vinne Press, 1912), 11–12.

187   **"the old crab":** Ibid., 10.

187   **"as great a tyrant":** "Journal of Samuel Cutler," June 3, 1777, *NDAR*, vol. 9, 376.

187   **According to a number of accounts:** Cohen, *Yankee Sailors in British Gaols*, 66–67.

187   **In Forton, for example:** Alexander, "Forton Prison," 380; and Applegate, "American Privateersmen in the Mill Prison," 312.

187   **"One of our men":** Paine, *The Ships and Sailors of Old Salem*, 134–35.

188   **Perhaps the most enthusiastic:** Sheldon S. Cohen, "Thomas Wren: Ministering Angel of Forton Prison," *The Pennsylvania Magazine of History and Biography* 102 (July 1979): 279–300.

188   **Various analyses:** See, for example Cohen, *Yankee Sailors in British Gaols*, 104–5; Alexander, "Forton Prison During the American Revolution," 384; Francis D. Cogliano, "'We All Hoisted the American Flag:' National Identity Among American Prisoners in Britain During the American Revolution," *Journal of American Studies* 32. No. 1 (April 1998), 32–33; Lemisch, "Listening to the 'Inarticulate,'" 17; and Applegate, "American Privateersmen in the Mill Prison," 319.

188   **"entered on board":** Caleb Foot, "Reminiscences of the Revolution: Prison and Sea Journal of Caleb Foote," *Historical Collections of the Essex Institute*, 1889, 97.

188   **"We, whose names are":** Herbert, *A Relic*, 208.

189   **Forton's American:** Alexander, "Forton Prison During the American Revolution," 385.

189   **"refused all the":** Benjamin Franklin, "August 7, 1787," *Documents Illustrative of the Formation of the Union of the American States* (Washington, DC: Government Printing Office, 1927), 875.

189   **"To-day being":** Paine, *The Ships and Sailors of Old Salem*, 125. See also Cogliano, "We All Hoisted the American Flag," 27–28.

189   **Although solid:** Alexander, "Forton Prison During the American Revolution," 382–83.

189 **It counts multiple:** See, for example, Samuel Cutler, "Prison Ships, and the 'Old Mill Prison,' Plymouth, England, 1777," *The New-England Historical and Genealogical Register* 32 (October 1878): 395–96; Connor, "A Yankee Privateersman," 347–48; Samuel Cutler, "Prison Ships, and the 'Old Mill Prison,' Plymouth, England, 1777," *The New-England Historical and Genealogical Register* 32 (July 1878), 307, 347; and Paine, *The Ships and Sailors of Old Salem*, 121–25.

189 **Another source estimates:** Lemisch, "Listening to the 'Inarticulate,'" 18, 18n59.

189 **"gold key":** Bethany Groff Dorau, "A Privateer's Private Side: Offin Boardman's Lost Diary Resurfaces," *Historic New England*, Winter 2018, 30.

190 **Many escapees . . . fifteen times:** Alexander, "Forton Prison During the American Revolution," 382; and Thomas C. Parramore, "The Great Escape from Forten Gaol: An Incident of the Revolution," *The North Carolina Historical Review* 45 (October 1968): 354.

190 **"black hole":** "Journal of Dr. Jonathan Haskins (Mill Prison, Plymouth, April 1778)," *NDAR*, vol. 12, 541; and Cohen, *Yankee Sailors in British Gaols*, 68–69.

190 **One lucky prisoner:** Background for Cutler and his escape comes from Samuel Cutler, "Prison Ships, and the 'Old Mill Prison,' Plymouth, England, 1777," *The New-England Historical and Genealogical Register* 32 (1878): January, 42–44; April, 184–88; July, 305–8; October, 395–98.

191 **One of the largest:** Background for this escape comes from Luke Matthewman, "Narrative of Lieut. Luke Matthewman of the Revolutionary Navy," *Magazine of American History* 2 (March 1878): 175–85, and Parramore, "The Great Escape from Forten Gaol," 349–56.

192 **While being a prisoner:** David Dzurec, "Prisoners of War and American Self-Image during the American Revolution," *War in History* 20, no. 4 (November 2013): 437; and Larry G. Bowman, *Captive Americans: Prisoners During the American Revolution* (Athens: Ohio University Press, 1976), 52.

192 **"Notwithstanding my long":** Paine, *The Ships and Sailors of Salem*, 129–30.

192 **After two and a half . . . September 16:** Ibid., 120, 139, 142.

192 **"I write with an":** Ibid., 169–70.

193 **But by far the worst:** Background for these ships comes from the following sources: Thomas Dring, *Recollections of the Jersey Prison-Ship*, ed. David Swain (Yardley, PA: Westholme, 2019); Hawkins, *The Adventures of Christopher Hawkins*; Robert P. Watson, *The Ghost Ship of Brooklyn: An Untold Story of the American Revolution* (New York: Da Capo Press, 2007); Thomas Andros, *The Old Jersey Captive: Or a Narrative of the Captivity of Thomas Andros on Board The Old Jersey Prison Ship at New York, 1781* (Boston: William Pierce, 1833); Ebenezer Fox, *The Adventures of Ebenezer Fox, in the Revolutionary War* (London: Charles Fox, 1848); Danske Dandridge, *American Prisoners of the Revolution* (Charlottesville, VA: The Michie Company, 1911); and Edwin G. Burrows, *Forgotten Patriots: The Untold Story of American Prisoners During the Revolutionary War* (New York: Basic Books, 2008).

193 **All told, there were seventeen:** Watson, *The Ghost Ship of Brooklyn*, 241–42.

193 **Edwin G. Burrows:** Burrows, *Forgotten Patriots*, 200.

194 **"Such an accumulation":** Fox, *The Adventures of Ebenezer Fox*, 141–42.

194 **"Hell Afloat":** Fox, *The Adventures of Ebenezer Fox*, 96.

194 **had been a fourth-rate:** Lincoln L. Paine, *Warships of the World* (Boston: Houghton Mifflin Company, 2000), 86.

194 **Before the start . . . 1,200 prisoners:** Watson, *The Ghost Ship*, 82–83, 242–43.

195 **"Never before or":** Dandridge, *American Prisoners*, 237.

195 **According to Thomas Dring:** Background for Dring's observations and all the quotes come from Dring, *Recollections of the Jersey Prison-Ship*, 20–22.

196 **Between six and twelve:** Watson, *The Ghost Ship*, 123–24.

196 **"there would be":** Testimony of Thomas Philbrook in Hawkins, *The Adventures of Christopher Hawkins*, 283.

197 **"There were about"**: See Dandridge, *American Prisoners of the Revolution*, 252–53.

198 **Because only two . . . bottom rung**: John O. Sands, "Christopher Vail, Soldier and Seaman in the American Revolution," *Winterthur Portfolio* 11 (1976): 71; and Hawkins, *The Adventures of Christopher Hawkins*, 19.

198 **"bloody and"**: Hawkins, *The Adventures of Christopher Hawkins*, 19.

198 **Some men, driven by**: Ibid., 71–72.

198 **"moldy and filled . . . a phenomenon"**: Fox, *The Adventures of Ebenezer Fox*, 102–5.

198 **"unsavory"**: Ibid., 103.

198 **"was so rank"**: Dring, *Recollections*, 31.

198 **During New York City's**: Burrows, *Forgotten Patriots*, 136–38.

199 **It was not only**: Ibid., 105–7.

200 **"was nauseous . . . in nature"**: Dring, *Recollections*, 61.

200 **"as fine water"**: Alexander Coffin, "The Destructive Operation of Foul Air, Tainted Provisions, Bad Water, and Personal Filthiness, Upon Human Constitutions," *The Medical Repository, Comprehending Original Essay and Intelligence Relative to Medicine, Chemistry, Natural History, Agriculture, Geography, and the Arts*, vol. 5 (New York: T. & J. Swords, 1808), 262.

200 **"the whole ship"**: Andros, *The Old Jersey Captive*, 16.

200 **"among a collection"**: Fox, *The Adventures of Ebenezer Fox*, 99–100.

200 **The sickest of prisoners**: Watson, *The Ghost Ship*, 125.

201 **"sought after by"**: Dring, *Recollections*, 53.

201 **"a very corpulent . . . after supplied"**: Ibid., 62–63.

202 **"If there was"**: Andros, *The Old Jersey Captive*, 18. See also Dzurec, "Prisoners of War," 444–45.

202 **Being placed on . . . strike a deal**: Betsy Knight, "Prisoner Exchange and Parole in the American Revolution," *William and Mary Quarterly* 48, no. 2 (April 1991): 201–22; Burrows, *Forgotten Patriots*, 81–82, 125–27, 152–53; Eugene L. Armbruster, *The Wallabout Prison Ships, 1776–1783* (New York: Privately printed, 1920), 24; and Bowman, *Captive Americans*, 103–13.

203 **"rueful countenances"**: Dandridge, *American Prisoners*, 98.

203 **Twenty prisoners**: Dandridge, *American Prisoners*, 98; and Connecticut Daughters of the American Revolution, *Chapter Sketches, Patron Saints*, ed. Mary Philotheta (New Haven, CT: Edward P. Judd, 1901), 339–40.

203 **chosen by Christopher Hawkins**: Background for Hawkins's escape and all quotes come from Hawkins, *The Adventures of Christopher Hawkins*.

206 **"officers, soldiers, and"**: "Friday, April 18, 1777," *Journals of the Continental Congress, 1774–1789*, vol. 7, 277–78.

206 **"that notwithstanding"**: "Friday, January 5, 1781," *Journals of the American Congress, from 1774 to 1788*, vol. 3, 562.

206 **The reports were**: Watson, *The Ghost Ship*, 184–85; Dzurec, "Prisoners of War," 440–44; and Burrows, *Forgotten Patriots*, 72–73, 82–84.

206 **Born in New York in 1752**: Background for Freneau and all quotes pertaining to his imprisonment come from Philip Freneau, *Some Account of the Capture of the Ship 'Aurora'* (New York: M. F. Mansfield & A. Wessels, 1899).

208 **"The various horrors"**: Philip Freneau, "The British Prison Ship," *Poems Written and Published During the American Revolutionary War*, vol. 2 (Philadelphia: Lydia R. Bailey, 1809), 41, 44, 51–52.

209 **"some idea of"**: John Adams to Abigail Adams, April 27, 1777, *FONA*, https://founders.archives.gov/documents/Adams/04-02-02-0170, accessed May 11, 2021.

209 **"As to our":** Benjamin Franklin to David Hartley, October 14–December 11, 1777, *FONA*, https://founders.archives.gov/documents/Franklin/01-25-02-0036, accessed May 11, 2021.

209 **"The prison ships":** Watson, *The Ghost Ship*, 184.

211 **"It is better to be":** "Westchester County in 1777, From the *Freeman's Journal*, or *New-Hampshire Gazette*, February 18, 1777: Extract of a Letter from Peekskill, dated January 19, 1777," *The Historical Magazine*, December 1870, 370–71.

CHAPTER 9: THE HOME FRONT

213 **"the most baneful . . . American flag":** William Whipple to Josiah Bartlett, June 1, 1778, *The Papers of Josiah Bartlett*, ed. Frank C. Meyers (Hanover, NH: University Press of New England, 1979), 182–83.

213 **"I cannot be":** Josiah Bartlett to William Whipple, June 20, 1778, *The Papers of Josiah Bartlett*, 186–87.

214 **"I agree with . . . accept a commission":** William Whipple to Josiah Bartlett, July 12, 1778, *The Papers of Josiah Bartlett*, 195–97.

215 **Ending the debate:** Josiah Bartlett to William Whipple, July 27, 1778, *The Papers of Josiah Bartlett*, 202.

216 **That caused serious:** See, for example, Crawford, "The Hawke and the Dove," 49–66; Morse, "New England Privateering," 404–5; and Paullin, *The Navy of the American Revolution*, 273–74.

216 **Far from demonstrating:** See, for example, Morse, "New England Privateering," 71–74; Crawford, "The Privateering Debate," 227–28; and Morgan, "American Privateering in America's War," 79.

216 **Although Whipple didn't:** See, for example, Secret Committee of the Continental Congress to Governor Nicholas Cooke, November 15, 1776, *NDAR*, vol. 7, 181.

216 **"in a ruffian":** William Rotch to Nicholas Brown, November 26, 1776, *NDAR*, vol. 7, 292.

216 **But what is clear:** Crawford, "The Privateering Debate," 228.

217 **Though it was also:** Fowler, *Rebels Under Sail*, 273.

217 **Privateering was indeed:** Fowler, *Rebels Under Sail*, 281–83; and Commodore Esek Hopkins to the Continental Marine Committee, November 2, 1776, *NDAR*, vol. 7, 17.

218 **"the privateers entice . . . all the prizes":** John Paul Jones to Robert Morris, October 17, 1776, in Sherburne, *Life and Character*, 21.

218 **Some, such as . . . price gouging:** James B. Hedges, *The Browns of Providence Plantations: Colonial Years* (Cambridge, MA: Harvard University Press, 1952), 269–76.

219 **There were roughly:** "Vessels of the Continental Navy," Naval History and Heritage Command, https://www.history.navy.mil/research/library/online-reading-room/title-list-alphabetically/v/vessels-of-the-continental-navy.html, accessed April 15, 2021; and John B. Hattendorf, *Talking About Naval History: A Collection of Essays* (Newport, RI: Naval War College Press, 2011), 199. General background for this section on the Continental navy comes from Fowler, *Rebels Under Sail*.

219 **The cost of fielding:** Fowler, *Rebels Under Sail*, 70–71; and William S. Dudley and Michael A. Palmer, "No Mistake About It: A Response to Jonathan R. Dull," *The American Neptune* 45, no. 4 (Fall 1985): 246n8.

220 **Nevertheless, the navy managed:** Maclay, *A History of American Privateers*, 216–17; and Edgar Stanton Maclay, *A History of the United States Navy from 1775 to 1894*, vol. 1 (New York: D. Appleton and Company, 1895), 150–51.

220 **While the navy performed:** Jonathan R. Dull, "Was the Continental Navy a Mistake?," *The American Neptune* 44, no. 3 (Summer 1984): 169; Dudley and Palmer, "No Mistake

About It," 245; Evan Thomas, *John Paul Jones: Sailor, Hero, Father of the Navy* (New York: Simon & Schuster, 2003), 64–66; and Paullin, *The Navy of the American Revolution*, 168–74, 236–37.

220 **"We cannot with":** William Ellery to William Vernon, March 16, 1778, *NDAR*, vol. 11, 661.

221 **Only seven of:** Winthrop L. Marvin, *The American Merchant Marine* (Boston: Wright & Potter, 1917), 5; Hattendorf, *Talking About Naval History*, 197–98; Fowler, *Rebels Under Sail*, 246; and Nathan Miller, *The U. S. Navy: A History* (Annapolis, MD: Naval Institute Press, 1997), 19.

221 **The navy's only:** Fowler, *Rebels Under Sail*, 247–52.

221 **capturing roughly:** Maclay, *A History of American Privateers*, viii–ix.

221 **"The Continental Navy did not represent":** William James Morgan, *Captains to the Northward: The New England Captains in the Continental Navy* (Barre, MA: Barre Gazette, 1959), 221.

222 **Even Jones's . . . got away:** Thomas, *John Paul Jones*, 178–98; Morison, *John Paul Jones*, 221–44; and Craig L. Symonds, *The U.S. Navy: A Concise History* (New York: Oxford University Press, 2016), 8–9.

222 **"In looking over":** John Adams to the President of Congress, July 6, 1780, *The Revolutionary Diplomatic Correspondence of the United States*, vol. 3, ed. Francis Wharton (Washington, DC: Government Printing Office, 1889), 833.

222 **"Despite a few glittering":** William Fowler Jr., *Jack Tars and Commodores: The American Navy, 1783–1815* (Boston: Houghton Mifflin, 1984), 1. See also Fowler, *Rebels Under Sail*.

223 **Whipple was focused:** Background for this section on how the army was affected by privateering and on the embargoes comes from Morse, "New England Privateering," 141–43, 193–208.

223 **As with the navy:** Advertisement, *Connecticut Gazette*, December 18, 1778; Advertisement, *Connecticut Gazette*, July 25, 1777; and Benjamin Rush to Richard Henry Lee, December 21, 1776, *Memoir of the Life of Richard Henry Lee*, vol. 2 (Philadelphia: H. C. Carey and I. Lea, 1825), 161.

223 **"As the whole":** Charles Lee to the New England Governors, November 27, 1776, *Collections of the New-York Historical Society for the Year 1872* (New York: Printed for the Society, 1873), 318–19. See also Isaac Smith to John Adams, August 6, 1776, *NDAR*, vol. 6, 77.

223 **Privateer owners—wealthy men:** Morse, "New England Privateering," 193–200.

223 **"I hope your":** John Adams to James Warren, April 6, 1777, *NDAR*, vol. 8, 262.

223 **"The amazing":** James Warren to John Adams, April 23, 1777, *NDAR*, vol. 8, 405.

223 **While some shipowners:** Winslow, *"Wealth and Honour": Portsmouth During the Golden Age of Privateering, 1775–1815*, 32–33.

224 **At the end of March:** Acts and Resolves of the Massachusetts General Court, March 26, 1777, *NDAR*, vol. 8, 203.

224 **"the great necessity":** Morse, "New England Privateering," 202.

224 **Even as it was:** See, for example, John J. McCusker and Russell R. Menard, *The Economy of British America, 1607–1789* (Chapel Hill: University of North Carolina Press, 1991), 362–63.

224 **"Your brethren":** Thomas Cushing to Robert Treat Paine, September 9, 1776, *NDAR*, vol. 6, 756.

225 **"The town was":** Charles H. Webber and Winfield S. Nevins, *Old Naumkeag: An Historical Sketch of the City of Salem* (Salem, MA: A. A. Smith & Company, 1877), 232.

225 **"as a token of their":** *New-Jersey Gazette*, January 21, 1778.

226 **Each prize auction:** See, for example, James Warren to John Adams, August 11, 1776, *NDAR*, vol. 6, 143; "Mr. Gill. Be Pleased to Give the Following Lines"; "To the Printer"; and James Warren to Samuel Adams, August 15, 1776, *NDAR*, vol. 6, 191.

226   **On board were 57,000 pounds:** "Boston, October 10," *Independent Chronicle*, October 10, 1776.

226   **"rendered us":** "From the Pennsylvania Packet, August 7," *The New-York Gazette: and The Weekly Mercury*, August 16, 1779. See also Abraham Ten Broeck, "An Address of the Convention of the Representatives of the State of New-York to Their Constituents," December 23, 1776, in *American Archives: Fifth Series*, vol. 3, 1386.

226   **"Money is now . . . among us":** "Mr. Gill. Be Pleased to Give the Following Lines."

229   **One of the most prominent losers:** Scott D. Wagner, "For Country, Liberty, and Money: Privateering and the Ideologies of the American Revolution" (senior independent study thesis, The College of Wooster, 2017), 85–87; and Patton, *Patriot Pirates*, 208–13.

229   **"It seems that fortune":** Nathanael Greene to Christopher Greene, January 5, 1778, *The Papers of General Nathanael Greene*, vol. 2, ed. Richard K. Showman (Chapel Hill: University of North Carolina Press, 1980), 247.

229   **"some are wallowing":** Samuel Curwen to William Browne, February 10, 1780, in George Atkinson Ward, *Journal and Letters of the Late Samuel Curwen* (New York: C. S. Francis and Co., 1842), 233–34.

229   **"still drudging at":** James Warren to John Adams, June 13, 1779, *Warren-Adams Letters*, vol. 2 (Boston: Massachusetts Historical Society, 1925), 105.

230   **"It has been":** Ezra Stiles, *The Literary Diary of Ezra Stiles, D.D., LL.D*, vol. 2, ed. Franklin Bowditch Dexter (New York: Charles Scribner's Sons, 1901), 77.

230   **"It is scarcely":** Marquis de Chastellux [François Jean de Beauvoir], *Travels in North-America in the Years 1780–81–82*, trans. "by an English Gentleman" (New York: White, Gallaher, and White, 1828; orig. 1788), 98–99.

231   **Other privateer owners who became rich:** Gustavus Myers, *History of the Great American Fortunes* (New York: The Modern Library, 1907), 59–60.

231   **"conspicuous among those":** John W. Tyler, "Persistence and Change Within the Boston Business Community, 1775–1790," *Entrepreneurs: The Boston Business Community, 1700–1850* (Boston: Northeastern University Press, 1997), 116.

231   **Newburyport's Nathaniel Tracy:** Smith, *History of Newburyport*, 107.

232   **"the greatest and":** "The Plan of the Bank of Pennsylvania," *Pennsylvania Packet*, June 27, 1780. See also Ramsay, *The History of the American Revolution*, vol. 2, 189.

232   **Focusing on the most:** See, for example, *Pennsylvania Gazette*, October 9, 1776; "Boston, August 2," *Pennsylvania Evening Post*, August 16, 1779; *Pennsylvania Gazette*, August 22, 1781.

232   **"The easiest":** "Mr. Printer," *New-Jersey Gazette*, January 31, 1781.

233   **"His Britannic Majesty":** Avalon Project, Yale Law School, "British-American Diplomacy Preliminary Articles of Peace; November 30, 1782," https://avalon.law.yale.edu/18th_century/prel1782.asp, accessed April 22, 2021.

233   **For one ill-fated . . . April 3:** Peabody, *The Log of the Grand Turks*, 29–32.

233   **The *Pompey*'s captain:** "Commonwealth of Massachusetts, Middle District," *The Independent Chronicle and Universal Advertiser,* April 23, 1783.

234   **On April 6, 1783:** James Lenox Banks, *David Sproat and Naval Prisoners in the War of the Revolution* (New York: The Knickerbocker Press, 1909), 102–3.

235   **"respective places":** Ibid.

235   **British authorities had:** Prelinger, "Benjamin Franklin and the American Prisoners of War in England during the American Revolution," 290–91; and Bowman, *Captive Americans*, 113–14.

235   **When Sproat boarded:** Burrows, *Forgotten Patriots*, 195.

235   **"three huzzahs":** Ibid.

235 **The best and most often:** Watson, *The Ghost Ship*, 211–17; Burrows, *Forgotten Patriots*, 197–201; and "An American," *Continental Journal, and Weekly Advertiser*, April 17, 1783. There has been considerable debate over how many men died on the prison ships, which is chronicled in these sources. Over the years, some have claimed that the number of dead on the *Jersey* was less than 11,500, while others believe it was more. All estimates, however, are horrifically large.

235 **By comparison:** "American Revolution Facts," American Battlefield Trust, https://www.bat tlefields.org/learn/articles/american-revolution-faqs#:~:text=Throughout%20the%20course %20of%20the%20war%2C%20an%20estimated%206%2C800%20Americans,died%20while %20prisoners%20of%20war, accessed April 22, 2021; Spencer C. Tucker, "Casualties," in *American Revolution: The Definitive Encyclopedia and Document Collection*, ed. Spencer C. Tucker, vol. I (Santa Barbara, CA: ABC-CLIO, 2018), 246; and "America's Wars" (fact sheet), Department of Veterans Affairs (May 2021).

235 **"What Andersonville":** Commager and Morris, *The Spirit of 'Seventy-Six*, 854.

235 **Around the time . . . late spring or early summer:** Cohen, *Yankee Sailors in British Gaols*, 207.

EPILOGUE: A FEW MORE ROUNDS

238 **"It is for the interest . . . finally ruins them":** Benjamin Franklin to Richard Oswald, January 14, 1783, *The Diplomatic Correspondence of the American Revolution*, vol. 4, ed. Jared Sparks (Boston: Nathan Hale and Gray & Bowen, 1829), 67–68.

238 **"privateering success in":** Benjamin Franklin to David Hartley, May 8, 1783, *FONA*, https://founders.archives.gov/documents/Franklin/01-39-02-0372, accessed May 11, 2021. For another version of Franklin's aversion to privateering, see Benjamin Franklin, "On the Criminal Laws and the Practice of Privateering," March 14, 1785, *The Works of Dr. Benjamin Franklin, Consisting of Essays* . . . (London: C. Whittingham, 1824), 216–23.

239 **"If virtue is the doing":** Drowne, *Journal of a Cruise in the Fall of 1780 in the Private-Sloop of War, Hope*, 9.

239 **Under the treaty's:** Treaty of Amity and Commerce Between His Majesty the King of Prussia, and the United States of America; September 10, 1785, Avalon Project, Yale Law School, https://avalon.law.yale.edu/18th_century/prus1785.asp, accessed April 28, 2021.

240 **America had a puny:** Stark, *The Abolition of Privateering*, 127.

240 **"I hope we shall:"** Thomas Jefferson to Tadeusz Kościuszko, June 28, 1812, *FONA*, https://founders.archives.gov/documents/Jefferson/03-05-02-0153, accessed May 11, 2021.

240 **Around a month:** Hezekiah Niles, "Privateering," *The Weekly Register*, August 15, 1812, 396–97.

241 **"were of incalculable":** Theodore Roosevelt, *The Naval War of 1812* (New York: G. P. Putnam's Sons, 1882), 416.

241 **Indeed, the vociferous:** George C. Daughan, *1812: The Navy's War* (New York: Basic Books, 2001), 23–24, 39–40, 147–48, 197–98, 323–24; Stark, *The Abolition of Privateering*, 127–36; Jerome R. Garitee, *The Republic's Private Navy: The American Privateering Business as Practiced by Baltimore During the War of 1812* (Middletown, CT: Wesleyan University Press, 1977), 244; Frederick C. Leiner, "Yes, Privateers Mattered," *Naval History Magazine* 28, no. 2 (March 2014), https://www.usni.org/magazines/naval-history-magazine/2014/march/yes-privateers-mattered, accessed April 28, 2021; and Faye M. Kert, *Privateering: Patriots and Profits in the War of 1812* (Baltimore: Johns Hopkins University Press, 2015), 9.

242 **In the decades . . . in future wars:** Stark, *The Abolition of Privateering*, 42–43, 139–52.

242 **A few years later:** The background for this discussion of Confederate privateers comes
     from J. Thomas Scharf, *History of the Confederate States Navy from Its Organization to the
     Surrender of Its Last Vessel* (New York: Rogers & Sherwood, 1887), 53–93; William Mor-
     rison Robinson Jr., *The Confederate Privateers* (New Haven, CT: Yale University Press,
     1928), 1–24, 56–78; Maclay, *A History of American Privateers*, 505–6; Abraham Lincoln, "A
     Proclamation," April 19, 1861, *Public Laws of the United States of America Passed at the First
     Session of the Thirty-Seventh Congress; 1861*, ed. George P. Sanger (Boston: Little, Brown
     and Company, 1861), 330.

242 **To justify their:** Spencer C. Tucker, *Blue & Gray Navies: The Civil War Afloat* (Annapolis,
     MD: Naval Institute Press, 2006), 73.

SELECT BIBLIOGRAPHY

This bibliography contains but a small fraction of the sources cited in this book. It is intended as a starting point for the general reader who wants to learn more about the history of privateers in the American Revolution. For additional information about specific topics and events covered in the text, please refer to the endnotes.

Alberts, Robert C. *The Golden Voyage: The Life and Times of William Bingham, 1752–1804*. Boston: Houghton Mifflin Company, 1969.

Allen, Gardner W. *A Naval History of the American Revolution*, 2 vols. Boston: Houghton Mifflin Company, 1913.

Andros, Thomas. *The Old Jersey Captive: Or a Narrative of the Captivity of Thomas Andros on Board the Old Jersey Prison Ship at New York, 1781*. Boston: William Pierce, 1833.

Burrows, Edwin G. *Forgotten Patriots: The Untold Story of American Prisoners During the Revolutionary War*. New York: Basic Books, 2008.

Clark, William Bell. *Ben Franklin's Privateers: A Naval Epic of the American Revolution*. Baton Rouge: Louisiana State University Press, 1956.

———. "That Mischievous *Holker*: The Story of a Privateer." *The Pennsylvania Magazine of History and Biography* 79 (January 1955).

Cohen, Sheldon S. *Yankee Sailors in British Gaols: Prisoners of War at Forton and Mill, 1777–1783*. Newark: University of Delaware Press, 1995.

Crawford, Michael J. "The Privateering Debate in Revolutionary America." *The Northern Mariner* 21, no. 3 (July 2011).

Dandridge, Danske. *American Prisoners of the Revolution*. Charlottesville, VA: The Michie Company, 1911.

Dring, Thomas. *Recollections of the Jersey Prison-Ship*. Edited by David Swain. Yardley, PA: Westholme, 2019.

Fowler, William M., Jr. *Rebels Under Sail: The American Navy During the Revolution*. New York: Charles Scribner's Sons, 1976.

Fox, Ebenezer. *The Adventures of Ebenezer Fox, in the Revolutionary War*. London: Charles Fox, 1848.

Griswold, Wick. *Connecticut Pirates & Privateers: Treasure and Treachery in the Constitution State*. Charleston, SC: The History Press, 2015.

Hand, J. P., and Daniel P. Stites. *The Cape May Navy: Delaware Bay Privateers in the American Revolution*. Charleston, SC: The History Press, 2018.

Hawkins, Christopher. *The Adventures of Christopher Hawkins*. Edited by Charles I. Bushnell. New York: Privately printed, 1864.

Herbert, Charles. *A Relic of the Revolution*. Boston: Charles H. Pierce, 1847.

Howe, Octavius Thorndike. *Beverly Privateers in the American Revolution.* Cambridge: John Wilson and Son, 1922.

Kuhl, Jackson. "The Whale-Boat Men of Long Island Sound." *Journal of the American Revolution,* November 1, 2013. https://allthingsliberty.com/2013/11/whale-boat-men-long-island-sound/.

Leamon, James S. *Revolution Downeast: The War for American Independence in Maine.* Amherst: University of Massachusetts Press, 1995.

Leiner, Frederick C. "Yes, Privateers Mattered." *Naval History Magazine,* March 2014. https://www.usni.org/magazines/naval-history-magazine/2014/march/yes-privateers-mattered.

Lydon, James G. *Pirates, Privateers, and Profits.* Upper Saddle River, NJ: The Gregg Press, 1970.

Maclay, Edgar Stanton. *A History of American Privateers.* London: Sampson, Low, Marston & Co., 1900.

McBurney, Christian. *Dark Voyage: An American Privateer's War on Britain's African Slave Trade.* Yardley, PA: Westholme Publishing, 2022.

McManemin, John A. *Captains of the Privateers During the Revolutionary War.* Spring Lake, NJ: Ho-Ho-Kus Publishing Company, 1985.

Morse, Sidney G. "The Yankee Privateersman of 1776." *New England Quarterly* 17, no. 1 (March 1944).

Nelson, James L. *George Washington's Secret Navy: How the American Revolution Went to Sea.* New York: McGraw Hill, 2008.

Patton, Robert H. *Patriot Pirates: The Privateer War for Freedom and Fortune in the American Revolution.* New York: Vintage Books, 2008.

Paullin, Charles O. *The Navy of the American Revolution: Its Administration, Its Policy and Its Achievements.* Chicago: The Burrows Brothers Company, 1906.

Powell, Walter L. *Murder or Mayhem? Benedict Arnold's New London, Connecticut Raid, 1781.* Gettysburg, PA: Thomas Publications, 2000.

Prince, Christopher, *The Autobiography of a Yankee Mariner: Christopher Prince and the American Revolution.* Edited by Michael J. Crawford. Washington, DC: Brassey's, Inc., 2002.

Sherburne, Andrew. *Memoirs of Andrew Sherburne: A Pensioner of the Navy of the Revolution.* Providence, RI: M. M. Brown, 1831.

Shomette, Donald Grady. *Privateers of the Revolution: War on the New Jersey Coast, 1775–1783.* Atglen, PA: Schiffer Publishing, 2016.

Starkey, David J. *British Privateering Enterprise in the Eighteenth Century.* Exeter, UK: University of Exeter Press, 1990.

Watson, Robert P. *The Ghost Ship of Brooklyn: An Untold Story of the American Revolution.* New York: Da Capo Press, 2007.

Williams, Gomer. *History of the Liverpool Privateers and Letters of Marque.* London: William Heinemann, 1897.

Willis, Sam. *The Struggle for Sea Power: A Naval History of the American Revolution.* New York: W. W. Norton, 2015.

Winslow, Richard E., III. *"Wealth and Honour": Portsmouth During the Golden Age of Privateering, 1775–1815.* Portsmouth, NH: Portsmouth Marine Society, 1988.

ILLUSTRATION CREDITS

Frontispiece: Courtesy Mariners' Museum and Park

page xi: Courtesy Peabody Essex Museum, Salem, MA. Photograph by Walter Silver

page xiii: Courtesy Peabody Essex Museum and U.S. Naval History and Heritage Command

page xv: Octavius T. Howe, "Beverly Privateers in the American Revolution," *Publications of the Colonial Society of Massachusetts*, vol. XXIV (January 1922)

page xvii: Courtesy Peabody Essex Museum, Salem, MA

page xxii: Courtesy Library of Congress

page 1: Courtesy Library of Congress

page 2: W. D. Cooper, *The History of North America* (London: E. Newberry, 1789)

page 4: Courtesy Miriam and Ira D. Wallach Division of Art, Prints and Photographs: Print Collection, New York Public Library. New York Public Library Digital Collections

page 5: Courtesy Library of Congress

page 7: Courtesy Library of Congress

page 8: Courtesy Norman B. Leventhal Map & Education Center

page 12: Courtesy Library of Congress

page 13: Courtesy Library of Congress

Page 18: Howard Pyle, *Howard Pyle's Book of The American Spirit*, ed. Francis J. Dowd (New York: Harper & Brothers, 1923)

page 20: Ebenezer Fox, *The Adventures of Ebenezer Fox in the Revolutionary War* (Boston: Charles Fox, 1848)

page 26: Courtesy Marblehead Museum

page 30: Courtesy U.S. Naval History and Heritage Command

page 33: Courtesy State Archives of North Carolina

page 35: Courtesy Library of Congress

page 36: Courtesy Library of Congress

page 39: Courtesy Library of Congress

page 42: Courtesy Library of Congress

page 46: Courtesy U.S. Naval History and Heritage Command

page 48: Courtesy Library of Congress

page 49: Courtesy Library of Congress

page 50: Courtesy Library of Congress

page 56: Courtesy U.S. Naval History and Heritage Command

page 57: Courtesy U.S. Naval History and Heritage Command

page 58: (Barney) Courtesy U.S. Naval History and Heritage Command

page 58: (*Hyder Ally*) Courtesy United States Naval Academy Museum

page 65: Courtesy Library of Congress

page 69: Courtesy Peabody Essex Museum, Salem, MA. Photograph by Dennis Helmar

page 71: (Saker cannon) Courtesy International Military Antiques, Inc.

page 71: (swivel gun) Courtesy Naval War College Museum

page 77: From the diary (Tagebuch) kept by Andreas Wiederholdt (Wiederhold) from 7 October 1776 to 7 December 1780. Courtesy Collection on the participation of German soldiers in the American Revolution, 1776–1885, Ms. Coll. 773, Kislak Center for Special Collections, Rare Books and Manuscripts, University of Pennsylvania

page 89: (Bingham) Courtesy Miriam and Ira D. Wallach Division of Art, Prints and Photographs: Print Collection, New York Public Library. New York Public Library Digital Collections

page 89: (Martinique) Courtesy John Carter Brown Library, Brown University

page 91: Courtesy Library of Congress

page 94: Courtesy Library of Congress.

page 95: Courtesy Library of Congress

page 96: O. L. Holley, *The Life of Benjamin Franklin* (Boston: John Philbrick, 1854)

page 98: © Trustees of the British Museum

page 99: Courtesy Library of Congress

page 100: Courtesy Library of Congress

page 105: Courtesy U.S. Naval History and Heritage Command

page 110: Courtesy Historic Beverly

page 112: Courtesy Newburyport Public Library

page 117: Courtesy Library of Congress, Geography and Map Division

page 120: John Greenwood, *The Revolutionary Services of John Greenwood of Boston and New York*, 1775–1783, ed. Isaac J. Greenwood (New York: De Vinne Press, 1922)

page 125: Courtesy Mount Vernon Ladies' Association

page 131: Courtesy Norman B. Leventhal Map & Education Center

page 132: Courtesy Peabody Essex Museum, Salem, MA

page 135: "The Trial of Captain Luke Ryan," *Hibernian Magazine* (April 1782)

page 142: Mariners' Museum and Park

page 144: Courtesy United States Naval Academy Museum

page 148: Courtesy Rumsey Map Collection

page 149: Courtesy Miriam and Ira D. Wallach Division of Art, Prints and Photographs: Print Collection, New York Public Library. New York Public Library Digital Collections

page 160: Courtesy Library of Congress, Geography and Map Division

page 167: Courtesy U.S. Naval History and Heritage Command

page 168: Courtesy Miriam and Ira D. Wallach Division of Art, Prints and Photographs: Print Collection, New York Public Library. New York Public Library Digital Collections

page 169: Courtesy Library of Congress, Geography and Map Division

page 171: Courtesy Library of Congress, Geography and Map Division

page 178: Courtesy Nova Scotia Archives

page 182: Courtesy Library of Congress

page 195: Courtesy Library of Congress

page 197: Courtesy National Portrait Gallery

page 199: Courtesy National Portrait Gallery

page 207: Courtesy Miriam and Ira D. Wallach Division of Art, Prints and Photographs: Print Collection, New York Public Library. New York Public Library Digital Collection

page 210: Courtesy Library of Congress

page 214: Courtesy Miriam and Ira D. Wallach Division of Art, Prints and Photographs: Print Collection, New York Public Library. New York Public Library Digital Collections

page 215: Courtesy Miriam and Ira D. Wallach Division of Art, Prints and Photographs: Print Collection, New York Public Library. New York Public Library Digital Collections

page 217: Courtesy Library of Congress

page 220: Courtesy National Museum of the U.S. Navy and U.S. Naval History and Heritage Command

page 225: Courtesy NSCDA-MA, Quincy Homestead, Quincy, Massachusetts

page 228: Octavius T. Howe, "Beverly Privateers in the American Revolution," *Publications of the Colonial Society of Massachusetts*, vol. XXIV (January 1922)

page 230: Courtesy Library of Congress

page 237: Courtesy Library of Congress

page 239: Courtesy Brown University Portrait Collection, BP.21

page 243: Courtesy Library of Congress

INSERT

1. Courtesy Worcester Art Museum, Massachusetts, USA© Worcester Art Museum / Museum purchase / Bridgeman Images
2. Courtesy Franklin D. Roosevelt Presidential Library and Museum, Hyde Park, NY
3. Courtesy Freeman's
4. Courtesy Peabody Essex Museum, Salem, MA. Photograph by Mark Sexton and Jeffrey R. Dykes
5. Courtesy Frank E. Schoonover Fund, Inc.
6. Courtesy Christian McBurney Collection
9. Courtesy © National Maritime Museum, Greenwich, London
10. Courtesy Beverley R. Robinson Collection, U.S. Naval Academy Museum
11. Courtesy Historical Society of Pennsylvania
12. Courtesy Prints, Drawings and Watercolors from the Anne S. K. Brown Military Collection. Brown Digital Repository. Brown University Library
13. Courtesy Prints, Drawings and Watercolors from the Anne S. K. Brown Military Collection. Brown Digital Repository. Brown University Library
14. Courtesy United States Naval Academy Museum
15. Courtesy Cape Ann Museum, gift of Alfred Mansfield Brooks and Ruth Steele Brooks 1971

INDEX

═══

ABOUT THE AUTHOR

===

Eric Jay Dolin is the author of *Leviathan: The History of Whaling in America*, which won the 2007 John Lyman Award for U.S. Maritime History and was chosen as one of the best nonfiction books of 2007 by the *Los Angeles Times*, the *Boston Globe*, and the *Providence Journal*; and *Black Flags, Blue Waters: The Epic History of America's Most Notorious Pirates*, a finalist for the Boston Authors Club's Julia Ward Howe Award in 2019 and designated a "Must Read" by the Massachusetts Center for the Book. Other books include *Fur, Fortune, and Empire: The Epic History of the Fur Trade in America*, winner of the New England Historical Association's James P. Hanlan Book Award and chosen by the *Seattle Times* as one of the best nonfiction books of 2010; *When America First Met China: An Exotic History of Tea, Drugs, and Money in the Age of Sail*, named one of the 100 Best Nonfiction Books of the Year in 2012 by *Kirkus Reviews*; and *Brilliant Beacons: A History of the American Lighthouse*, chosen by the website gCaptain and by *Classic Boat* magazine as one of the best nautical books of 2016 and selected as a "Must Read" for 2017 by the Massachusetts Center for the Book. Dolin's *Furious Sky: The Five-Hundred-Year History of America's Hurricanes* (2020) was selected by the *Washington Post* as one of the year's 50 Notable Works of Nonfiction; by *Kirkus Reviews* as one of the Best Nonfiction Books (in addition to being a Kirkus Prize finalist); by *Library Journal* and *Booklist* as one of the Best Science & Technology Books; by the *New York Times Book Review* as an "Editors' Choice"; and by the Massachusetts Center for the Book as a "Must Read." A graduate of Brown, Yale, and MIT, where he received his PhD in environmental policy, Dolin lives in Marblehead, Massachusetts, with his family. For more information on his background and books, visit his website, ericjaydolin.com. You can also follow his posts on his professional Facebook page, Eric Jay Dolin, or on Twitter, @EricJayDolin.